COMPANY MANNERS

COMPANY MANNERS

An Insider Tells How to Succeed in the Real World of Corporate Protocol and Power Politics

LOIS WYSE

McGraw-Hill Book Company

New York   St. Louis   San Francisco
Toronto   Hamburg   Mexico

1 2 3 4 5 6 7 8 9 D O C D O C 8 7 6

ISBN 0-07-072193-9

LIBRARY OF CONGRESS CATALOGING-IN-PUBLICATION DATA

Wyse, Lois.

  Company manners.
  1. Success in business.   2. Business etiquette.
3. Office politics.   4. Business entertaining.
I. Title
HF5386.W97   1987   395'.52   86-7394
ISBN 0-07-072193-9

BOOK DESIGN BY PATRICE FODERO

For those who taught me

Contents

Prologue

Let me begin at the beginning.

It all started a month or so ago when the executive vice president of a Fortune 500 company invited me to lunch in the company's corporate dining room four weeks hence. "It's time we did some things together," he said.

For four weeks I smiled a lot. Oh, what a chance this was. Me, the president of Wyse Advertising, one of the 100 largest advertising agencies in the United States, sought as a major client's luncheon guest.

Of course, I had been invited to corporate dining rooms before. I had even been invited to this corporation's dining room by persons higher on the ladder than the man who invited me. But my earlier visits to this company had been ceremonial, the kind of president-to-president visit that happens regularly in executive life. In our years in the advertising business, our agency has been involved with Fortune 500 companies, interesting entrepreneurial companies, and a collection of power people from New York to California, from Europe to Australia.

We have worked for the best of the beauty advertisers like
Revlon and Clairol, for the giant conglomerate TRW and the giant
American Express. We have been the advertising agency for companies as diverse as Maidenform and Seagram's. And we are the
advertising agency that, more than twenty years ago, launched a
campaign for a little jellymaker in Ohio with the line, "With a
name like Smucker's it has to be good."

Still, despite our credits, an invitation to a nonclient's executive
dining room was not an everyday occurrence. In my business you
know you are wanted when the client comes after you. Usually it
is the other way around.

I was excited by the possibilities of this new piece of business,
and my enthusiasm was contagious. Everybody in the office shared
my anticipatory high. Each day my associates and I regaled one
another by imagining still more amazing opportunities we would
be offered. It seemed that every sentence we uttered began with,
"What if . . . ." After all, could an executive vice president (forget
for a minute that Fortune 500 companies have more executive
vice presidents than we have secretaries)—could an executive vice
president not be inviting me to lunch because he had an incredible
assignment that would heap new riches on Wyse Advertising and
make us eligible for still more kudos and Clios?

The night before the luncheon I laid out my clothes. No last
minute stands at the closet for me. No, I'd be preprogrammed.
Nothing like an uneven hem or a spot on a jacket would stop
me.

I took out a little Adolfo. I figured if it's good enough for
Nancy Reagan, it would work for me.

I took out the little Chanel bag and hat.

I put out the right pantyhose and the shoes.

I was up at 6 A.M., dressed, and in the office at 7:30 waiting
for lunchtime.

And, at noon, like a shot, I ran up the street to my executive
vice president and lunch in the executive suite.

There were two men at the luncheon, one executive vice president, one divisional president. (In that dizzying world of corporate jungle gyms, there are many presidents who are lesser persons than the executive vice presidents. This was one of those instances.)

The men were charming—as are all men who are about to give you business—and we went through the ritual of the drink, the ordering, and the conversation. The conversation was incredible. It was crossed with promises and dotted with premises. If the company made this—how would we sell it? What did we think of the A strategy versus the B strategy? I was really getting into it now. I told them. I really told them. I gave them ideas I didn't even know I had. It was one of the greatest idea exchanges-cum-luncheons I had ever attended.

Then, at the end—you always know when the end of a luncheon is near because the host looks at his watch—at the end, the host said, "This has been fascinating, Lois. I just wish we had an assignment for you."

I choked. "Do you mean—do you actually mean—you have nothing for us?"

Large sigh from second man. "Too bad, isn't it?"

Me, turning purple. "Too bad? You think it's too bad. Then why am I here?"

Man One, "We wanted to get to know you better."

Me, "Why?"

Divisional president, "We like to know what talent is available in case we need it."

I stood up, straightened my Chanel and Adolfo parts, and said in my frostiest tone, hoping all the while that the sarcasm would not be lost on them, "Thank you."

And then I left.

And as I walked back to my office, I thought . . . those men are coarse and cruel. I don't care what clubs they belong to and how golden their parachutes may be.

How could they invite me, ostensibly for an assignment, let me think for ninety minutes that they planned to hire us, ask

me for ideas and innovative marketing perceptions, and then—
thunk!

How dare they!

What made them think that working for a big company was
a reason to have little courtesy and concern for others.

These men—why these men had no manners.

And then I realized that, of course, they had manners.

They had company manners. They met life's exigencies with
let-me-do-what's-best-for-me as the Number One Priority.

Company manners is the protocol by which one saves one's
self in business.

In the corporation for which these men worked—in the corporate world *the corporation* means one significant executive at
corporate level—well, one high-ranking executive liked the work
of our company and wanted to see our agency hired.

And that scared these men.

Hire someone because a key executive on the forty-fourth
floor thought it would be a good idea?

If they let us in, who knew what the corporation would ask
next? More important, who knew what secrets we would take back
to headquarters? Would they be second-guessed at every turn?
Could we influence titles, spheres of influence, and salaries? And,
if we did, who knew when their heads would be the next to
roll?

No, their interpretation of company manners called for dis-
posing of corporate wishes neatly. No blood on the rug; no bodies
in the hallway. How could I complain when I had been wined
and dined so politely? Wouldn't I sound like an emotional spoil-
sport if I were to complain?

Besides, what was there to complain about?

Hadn't the wine been chilled and the hosts warm?

It was nothing I could explain without whining. The hired
assassins had done a very neat job in the corporate dining
room.

And I had been hooked, snookered, and discarded.

Why hadn't I realized in advance what was about to happen?

What made me think that simply because so many corporate executives in my business life have treated me with courtesy and kindness that all would?

Why did I think people in business always meant what they said?

Because no one told me they didn't.

We simply don't tell each other about the booby traps, the secret words, the clubby attitudes that make up company manners. We slog along thinking everyone will learn for himself.

But I think it is high time that those of us who care about the way people treat one another in business recognize some company manners for the impious, time-wasting, money-wasting, career-busting maneuvers they often are.

I think it's about time someone told what goes on in the name of business, profits, and style.

So I have put together some of the things I have learned in working with some of the best-known corporate people in America.

I am recounting these stories because when you know what can happen, you can respond with appropriate action.

All company manners are not nefarious.

Nor are all companies and their operating executives.

But remember, nothing defangs a potential corporate tiger more swiftly than a person on the other side of the desk who understands what the Man with the Golden Parachute means— no matter what he says.

So welcome to Manners à la Business.

Every day another company is merged or submerged with another company. Every day senior people who thought they would go on doing whatever it is they were doing until nature stopped them now find that they are stopped by man.

These are the things no one wants to talk about—at least not out loud.

Company Manners is based on real experiences and real solutions. And, considering that much of our business life is disguised as a social life and takes place outside of traditional business settings, this book talks about those times and places, too.

There are only two things people ask when they meet you, "What is your name?" followed by, "What do you do?" And very often they don't listen to your name until the second question is answered—and to their liking.

Business has become the central force in the lives of women as well as men. In the 1950s and 1960s men were identified by their jobs, and women were identified by their husband's work. Now each of us is known more as an individual and less as a spouse. From the business center of our lives we now create the pattern for behavior in other areas.

The way we do business is the way we live.

The waters are rough out there; survival is not enough, for there is no joy simply in surviving. Survival must be done with panache, with style, and that is what truly separates the top quality person, not just the top title, from the middle.

As for those two corporate executives who invited me to lunch in order to tell me that they had nothing for me, both have since learned that their corporation has nothing for them. What then becomes the fallback position for people with no company manners?

I have learned that style counts in the workplace.

I have learned that the style which I call company manners permits talent to flourish because the more we do to create a warm atmosphere, the better our talent grows.

This is the Age of Anxiety, the Century of Stress, the Era of Fear. If we develop a personal code of company manners in all parts of our lives, if we relieve the stress, we protect our greatest assets, our talents. In this way company manners becomes a kind of constant insurance policy for those things which we hold most dear.

I have learned that in business everyone is looking for someone to trust, and the secret to moving ahead is to gain the confidence of one's superiors and one's peers. What better way than with exemplary company manners?

Exemplary company manners are made of more than caring for others. Caring is the beginning, but caring is not enough.

The way we communicate the caring is what it's about.
A generation ago we heard that the medium is the message.
Now the style is the manners.
Style is at the heart of company manners.
It is at the heart of the secrets I am about to tell.

The Elements of Style

The style is the man himself.

George Louis, Comte de Buffon, 1753

CHAPTER 1

Establishing Company Manners

The power drive in America starts at 7:30 each weekday morning and ends at 9 A.M.

It begins as chauffeurs in carefully cooled (or heated) conservative luxury cars (small Cadillacs, Lincolns, Mercedes, BMWs, or Jaguars) wait in front of Park Avenue and Fifth Avenue apartments, in the sheltered drives of Potomac estates, on side streets lining Chicago's Gold Coast, in the six-car garages of Texas ranches and car ports of California beach houses. The gold-plated passengers who will slide into the backseats laden with newspapers, reports, and easy access to a car phone are the people who within eight hours will be making the moves that will ultimately run, power, and take over much of the business world.

Their cars, like most of their life, are a business expense.

They are identified, these many men and few women, more by their titles than their given names. The exceptions are those instances where their names mean their businesses (Ivan Boesky, arbitrage; Carl Icahn, takeover; Ted Turner and/or Rupert Murdoch, communications).

The offices where they are headed are as varied as their cars are similar. Once an executive steps into his office, the company thrums with life. Top people set the style that the rest of the company adopts. The CEO's politics and policy, politeness and performance—those are the elements that make company manners vary from place to place.

And the company manners in each place of business are communicated through the corporate levels by style. Watch the style, and you get the pulse of the company. But don't be too judgmental. There is no right or wrong executive style.

The style begins with the person in the corner office who may be young or old, fat or thin, male or female. Understanding that style and the ways it filters through a company is often the single most important key to a successful relationship with that company.

Warren Bennis, a University of Southern California management professor, says, "The chief executive is the major determinant of the stock price."

In 1985 when American Express's Fireman's Fund Insurance Co. was resuscitated with its third multimillion dollar infusion, the stock dropped only one-quarter point because John Byrne, characterized by *USA Today* as a "Wall Street darling" was named chief executive.

Sometimes analysts are impressed by an executive's ability to change his mind, so long as the change is accompanied by a profit turnaround. When Samuel J. Heyman won control of GAF Corporation after a lengthy and difficult proxy battle, Heyman vowed to sell many of the company's operations, particularly the core chemical business.

But once he viewed the company from the inside, Heyman's strategy changed.

Instead he poured millions into the company's chemical holdings, instituted rewards for innovative thinking, and within two years the stock doubled. A favorite of Wall Street, Heyman is in his midforties and has no conventional management experience.

Generally the unconventional entrepreneur runs a private company, for—contrary to the daily financial pages which are filled with stories of takeovers—private enterprise is not diminishing. It is, in fact, increasing. The chief external difference between the public company and the private company is size. The 400 largest private companies in the United States, according to *Forbes*, have combined sales of $340 billion, which is one-seventh of the combined sales of the 400 largest public firms.

Private firms, however, represent 98 percent of all U.S. companies in number and are responsible for one-third of U.S. production. Among the private companies are Estée Lauder (reputed to have sales over $1 billion) and Hallmark (both companies today have presidents who are sons of the founders), Uniroyal, S. C. Johnson, Levi Strauss.

Generally, what private companies and public companies have in common is a sexy CEO.

The Sexy CEO

The chief executive officer (CEO) of the public company is usually male; the female CEO of a public company is such an anomaly that it is impossible to draw a profile in the corporate world. Woman is still like the talking dog—it does not much matter how she does it; the wonder is that she does it at all. There are, however, an increasing number of female entrepreneurs, women who own smallish businesses and are part of the private company explosion.

In the corporate world the definition of a sexy CEO changes with the season; now the sexy CEO is one who can charm Wall Street and so help overcome almost anything, even reduced or poor profits.

A sexy CEO is not necessarily handsome, although that is no drawback, but it is more important that he project intelligence, integrity, warmth, forthrightness.

A kind of corporate Robert Redford would fit the bill today.

Roberto Goizueta, despite Coca-Cola's marketing blunders, is a persuasive performer at analysts' meetings.

Charles Wohlstetter, who strung together a series of independent telephone companies and created Contel, a multibillion dollar telecommunications empire, is a highly literate and effective performer at analyst's meetings. Drama seems to follow him. Once, at a New York stock analysts' meeting, he was called to the telephone and came back beaming. "I couldn't have staged this better," he confided. "That was a call giving us the go-ahead. . . ." He then outlined briefly the details of a major government contract.

The entrepreneur in the privately held company plays a different game from the entrepreneur in the publicly held company. In the public company the name of the game is earnings. In the private company the entrepreneur seeks asset enhancement.

But what all entrepreneurs seek is their own style, their own way of facing problems and victories.

Not all of them know how to project a desired company manner, nor indeed do some even think about it.

In their determination to run no-nonsense, profitable companies some executives come down hard on associates; some uplift the people in their employ and serve as a role model.

During Charles Revson's reign at Revlon, company manners called for the sacrifice of any private life for the sake of the company. This attitude of sacrifice prevailed and resulted in people working late into the night, forcing others to wait for hours despite scheduled appointments. It caused regular rudeness and belittling of executives in meetings. Courtesy was low on the list of corporate qualities. But everything was done in what became the Revlon company manner: tough, hard, competitive action.

Ronald Perelman, whose company Pantry Pride acquired Revlon despite the fight led by Charles Revson's hand-picked successor Michel Bergerac, is quiet, self-effacing, and courteous. His written thank-you comes almost before the action he is acknowledging.

Paul Smucker, the chairman of the J. M. Smucker Co., is punctilious about every aspect of the business started by his grandfather. Each aspect of growth is credited to "the team," headed by his sons Tim and Richard. Everyone who does business with the company, customer or supplier, is treated with equal consideration. And if Mr. Smucker takes a jar of jelly home, he pays for it. That sets the company style.

George Jenkins's Publix Super Markets in Florida make up a closely held $3.2 billion company. Employees, including bagboys, own 62 percent of the stock and get back 20 percent of the profits. Workers wear badges that say, "I am a Publix stockholder," and headman Jenkins still makes sure the strawberries aren't too expensive. He checks quality and prices in his stores and even pokes around to be certain the floors are clean and the service fast.

Stephen D. Hassenfeld, the chairman of Hasbro, Inc., the toy and game makers, describes himself as a person who "drives the dialogue" and questions associates endlessly on various aspects of a business plan. He will take twenty to thirty minutes to poll every person in a room on opinions of a new toy. Some unnamed executives admit that the style drives them crazy.

But the corner office has room for idiosyncrasies.

The ultimate entrepreneur is the artist whose talents form the basis for his business. No one is freer of convention and restrictions than artists. James Rosenquist, one of the most acclaimed contemporary painters, once went to a black-tie formal dinner with many of New York's Anonymous Rich as well as Tisches, Rudins, and Papamarkous. For his black tie Rosenquist wore an old Brillo pad.

Margaret Harold Whitehead, who founded *New Woman* magazine, listed as two staff members on the masthead Harold P. Whiswell III and Pippin von Schpringentail—her dogs.

Sigmund Warburg, head of the famous banking house, never hired anyone—including top executives—without having the person take a handwriting test. The handwriting sample was then sent to Zurich for analysis of traits that would make the prospective banker worthy of hiring.

The only mistake ever made as a result of this practice, according to Warburg, was the time the advice of the handwriting expert was ignored and the wrong person hired.

Setting the style

In the last quarter of the twentieth century style is what each of us makes it.

One man's table is another man's desk.

One woman's Coco Chanel is another's Liz Claibourne.

One executive's light reading is another's weighty thought provoker.

There is no price tag, no intelligence quotient, no mandate.

Style does not follow the rules; style makes the rules that become fashion—and fashion is what people follow.

No two persons run a business the same way; style separates us all.

The first thing that contributes to style is power.

In order to have power, one must have a job.

A job gives one access to privileged information. Part of executive style is being among the first to know. As Irving Shapiro said when his tenure as chairman of DuPont ended, "What I miss most is the grapevine. Nobody calls."

No one is less interesting to movers and shakers than ex-tycoons. Like old movie stars, ex-bosses are remembered only as, "Didn't he used to be. . . ." The real attitude toward the unemployed was best expressed by two corporate heads lunching in the restaurant "21." They were seated on the first floor in the generally accepted A area and looked across the room into the B area. Said the first man, "There's Bill X over there. What is he doing now that his company has been sold?"

"Not much," said the second. "Nowadays Bill is just another guy in New York with $20 million and nothing to do."

Which is more important to executive style, $20 million or a job?

That's easy.
A job is more important.
Nothing is more stylish than power.
Power is not in the net worth, nor is it in a title.
All power is in the job.

This is a story about the officers of a conglomerate who learned that the hard way.

It all began one pleasant June morning with a review of all divisions by the corporate president and executive vice-president. A few minutes before the meeting was to begin, all the divisionals had assembled. Only the corporate president was missing. Joy, a divisional president, was getting nervous. Where was Alfred, the president? She had scheduled back-to-back meetings and wanted to start this one on time. She turned to Frederic, the executive vice-president, "Have you called Alfred to remind him? Sometimes corporate presidents forget. . . ."

Frederic's back stiffened, and he spoke through lips that scarcely moved. "Alfred and I are not talking. We haven't spoken for four days."

Joy couldn't believe her ears, but she simply went to the telephone, called Alfred's office, and informed him that a group was waiting. Within two minutes the meeting began with all principals in attendance. Joy noticed that Alfred said not one word to Frederic, and the chilling silence was returned with chilling silence.

"This cannot continue," Joy thought—but true to her company manners—she said nothing aloud.

Three weeks later at the company golf outing everyone was aware of the rift between Alfred and Frederic. At the dinner following the golfing, the corporate chairman sat between the two warriors.

"Will you ask Alfred to pass the butter?" Frederic said to the chairman.

Now, thought Joy, they have gone too far.
And so they had.

Within a month the financial journals announced the resignation of Frederic "to pursue personal business interests."

Joy knew better.

"Frederic never understood the unwritten rule of the corporation," she said. "He thought the best way to become chairman was to become executive vice-president. So he decided to give up the presidency of the software company that he had founded, the company the parent company acquired when he came to work here. Once Frederic was operating without a power base he was vulnerable. Poor Frederic. He just didn't understand that in reaching for the king's throne, you have to do so from your own territory.

"Keep your power base. That's the number one rule in business. Of course," she added ruefully, "by the time you learn that you're usually out."

Staying in, however, is the only way to pursue the power style.

How do you stay in, assuming that you have talent and that there is a job for you?

One must assume that, in addition to your talent and the company's need, you have a pleasant personality, do not announce your immediate accomplishments every fifteen minutes, and are intelligent in your choice of office friends.

How then do you stay in and move up?

What are the secrets no one will tell you?

Language is one secret. You can move faster when you know the motivating phrases, the buzzwords currently in use. Nothing is more correct than this year's key words; nothing is more dated than last year's.

You need also to know, understand, and have the ability to adopt the clubby attitudes which indicate that you belong—or are about to belong—to top management.

And, finally, you must recognize and avoid the booby traps that are put in your path both wittingly and unwittingly.

Now let us take a closer look.

Learning the secret words

Most large corporations, and smaller companies as well, have ways they like to describe themselves and think of their products, services, and employees. These descriptive words are the current passport, and—like a passport—they need renewing.

The secret words vary from business to business and from company to company.

In one company the secret word may be "innovative." This means simply that this is the year that the company's focused commitment is to innovate people, product, and performance.

You may not always know the reason for the choice of secret words. We once worked with a company where the operative word was "new." Everything "new" was given an automatic good. Everything from "last year" was a disaster. In that case, it was easy to understand the reason. The company had a new president, and last year's president had been a disaster.

The faster you learn the code words, the less likely you are to make mistakes.

The fastest way to learn individual company code words is to lunch with the president's secretary.

A secretary is one of those persons with regular access to the power people, and a new person can learn the most about current buzzwords and protocol from someone who not only observes at close range but generally has good reportorial skills.

Further, secretaries are those who are frequently willing to impart information because they are not vying for top positions. The more questions a new person asks of an upper middle management person (an UMM), the less he is likely to learn. UMMs have many fears.

There are some secret words that everyone headed for the top should recognize. One of the phrases is "no problem" or its corporate equivalent in your environment.

Lawrence and Ben both joined the sales department of a greeting card company the same year. Lawrence was assigned to the midwest, Ben to the southeast. The first time the sales manager gave price changes to the sales force, Lawrence made the changes and got the business expected of him. Ben also made the changes and not only got the expected business but went slightly ahead of plan.

The second time price changes were made, Ben picked up the phone and called his supervisor. "Why these price changes?" he asked. "Isn't business tough enough without you guys adding to my problems?" To underscore his complaint, he then sent a letter repeating his annoyance. Still, despite his protests, he again went ahead of plan.

Lawrence, on the other hand, said, "OK. If that's what we have to do, then we'll make the changes. No problem." His final figures that month were not as impressive as Ben's.

Each time that a supervisor made changes, Ben grudgingly accepted, although he performed well above average. Lawrence accepted cheerfully, although his performance was only average.

The following year a regional sales manager in the west left the company, and the choice for replacement was between Ben and Lawrence.

Management did not delay in naming Lawrence. He was considered "cheerful, able to lead others," while Ben was characterized as "a salesman who is more concerned with his ease in doing things than he is in the company."

The ability to sell is not always all that counts en route to a top sales job.

While Ben was unable to challenge management in a constructive manner, it is possible to question actions in a way that brings favorable attention to the challenger.

Ruth Block started as a statistical clerk with the Equitable Life Assurance Society of the United States in 1952 and ultimately became the third-ranking executive in the company.

"I was there when computer technology came into being," she recalls, "and I moved up because I constantly challenged the status quo. I never challenged by defying others; I challenged by asking, 'Why?' My question was always, 'What would happen if we did the opposite thing? What are the alternatives?' I have never accepted the words, 'That's the way it's always been.' "

While individual company and industry buzzwords are important, the biggest overall business secret that no one wants anyone to know is simply that all business is a lot easier than it looks from the outside.

Once you get into any business, you learn that the similarities to other businesses far outweigh the differences.

The gizmo in one company is the widget in the next.

If you are the new person on the block, you will know everything you need to know about almost any company when you know the following:

1. Costs of manufacturing
2. Methods of selling
3. Profit structure

The most important word to learn in any company is the pronoun "we."

Forget "I" until you make it all the way to the top. By then, however, you'll probably be so accustomed to the editorial "we" that you will have difficulty saying "I."

The word to avoid at all costs is "they."

In business "they" refers to the competition or any place where you used to work. The first six weeks on a new job, one is permitted an occasional "they," but after that period of grace, remember that the moment you call your coworkers "they" is the day you'd better get your résumé together.

Clubby attitudes

Clubby attitudes are those business styles affected in order to conform to the attitudes of the corporations.

You don't need to walk around in the company sweatshirt in order to let everyone know that you are part of the team. But you do have to act in business the way top management does if, indeed, you want to become a member of top management.

Elliot was director of European sales for a housewares company and left to accept the job of marketing director with a manufacturer of fine china. He spent the first two weeks in a crash training program learning how the company went from design to finished product. At the end of two weeks he was driving home to the suburbs with the president of the company.

"How are things going?" the president asked.

"I had a disastrous meeting today," Elliot said. "We had a product meeting, and everything was wrong."

The president cleared his throat and said quietly, "That is not the way we operate. We never have a disastrous meeting because we never permit a meeting to go the level where people can feel everything is wrong. When you sense that you are not going to get what you think you should have, go back to the basics. Ask the primary questions: Is this product supposed to achieve x or y? Are the costs in line? In this company there is no such word as disastrous. No one here complains; everyone here performs."

Lili was considered one of the best presenters in the advertising agency where she worked in the marketing department, and when she went to work for the market research company, she knew she would be applauded for her presentation skills.

At the first meeting with a client, a shoe manufacturer, she felt confident.

She had her facts.

She had the authority of a top company behind her, and as a plus for her presentation, she wore and liked the product she was trying to help the client sell.

But the presentation was not ten minutes old before she knew that something was wrong.

There was a distinct chill in the room.

What's wrong, she wondered.

To compensate, she talked faster and a bit louder.

The chill now felt more like icy blasts coming from the client side of the table.

Thirty minutes later—it seemed like thirty hours—the people from the research firm left.

"What did I do wrong?" Lili moaned as they climbed into the station wagon for the trip back to the office.

"Wrong? You were fantastic," said Lili's new employer.

"B-b-b-but they hated me," Lili stammered.

"They loved you. Didn't you see how they kept their distance?"

"Whaaaaat?" she wailed.

The president of the research company laughed. "You have to learn to read people better. These are sober-sided people, and they are composed and correct in all their dealings. When they don't like something you present, or when they don't like someone, they are very sweet. They say things like, 'How kind of you to go to all this bother.' When something really reaches them, they don't want anyone to understand that they are deeply interested or affected or that what they are hearing is so important that they may even change their way of doing business. So instead of being warm and excited, they get cold and distant. The colder the meeting, the hotter the possibilities for change."

"Are all your clients like this?" Lili asked.

"Of course not," the president said, "but until you learn to read the unspoken signals of the company where you want to do business, you'll never be able to do business. And of all the unspoken signals, the most important ones are those the people on the inside exchange."

Power people don't always act like power people. Only a few are like Charles Revson, who always acted like someone who expected to get his own way.

I was once interviewed by an officer of a Fortune 500 company. He was so mild-mannered and unprepossessing that halfway through the interview, I began to interview him. "What is your job and what responsibilities do you have?" I asked.

"I am president and CEO," he said.

I didn't believe him until I went back to my office and checked with his company.

He was the president. He was the CEO. But I would have been equally convinced had he told me he was a third assistant vice president.

Of course, there are people whose confidence seems to come with the genes—like blue eyes or curly hair.

When *New York Magazine* asked a writer to profile Joni Evans, the president of Simon & Schuster, the writer went to Phyllis Levy, the person who gave Ms. Evans her first job after college.

"As the interviewer talked to me about Joni," Ms. Levy said, "I realized something I had never thought about in all the years I have known her. I knew for the first time that when Joni came to see me, just fresh from college, she looked and talked exactly the way she does now. Her clothes may be made by a more famous designer today, but the look is the same. Her hair may be cut by a leading stylist now, but still she looks the same. When I hired her, there were twenty or thirty applicants for the job as my assistant—I was then the fiction editor of a women's magazine—but there was never any doubt in my mind. Joni was just so confident I had to hire her. She was successful before she was successful."

Booby traps

Of the many booby traps that companies keep secret is one called friendship.

Friendship is the two-way street of business.

It is a two-way street because it can work both for and against you, and the way it works for or against you will depend on the company style, not on you.

Our agency has been booby-trapped by friendship many times.

Certainly the story about the executive vice president who would not hire us because we were too well-connected higher up for his comfort was one example.

Another time we were working for a client and doing an excellent job, according to everyone on the client side, when suddenly the company changed presidents. The new president, anxious to make a strong first move, immediately fired our agency and hired an agency he had worked with eighteen years previously. "My closest friend in the world is at that agency," he explained, "and he understands me, so I want to work with him."

Never mind that his closest friend in all the world had not worked on this account for eighteen years.

Never mind that we were doing a creditable job.

Friendship came first.

Friendship has worked the other way for us, too. We have been called in by one-time clients who moved to other companies.

We have been called in by those who know us socially.

But to this day we never know when friendship will work in our favor and when it won't.

It is easy to be booby-trapped by virtues.

Just as "friends" can do you in, so can rectitude.

Mandy had been working for a small cosmetics company. As advertising director, she had no budget for research. Instead she practiced a number of ploys that both she and her employer considered resourceful.

When some months later, Mandy went to work in the advertising department of a large cosmetics company and was approached by her boss and asked to find everything she could about another large cosmetics firm, she remembered one of her previous tactics.

Using her best English accent, Mandy picked up the telephone and called the competitive firm. "I am here from England and am working on my master's thesis. Can you give me some information about your company?"

She dutifully recorded what she was told and turned it in to her superior.

"How did you learn this?" she was asked.

Mandy recounted her resourceful action.

Her superior paused for a moment. "Did you misrepresent yourself and our company?" she was asked.

"Well, yes, I guess I did," Mandy said.

"We operate with trust and with honesty," her superior said.

Mandy was contrite. "I guess I made a judgment error," she whispered.

"No," she was told. "You did not make a judgment error. You made a character error. This company is characterized by its integrity and its ability to operate with honesty. You misjudged our character."

Mandy is learning what everyone eventually learns in business—each company has its own code of ethics and defines its own morality in terms of its business.

To do business the company way requires early knowledge of that specific aspect of company manners.

Conforming to the corporate culture does not mean giving up one's identity and becoming a company clone.

Certainly company manners requires conformity in many situations because conformity of goals and styles gets the job done faster.

But company manners does not mean bowing down to false idols. Instead it means standing up with grace and dignity.

John Johnson, the founder of *Ebony* magazine, tried for many years to get the white advertising community to accept and advertise in his black publications. But these were the early 1960s, and no one was interested.

Advertisers and agencies, however, were interested in maintaining cordial relationships in the black community, and each year Mr. Johnson was invited by the chairman of a large Chicago advertising agency to come to tea in his office. The invitation was always extended during Brotherhood Week.

Finally, one year as the pleasant tea was concluded, Mr. Johnson walked to the door of his host's office. At the door the chairman put his arm around Mr. Johnson's shoulders and started to say his good-byes.

Mr. Johnson took two steps back, unwound the chairman's arm from his shoulder, and said, "Sir, you don't have to love us. Just give us your business."

Those company manners eventually won him much of what he wanted.

CHAPTER

2

The Maverick and the Entrepreneur

At the turn of the century when the original Dixieland Band was first booked by Reisenweber's Restaurant in New York, the restaurant owners were shocked to see that the band members arrived with no music.

Musicians without music?

Impossible!

"No, we don't use sheet music," the jazzmen explained. " 'Cause if we did, what would we do if the lights went out?"

That famous old jazz story is what mavericks are about. Mavericks are the people who operate in business without sheet music. But you have to know the music well before you can perform in public without it.

Mavericks are those who have talent and authority that goes beyond all rules. And, like Picasso, mavericks can break the rules because they know both the rules and the rules' limitations.

Power mavericks, however, do not break the basic power rules. Marvin Davis, whose net worth is believed to be in excess of $1 billion and whose holdings include real estate, oil, and communications, is considered a risk taker, "but not a foolish risk taker," according to those who do business with him. Further, his reputation is such that it is said, "With Davis, a deal is a deal."

The late Bill Veeck, the baseball owner, was an authentic maverick. He wore no neckties in a button-down world of businessmen. He sat in the bleachers with the fans while the other ball club owners sat in their comfortable boxes.

When I first met Bill Veeck, I was a teenage stringer for *Life* magazine, and Mr. Veeck was in Cleveland's University Hospital following a further amputation of his leg as the result of a World War II injury.

As a young, aggressive reporter, I had a question I wanted to ask, but I didn't know quite how to phrase it, so I asked it bluntly. "Mr. Veeck, do you think your handicap will keep you from running the ball club?"

He looked at me from his hospital bed. "Handicap? What handicap?" he asked pointing to the place where his leg should have been. "I don't have any handicap. I like people. The only ones who have a handicap are those who can't get along with others."

Bill Veeck went on to become one of the most successful mavericks in baseball history. He hired the first black player in the American League (Larry Doby), put a midget in as a batter in order to confuse everyone about the batting zone, hired Satchel Paige at a time when he was probably twice the age of most of the players on the team.

But Bill Veeck, like every true maverick, knew that you had to have talent, knowledge, and authority before you could make waves.

John Kluge, ranked by *Forbes* as one of the 400 richest individuals in the United States, came to Cleveland one day to buy a radio station.

At the end of the day he invited some people from our agency to join him for a drink at a local bar.

As we were waiting for our order, Mr. Kluge told us about himself. "I stand on my head every day," he said.

No one said anything.

Mr. Kluge repeated his statement.

Still no one spoke, but I did raise an eyebrow.

Mr. Kluge shook his finger in my direction. "You don't believe me. I know you don't believe me. I can always tell. I once told a woman in Washington that I stood on my head every day, and she looked at me just the way you're looking at me. So you know what I did? Exactly what I'm going to do now. Waiter," he called, "clear this table."

The table was cleared.

No one said a word.

John Kluge put his hands on the table, made certain it was steady, and then he lifted his legs off the floor and stood on his head on a tiny cocktail table in Cleveland, Ohio.

When John Kluge stood on his head that long-ago day, I should have understood that, like all mavericks, he was making a power statement.

And had I been older and smarter, I would have known instantly that I was looking at Power. I would have understood that Power, like opportunity, does not label itself when it comes calling.

And had I been not only older and smarter but also richer, I would have bought his Metromedia stock immediately.

But Mr. Kluge did not put his power into words, and it took time for me to understand and interpret nonverbal communication, to translate the action of the maverick, and decode his hidden agenda.

For, even though every maverick is not an executive, every maverick is an entrepreneur.

The Entrepreneur

Today I can walk into a company, watch the way a man walks, and tell if he owns the place—or acts as if he owns the place.

Not all bosses are entrepreneurs, but all entrepreneurs are bosses, and they are easy to spot.

Head straight ahead, purposeful quick steps, arms swinging.

Is that an entrepreneur?

Never.

The entrepreneur is the one who walks slowly, looks in every office, and sniffs the action—or inaction.

The entrepreneur is the one who has short meetings, short memos, and a short attention span.

The entrepreneur is the one who, when backed into a corner, makes sure it is a corner with a water view, a golden parachute, and a place where you can say "yes" as well as "no."

Being a boss has both pleasures and perils.

The applause is yours, and so are the dents in the image.

The big office is yours, and so is the responsibility for the rent.

But all can be managed with entrepreneurial style.

The entrepreneurial personality is recognizable at an early age. It does not suddenly appear at age 45. Carl Spielvogel, the chairman of Backer & Spielvogel, says that when he hires top-level persons for his advertising agency, he seeks those with entrepreneurial qualities that were demonstrated early: those who had a paper route as a child, the college student who started a computer business, wrote the neighborhood newspaper, organized neighborhood children, and sold grass-cutting and snow removal services.

Many entrepreneurs are salesmen; they not only had an idea, but they managed to sell it to a part of the world. That is why it is often easier to make a sale to an entrepreneur. He knows the satisfaction in hearing someone say "yes," and often he is secure in both his talent and his business. That is one of the primary differences between the corporate executive and the entrepreneur. The corporate executive has fought carefully and diligently to rise to his present position, and still he is nervous. The entrepreneur *enjoys* being where he is. He has created his own environment, as opposed to the corporate executive whose environment has been dictated by earlier regimes. The entrepreneur is more like an expansive, genial host at the party. The corporate executive is still afraid he will use the wrong fork—and blow the whole lifestyle from call cabs to corporate jets.

Since entrepreneurs are idea people, often with high energy levels, and are emotionally involved in their businesses (many know their employees better than their children), an entrepreneur is the most exciting kind of person with whom to share a lunch or a life. Entrepreneurs are never safety first people. They are gamblers, risk takers, those who live on the edge of the knife. Some become entrepreneurs because of a genuine desire to do it "my way." Some feel they are failures and are determined to show that they can be "somebody." Carol Goldberg, the president and chief operating officer of the Stop & Shop Companies in Boston, recalls that as a teenager she was turned down for membership in a girls' club; that was the turning point for her, the time when she made the decision, the promise to herself, that she would be successful.

Just as many comics and humor writers have had unhappy childhoods, so many entrepreneurs have built success on what they perceive to be early failure and the "I-want-to-be-somebody" dream.

The first thing you learn when you run a business is that not only are you "somebody," you are everybody. You cannot be above any job. Edward A. McCabe, the president of Cali, McCabe, Sloves, says, "The world is a better place as a result of Michelangelo not having said, 'I don't do ceilings.' "

In a small business you always know who the owners are. They are the ones who answer the telephones after 5:30.

Lillian M. Katz, chief executive of the Lillian Vernon Corporation, a mail-order catalog company she started, personally tests and approves every product she sells, despite the fact that her company now has sales in excess of $100 million a year. Even her competitors agree that her eye for salable merchandise puts her in the forefront in her field.

Charles P. Lazarus, the founder of the supermarket chain Toys R Us, has never been afraid to do things differently—particularly when it comes to buying and pricing merchandise. Instead of basing his selling price on the wholesale price, Lazarus looks at an item, decides at what price he can sell it in volume, and then decides what price to pay. Evidently this discipline with a difference has worked; company sales today are in excess of $2 billion.

Bossing in an entrepreneurial service business is no different from bossing in a product-oriented business. In order to be a good boss, regardless of the business, you must have a recognizable attitude toward the people and the work. When employees know the way you want things done, when they understand your style and your way of doing things, business life achieves a comfort level for both employee and employer.

But to reach the comfort zone, you have to make some bold moves and set the policy for entrepreneurial company manners.

Don't try to be a conformist

No business is built by people with cookie-cutter mentalities. Even the cookie business is not built that way.

When Debbie Fields, the owner and creator of Mrs. Field's Cookies, went into business, she disregarded all rules. It wasn't that she didn't study the corporate world—she did. But she decided to live by one self-imposed rule: make the finest quality cookies possible. Then, with that goal in mind, she listened to friends who told her that few persons wanted to eat twelve cookies at a time—but no one would feel guilty eating one. The result was a cookie which is thick, rich, chewy, and BIG.

But Mrs. Fields learned quickly that quality cookies were not enough—she was making the best cookies, but no one was coming to her store in Palo Alto to buy them. So she took trays of her cookies and gave them away at Stanford.

There was no book that told her to give away what she wanted to sell. But she did it because she thought it was the best way, and it worked.

One of the reasons that entrepreneurs can operate in the way they think best is that they are creators. And the creative mind is better able to see the unusual solution. Anyone can scratch his right ear with his right hand, but only the creative mind thinks of taking the left arm, bringing it up over the head, and scratching the right ear.

Don't treat your employees equally

The office is not a democracy, so why act as if it is?

After all, were you duly elected by your constituents with everyone having the same vote?

Of course not.

Besides, your employees don't all treat you the same way. Some are inventive and imaginative and work at levels far beyond any job description. Others give the word "minimalist" new meaning. So why should you knock yourself out for raises and bonuses just "to keep two people who have the same job equal?"

Salesmen on commission may have the same job, but they don't always get the same pay. So think about it. If your employees were all on commission, who would be starving and who would be buying his own Rolls Royces?

Equality also extends to meetings. Everybody at the same level does not have to attend meetings. Some attendees only add to the noise level in a vain attempt to prove their importance.

In truth, the best contribution many can make is not to appear at the meeting at all. It is a lot easier to sell a brilliant marketing team when it is not sitting in the same room looking at the ceiling or recovering from an allergy attack.

Don't have any employee as an intimate personal friend

Don't tell the world how you love him like a brother.

Don't tell the world about your parties he attends.

Don't tell the world that you vacation together.

Don't keep reminding yourself that you play golf together.

Stop announcing that his wife and your wife—

Got the picture?

Close personal relationships, relationships based on personal rather than business intimacy, between boss and employee, are death in an office.

They kill the spirit of others who are sure that the two of you are discussing them and their futures every moment. The employee gets the reputation of being able to get anything he wants from you by flattery. And you get a reputation for softness and favoritism. Of course none of that is true—but who believes you?

This is a story about one company where the employer and employee got close. It happened to a jobber of hardware supplies who became the best buddy of one of his salesmen. One day the salesman took a call from a customer. The customer was calling with an order. But instead of putting the order through regular channels, the salesman billed the customer through a company set up in his wife's name. The jobber didn't find out about it until the salesman had managed to put a few deals through the phoney company. The salesman thought his boss would overlook the transgression because, after all, weren't he and his boss like brothers?

What he forgot is that Cain and Abel were like brothers, too. Treachery does strange things to friendships. In the end the firing was painful and hurtful to both men, but it was even sadder for the boss because his trust was violated.

What many employees do not realize is that employers have feelings, too.

So don't play Big Daddy or Big Mommy to any employee.

Don't take any nonbusiness trips together.

Don't get enmeshed in the families of one another.

It all spells trouble with a capital T.

Don't give reasons for everything you do

One of the best things about running a company is that you do not have to be accountable in every instance to those who work for you.

John ran an auto parts company, and he was having a tough time meeting his payroll, but he didn't tell any employee because he knew that the best action for him was to sell his business. He also knew the company would be more valuable if he were able to keep his management team intact. It would be to the advantage of employees to hold on for the sale because they would be able to get an insider price on stock in the new company, and salaries would be adjusted upward to continue the business.

Despite the fact that he had heretofore told them nothing of the company woes, John thought that his people would be pleased to learn how he was planning their futures; he decided to make an insider group his confidantes.

He gathered them together and told them his plan. John was so excited himself that he didn't notice the pinched, nervous faces around him, especially the part about "it's been tough meeting payroll around here lately."

Within two weeks the key players had other jobs, and John lost his deal and eventually his company.

Had he held his cards close and kept his mouth shut, everyone would have done better. But the employees acted out of fear . . . news of a sale is always frightening because employees are concerned that new management will not appreciate them, and—in this case—fear of a nonsale was equally scary.

John thought he was being fair to his workers. He acted out of the belief that sharing is caring.

What he did not realize is that sometimes not sharing is even more caring.

Don't spend too much time making your move

If you are brought in to shake up a company, start mixing and matching as fast as you can.

When Robert Broadbent was made the chairman of Gimbels in New York, he knew that all the people in the department store were waiting for something to happen. He wanted them to know that something was on the way. Still he couldn't inaugurate services or make certain changes without more knowledge. There was one thing, however, that he could do to signal change was on the way.

He changed the direction of the escalators. When employees and customers came to the store one morning, they found that all the up escalators went down, and all the downs went up.

When customers asked what happened, salespersons said, "I guess the new chairman is going to change things."

And so he did.

To establish credibility as a leader, do at least three of the following as soon as possible:

1. Add a new division.
2. Consolidate or lop off a present department.
3. Add new people; reassign and reward present employees.
4. Get rid of the unfireables—the people who couldn't (but should) have been fired under previous management.
5. Change the method of accounting.
6. Do not change accountants, lawyers, advertising agencies, or other outside services for one year—they are your best eye on the inside.

7. Ask a lot of questions, and demand answers within a month—this will create a flurry of activity which is always a healthy sign in an office.

8. Contact key people in your industry, and arrange dates in your office or outside for luncheon, breakfast, tea, or a get-acquainted meeting—your staff will be impressed that you know the industry leaders and have access to them, and this will reinforce management's judgment.

9. Improve working conditions—add a lunchroom or a kitchen facility—but make sure that the improvement you institute is one that benefits all and not just the privileged few.

10. Update present benefit plans—and if you do that, you probably don't have to do the nine other things so far as employees are concerned.

Don't accept anything until you're sure it's the best

During the Tonkin Bay situation, Henry Kissinger asked an assistant to prepare an analysis. The assistant worked night and day for a week and put the document on Mr. Kissinger's desk only to receive it back within an hour. Affixed to the report was a note asking that it be redone. The assistant dutifully redid it; he slept a total of nine hours for a week. The document went on Mr. Kissinger's desk, and an hour later it was returned with a note from Mr. Kissinger assuring that he expected better and asking that the work be done again.

And so the assistant went back to the drawing board once more. Another week of intense work, and then the assistant asked if he might present it personally to Mr. Kissinger. When he came face to face with Henry Kissinger, he said, "Mr. Kissinger, I've spent another sleepless week. This is the best I can do."

Said Henry Kissinger, "In that case, now I'll read it."

Don't be proud of dumb things

It's dumb to be proud of production records rather than products.

It's dumb to be proud of a plant rather than the working conditions of your employees.

It's dumb to flaunt your wealth and then try to tell employees that times are tough, vacations must be canceled, etc.

It's dumb to ask employees to make any sacrifice you are not willing to make in kind. We have lived through a lot of tough times in our business. At one point in the 1970s things were really going downhill in our New York office, so we gave up our glamorous-view-of-the-river offices on Third Avenue and moved to tiny, cramped space on East 56th Street. I had an office that was reached only by walking through two other offices, and I shared a telephone with another writer. During the year we lived that way—until times improved—no one in the office ever complained. Once our office space grew, however, so did the demands.

Don't be afraid to gamble the irreplaceable things: Your popularity and your successful image in the business community

When James Wood took over the chairmanship of the Great Atlantic and Pacific Tea Company in 1980, the supermarket chain was limping toward oblivion. Within five years, Wood had not only recognized the problems, he had cured them.

In his first two years, James Wood closed more than 500 stores, eliminated 20,000 employees, and reduced corporate revenues by 50 percent. He announced that the company would be regional rather than local. Additionally he sought ways to make more employees entrepreneurs. He did it by creating a subsidiary, Super Fresh, that operates supermarkets in the Philadelphia area. If employees at Super Fresh keep labor costs down to a predetermined level, they share 1 percent of the sales in their stores.

A good entrepreneur knows that entrepreneurialism is not confined to the chairman or president of a company.

An entrepreneur, however, has to instill the entrepreneurial spirit in his associates.

Kent was the executive vice president of a tool and die company. J. R., the owner-boss, had an expansive personality. A kind of hail-fellow-well-met, he was everybody's friend. The company, in a small Michigan town, provided a fine income for J. R., a good income for Kent. J. R. belonged to the best country club in the next town and had both a tennis court and swimming pool at his home. Kent belonged to the small country club in the town where he lived, and his wife played golf there. One day she came home and reported to Kent, "I played with a woman today whose husband is very ill. It's so sad. I know they need to sell their company; I think it's a good fit for you."

Kent snorted. "The last time I tried to tell J. R. about anything, he told me point blank not to get involved in anything that wasn't my job."

Two weeks later in a staff meeting, J. R. said, "I wish we had known about that company in your town that was for sale, Kent. Our biggest competitor bought it."

Kent said nothing. But the problem was J. R.'s, not Kent's. J. R. never gave Kent the confidence to contribute outside his defined area of operation.

The company operated with a one-man success style.

It's important to remember that you don't have to hand down the mantle in order to hand down the right to wear it from time to time. There are days when anyone who wants should be able to borrow the king's crown and operate like an owner.

Never underestimate the contribution of a spouse

Depending on the state of the marriage, there is a greater or lesser willingness to value the advice a spouse can give an entrepreneur in running a business.

Meg was so pleased when she started her business. It was her first independent move since leaving college. Then she found that in order to get a loan, she needed her husband as a cosigner. Then she found in order to get a warehouse lease, she needed her husband as a cosigner. She was not only disappointed; she was angry. This was to be *her* business, *her* statement. As a result she was determined to run the business without his counsel. And so she did.

When her husband offered to introduce her to an associate of his who might have become her biggest account, she said, "No. No, I want to do it myself."

Six months later her business failed. It did not fail because she refused to meet that one man; it failed because she was too involved with the do-it-myself philosophy.

The lesson, of course, is that help can come from anywhere.

Why not let a spouse help you? The only thing in life that is really difficult is when no one helps you.

Arthur Carter, who founded Carter, Berlind, Weill, Levitt— the brokerage house that grew into American Express/Shearson-Lehman—says that the company never would have happened had his wife not been friendly with Joan Weill, the wife of Sanford Weill. "The two wives were best friends and brought us together," he admits easily.

Don't be everybody's mentor

Ever since mentor became a buzzword, men and women with an upward eye have been vying for mentors.

Mentoring is not really a new occupation for bosses; apprentices have been seeking guidance ever since the beginning of the guild and the world of bosses and employees began. But, as the employer, be careful not to play the role too well in your own office or you will make the rest of your staff sick with concern that you are paying too much attention to certain employees.

Mentoring, generally, is better when you confine it to people outside your own office, people who are not dependent on you for raises and promotions.

Of course, mentoring doesn't always begin that way.

Generally mentoring starts when someone who works with you graduates to a new job—and your interest continues.

A good mentor is not simply a listening post and a clucking, sympathetic person. A good mentor is tough.

When Helen Fisher was with McKinsey & Co., the management firm, she met Louis V. Gerstner, Jr., now president of American Express. After only two weeks with McKinsey, Ms. Fisher was sent on assignment to Philadelphia with Mr. Gerstner. After their day of work, he invited her to dinner. Ms. Fisher walked confidently into the restaurant; she was certain that she was going to hear how good she was. Instead Mr. Gerstner sat down to dinner and told her everything she was doing wrong. Ms. Fisher, who is now with *Fortune Magazine,* regards that meeting as a turning point, a time when she began to assess realistically her qualifications, talents, and aptitudes in the business world. Although she and Mr. Gerstner no longer work together, he has continued to play a mentoring role in her life.

Accept responsibility, but make sure you're not somebody's fall guy

Recent financial history is redolent with deception, double dealing, and intrigue, and it has all been detailed in stories that have grabbed headlines for days, weeks, and months. There is, in the background of all these stories, a villain.

There is always a villain, no matter what the story.

There were villains in mythology, in fairy stories, in the Bible, in Shakespeare. We seek culpability in all adventures; we want to identify the person responsible for the dastardly deed. The only difference between ancient history and the history we write is that now we work to create our own villains; we want to make someone the fall guy.

Regardless of the size of your company, make sure you do not become anybody's fall guy. You will not be the fall guy if

1. You do not grab the headlines and announce everything as a one-man band.

2. You do not assume sole financial responsibility for anything that happens in the company.

3. You appoint committees whose actions must be approved and made known.

4. You make sure that if anything goes wrong, there is someone who can immediately leave the company and become the fall guy, because, as you have probably noticed, many reports of financial misdeeds are followed by a CEO saying, "We didn't even know what was going on. It was all because of X, and he left the company ten months ago."

Pitfalls of the entrepreneur

When business is good, it's all fun. And even when business isn't good, it's another kind of fun. But because the entrepreneur is a unique personality, there are unique pitfalls:

1. The entrepreneur frequently is unable to delegate. Nobody ever does things with quite your entrepreneurial flair. I see it in our business when an account for whom I wrote the original copy now has its campaign written by another agency person. It's never written precisely the way I'd write it. I delegate, but not with joy.

2. Entrepreneurs become convinced of their own immortality. They are aware that others may be mortal; indeed the obituary columns are filled with stories about the brilliant lives of men and women who were alive yesterday. But even though the entrepreneur often recognizes the mortality of his associates, he cannot imagine his business with-

out his running it, and so with delusions of immortality, he creates no succession plan. "Next year I'll do something," he says.

He may have hundreds of employees, but in his opinion none is good enough to succeed him.

3.   Entrepreneurs, these idea persons and sales persons, frequently lack management skills. They are unable to build a staff and train that staff. An entrepreneur is frequently overdeveloped in one area and underdeveloped in another. His continual preoccupation with hands-on management makes him less than ideal in terms of training subordinates. The most damning statement about any business is, "Yes, but who is there beyond the president?"

4.   The small business person lacks capital for expansion, and often he or she is inexperienced in financing and, with the concern for self-image so common to entrepreneurs, does not seek the kind of professional help that will answer the problem.

5.   The success syndrome can make the business collapse ahead of its time. Daniel Scoggin, president of TGI Friday's, Inc., the theme restaurant chain, has found that when one of his restaurants opens, the employees are always gracious and the food excellent. But after the restaurant has been operating for a while, Daniel Scoggin notes that success changes the entrepreneur, and instead of being Plain Old Joe, a guy with a restaurant, he is now Mr. So-and-So.

And Daniel Scoggin has learned that Mr. So-and-So never has quite the same personal, caring quality toward the business as Joe.

Entrepreneurs are not always in charge of businesses that they own.

Entrepreneurs may work for others and are found in every business everywhere. Yet, regardless of the style or size of the business, the entrepreneurial personality emerges in many of the same ways, and both entrepreneurial employer and employee share the same concerns.

Problems of the entrepreneur

1. There is no real satisfaction for the entrepreneur because he can never find the perfect solution. He seeks only perfection, is not satisfied unless he feels he finds it—and, of course, he never finds it. There is always an unfulfilled restlessness about the entrepreneur; it is part of both his success and his frustration.

2. Success is never assured, and the entrepreneur cannot deal with anything but success. Whether an owner or a hired hand, he wants all decisions to be perfect; when they are not, he tends to reshape history until they are.

3. The entrepreneur frequently alienates his family and friends because he believes it is "right" to let the business come first and make the company his mother, spouse, child, and best friend. The missed family dinners, the postponed trips, the canceled plans are the marks and trademarks of the person who feels he is the only one who can solve the problems at hand.

    As a result the entrepreneur often feels lonely, complains that he has no one to talk to. He forgets that he has consciously reduced his audience and willingly bypassed those who would offer him emotional support.

4. The entrepreneur, the person who built the business, is a hands-on person. As the business prospers, he will lose the direct control. This is true of the person in the corporation who has entrepreneurial skills as well as the entrepreneur who found and directs his own business.

    The entrepreneur finds that, increasingly, he must become familiar with procedures that are "big business,"

procedures that give him more frustration and less satisfaction.

5. Many managers become experts not in MBO (manage-
    ment by objectives) but rather in MBE (management by
    event). Instead of making decisions, there are those who
    permit decisions to make themselves.

Donald was the hired editor-publisher of a city magazine. His
indecisiveness was visible to all the staff. They could see his desk
piled with six weeks' worth of trade publications, stacks of un-
answered mail, and invitations for last month's events. When the
magazine owners suggested that perhaps the publication needed
a new format, Donald said he'd look into it. When the owners
suggested that perhaps there was an opportunity for offering local
advertisers small-space ads at a special local rate, Donald said he
would look into it. Donald knew that eventually things would take
care of themselves.

And so they did.

The owners hired a new manager.

MBE is the greatest pitfall of the entrepreneur and a major
cause of underuse of executives and poor morale.

Style and energy start in the corner office with the entrepreneurial spirit of the person who runs things.

Every time you find a manager who thinks "it will all take care
of itself" when it comes to a succession plan or implementation
of new ideas or decisions on risktaking, you see an indecisive
manager and a business that is stuck in its own time warp.

True entrepreneurial style is exhibited by those who are not
afraid to make mistakes.

And in order to minimize the possibility for error and maximize the possibilities for success, there must be solid, well-
considered reasons for action and back-up positions for failure.

The Executive Style: The Yeses and Nos, the Hirings and Firings, the Criticizing and the Promotion to "Up There"

Executives are entrepreneurs who age well.

While genius may put a man or woman in the corner office, genius alone does not keep one there.

Steven P. Jobs was brilliant enough to cofound Apple Computer, but he was not brilliant enough to win a power struggle with John Sculley.

James L. Dutt made Beatrice Cos., Inc., the largest food and consumer products marketer in the nation, but he was ousted in a Saturday morning massacre at a special meeting of the Beatrice board. Wall Street greeted the news by driving the stock up $2 a share on Monday.

Following the meeting, it was generally agreed by members of the financial community that there was no disagreement concerning Mr. Dutt's strategy. It was his brusque style that did him in. A Merrill Lynch analyst said that institutions felt that Mr. Dutt was unapproachable and belligerent and saw his personality, not his market precepts, as the reason for his downfall.

An E. F. Hutton analyst remarked that while Mr. Dutt may

have been known for his arrogance, it is to be expected that you will step on a few toes when you run a $12 or 13 billion company.

It is, however, not necessary for executives to step on toes. It may even be dangerous to your corporate health because—thanks to green mail, junk bonds, mortgage-backed securities, Pac-Man defense, shark repellents, and white knights—it is possible for that little company you offended or ignored yesterday to be your employer tomorrow.

Therefore, what you say and the way that you say it is more important than ever.

The way you say "no" and the way you give criticism can come back to haunt you.

The Unspoken No

The single most dangerous word to be spoken in business is "no."

The second most dangerous word is "yes."

It is possible to avoid saying either, and this is done regularly as one of the unspoken but highly used techniques of company manners.

Derek was made president of the frozen foods division of a large food company. It was a job he had dreamed of getting for seven years, and he was astonished when, the first week in office, the chairman invited him to luncheon only to say, "Derek, my son-in-law is with one of the metals companies. Now let me give you his name. I'm sure you'll want to use his company for your packaging."

Derek was tempted to throw his napkin on the table and walk out of the company dining room.

But he was saved by his company manners.

He remembered that nothing said is nothing done.

And so Derek said nothing.

He did not say he would give the chairman's son-in-law the

business. He did not say that he would not. Instead he listened intently and nodded frequently. He even smiled twice.

At the end of the luncheon the chairman shook Derek's hand. "I am sure you're going to have a great run, Derek," he said as he slapped the new president on his shoulder.

The chairman strode back to his office, picked up the telephone, and phoned his son-in-law. "Call Derek," he instructed. "He is going to have some business for you."

When the son-in-law called, Derek was polite. He invited him to luncheon at a pleasant—but not overly expensive—French restaurant. The two men chatted amicably.

"I certainly hope we'll be able to work together," the son-in-law said.

Derek nodded. He said nothing.

Now, six months later, Derek has still given no business to the chairman's son-in-law. And the chairman, like most CEOs, is too busy putting out fires outside his window to remember that luncheon with Derek.

But Derek knows eventually he will remember and call him in. When he does, Derek knows what he will say. Derek will nod sagely and speak slowly, "I have several people looking at that. We are reviewing costs now."

Then Derek knows that he will wait for at least one more year before he says to the chairman, "I'd like to give your son-in-law the business, but my people feel the quality really isn't there . . . at least not for the price."

Derek will never say "no" to his chairman.

His company manners are too sharp for that.

Instead of a verbal "no," the best players in corporate roulette today offer the implied "yes."

The ability to avoid "no" is helping many people move up today.

Other lines that give the effect of "no" without the spoken "no" are

- May I think about that and get back to you?
- I'd like to do some research and find out what the consumer thinks.
- What a good idea! Let me see if Jim has room for it in his budget.

Just as "no" is frequently said without allowing anyone to lose face, so is criticism given without permitting people to feel so diminished that they are unable to function effectively afterwards.

Unlike the self-serving aspects of the unspoken no, the purpose of company manners criticism is to increase productivity, not to decrease self-esteem.

The Critical Abilities

A sign of comfort in the executive suite is evidenced by the ability to give criticism.

Criticism is one of the subtle arts of management, and it is increasingly being recognized as such.

When the Rhode Island School of Design was interviewing candidates for head of the Sculpture Department, one of the tests for applicants was to critique student work.

Administrators wanted to see if candidates were able to praise without deluding.

Were they able to criticize without dashing all hope of aspiring artists?

On what was criticism based?

With a contemporary businesslike attitude toward teaching, the eminent design school showed that it believes teaching is more than imparting old truths; it also includes the giving and accepting of criticism, the new truth.

What the Rhode Island School of Design discovered in their talent search was that many applicants with impressive work records, truly accomplished people, were sometimes inarticulate and unable to engage the students in productive dialogue.

* * *

The same thing happens in business.

There are people who do their jobs well who are unable to help others grow because they are incapable of instructing without offending or criticizing without alienating.

Good criticism can cause talented people to perform at a better level, and it can strengthen the relationship between the giver and the taker.

Most of us tend to have confidence in those who criticize us with both compassion and honesty; this communicates a kind of company manner that will work in any business.

The techniques of criticism can be developed with thought.

Watch your opening lines

I was in a client meeting one day when a product manager presented a market plan. He was four minutes into the plan when the executive vice president said, "That's ridiculous. We'll never do anything like that."

All of us from the agency were embarrassed for the product manager. What happened eventually was that the executive vice president was fired, a victim of his own critical style. The product manager had slunk away long before.

The message from this story comes through loud and clear: start all criticism in neutral. Don't go in blasting.

Start with simple, nonemotional phrases:

"I'd like to give this more time. Come back to me next week for a decision."

"Let's ask some other people for their opinions."

Don't make any criticism a personal criticism

It isn't always easy to walk that fine line because people who have to listen to criticism tend to believe that what supervisors say is personally directed. I think the height of diplomacy was reached in our office the time an art director designed a coupon ad with the ad in reverse; the type was in white on a black background. The art director simply said, "It looks very good. Now fill out the coupon for me." Of course, it meant a white pen was needed, so the whole idea was impossible to execute, and the gaffe was turned into an office joke. A touch of humor always relieves a bleak situation.

Because personal criticism is what employees fear, here are some other ways to communicate displeasure with the *idea* and not the *thinker:*

"I don't think the job will support this kind of budget." (Instead of, "You're out of line on finances.")

"Don't forget the person you want to reach—will this appeal?" (Instead of, "This copy is all wrong.")

Always give a reason for the criticism

The day of the supervisor who says, "I don't like it. I can't tell you why I don't like it. I just don't like it," is gone.

No business can afford to play the game of likes and don't likes.

We equate time with money, and it costs too much money for us to fail to pinpoint criticism.

Every good business relationship is a working partnership, and productivity will be increased the minute the employer levels with the employee and explains carefully what he likes and what he doesn't like—and why.

Remember, too, that the *why* is more important than the *don't like.*

Suggest a change if you can

If you have an idea that will make the project fly—give it. But, as a good boss, make sure that the person to whom you are giving the idea understands that it is only a suggestion. If it is a mandate, then tell him. And tell him in unmistakable terms. "This is what I want done, and I do not want to see any alternative suggestions."

Try to help solve the problem

Don't give all the reasons for your "no" and then turn your back.

There is a second step, the step that moves people in a good direction.

The second step is to ask questions.

This is particularly helpful to new employees who are truly trying their best to come up with solutions. Sometimes asking a few questions can put them on track quickly.

Questions that probe and help them think their way through a problem will increase a worker's confidence and trust in you. Questions such as

What do you want to happen?

Who is your audience?

What do you think personally is the way to do this?

What does the research tell you?

Can you find a similar experience in the marketplace?

All those questions can be used to begin a dialogue that can lead to a solution.

Don't follow criticism by doing the job yourself

A copywriter who came to work for us told us about her last boss. When a piece of copy was wrong, the boss put a piece of paper in the typewriter, wrote the copy himself, and then handed it to the person. "See how easy it is," he would add. "I don't know why you're having so much trouble."

Removing all initiative and not permitting someone to correct his own mistakes may be the worst thing you can do to a person of value.

If you are on the receiving end of criticism, understand what someone is trying to do by

Thanking the critic for both time and interest

Most of the time the hours spent with a critique can be used for other matters by the critic. The purpose is to make you better at what you do. Not a lot of people in business will take the time to try to make you better.

Be sure to say thank you.

This is the beginning of mentoring.

Redo the work and inform your critic

If the work does not have to pass over the critic's desk again, be sure that you let the critic know how you have used the help given.

Extra special is the person who also takes the time to write a thank-you note.

The business thank-you note is probably the most unexpected and most rewarding gesture of all. The greatest pro in note-writing history was Jacqueline Susann; she even wrote thank-yous to the teamsters who delivered her books.

Don't discuss criticism with the rest of the office

The produce buyer of a supermarket was called in by the president and chastised for buying practices that the president believed resulted in inferior produce.

When the buyer left the president's office, he was so angry that he told all his associates. Many of them were disappointed in the president's handling of the matter, but even more of them were surprised to find that the produce buyer didn't have the confidence of the president.

By the end of the day, the produce buyer didn't have the confidence of his associates either, and within days he was actively seeking another job.

*   *   *

Most people are more adept at praising employees. The only problem may be praising when there is no reason.

Walter Kerr, the eminent theater critic, once wrote, "Undeserved praise screws everything up."

A kind word, however, can be remembered forever.

When Edwin K. Hoffman was the president of the Higbee Co., we produced a Christmas catalog for the store. The day that the first copy came off the presses, I took the catalog to Mr. Hoffman's office. With me was my assistant, Jane Sherwin. We sat, Jane and I, side by side on a love seat while Ed Hoffman wordlessly turned the pages and read every word, looked at every picture. Finally he looked up. Still he said nothing. Then he stood, walked to the windows in his office, faced outside, and after what seemed like a small eternity, turned and faced us, "You will have a lot of clients in your business life, and you will not always make them happy. But I always want you to remember that at least once in your agency's history you made a client very happy." Then he walked to his desk and took an Indian icon from a pile of papers. "I want you to have this," he said to me. "It goes from my desk to your desk, and any time you fail to please a client, just look at that and say, 'Well, at least I did it once.' "

That Indian icon still sits on my desk.
Sometimes I look at it a lot.
And then there are times when I don't need it at all.

When I need it most is when I have to be the bearer of bad news.

The business definition of bad news is any information which will shake your confidence in yourself and your company and the confidence of the people who report to you.

Communicating bad news is a responsibility of management, and the single most difficult negative news to communicate is termination of employment of a person for whom you once had high hopes.

How do you fire without pain to the employee?

Without pain to yourself?

The answer is quite simple. You don't.

Even the most hardened employers, after years in business, feel remorse, regret, and a terrible sadness when an employee—whatever the reason—must be let go.

Termination is the ultimate bad news for an employee.

Firings, however, while the worst news for an individual, do not constitute all business bad news.

Losing a piece of business is medium bad news for an office.

Not getting a piece of business is disappointing, and depending on the order not won, can be anywhere from 1 to 10 on the bad news scale.

What can make bad news tolerable is the manner in which the company chooses to communicate the negative.

There are company manners for dealing with bad news.

One cannot make bad news better by putting it in a quasi-social situation such as lunch.

Indeed, no bad news should ever be delivered over lunch because the person on the receiving end should have the right to get out fast if he or she so wishes. Besides, you—as the message bearer—have no right to restrict the emotional or nonemotional reaction of the recipient by putting your drama in a public place.

In announcing bad news, there are some things to consider:

Don't put the blame on Mame

When the company loses a piece of business, you have to make certain that your best people don't begin to point fingers and begin to question their own abilities. The last thing you want to do is cause them to lose confidence and become less effective.

Because all the world really is a stage and because each of us thinks he is the only player, we all tend to blame ourselves when things go bad.

"If I hadn't . . . ."

"If I didn't . . . ."

In truth, each one of us is only a part of the reason the business didn't happen.

The most important first step is to notify your key players as a group. Have a meeting or gather them in an office or meeting room and give them the news.

Tell them what happened, why you think it happened, and repeat your confidence in their abilities as a team. It is important to keep the team spirit going when the team has just been pushed off the field.

In dealing with the group, watch for expressions on faces.

Who looks crushed?

Who has that I-knew-we'd-lose-this-if-no-one-listened-to-me look?

The job of the manager is to reinforce the confidence and good feeling of the person who seems most burdened by the loss.

Often the kindest thing to do when the business is lost is to get in touch as soon as possible with the person who seems most devastated by the news.

Bring him or her into your office, and give your additional reassurance and confidence by reminding him that had you been a winner, you wouldn't have given him all the credit. So now that you've lost, he has to stop putting himself in for all the blame. You share the blame, just as you would share the glory.

Then start asking, "Why?"

If "why" comes from a genuine desire to improve—and your associates have been reassured in terms of their own culpability— you may indeed be able to shore the company's vulnerable areas and come back a winner next time.

You're Fired!

Everyone has a horror story when it comes to firing.

There is the story of the man who was personnel director of a large steel company, and when the steel industry in the United States came on hard times, the personnel director was given the names of five people to fire immediately. Not only was he to fire them, but he was to ask them to clear their desks and be out of the building within one hour. The man gritted his teeth and did what he had to do. At the end of the day, with a heavy heart, he went to the president of the company and reported that he had done his job. "Very good," said the president. "Now pack up your things. You're fired, too."

Still another firing story is about the personnel director of an advertising agency who was delighted when he was told he was to fire one of the creative directors, a man the personnel director loathed. When the creative director came in, the personnel director couldn't resist adding an extra twist. Instead of saying simply, "You're fired," he said, "I don't like you, and I'm firing you."

The creative director took two steps back, said not one word, but instead picked up the marble top from the personnel director's desk and threw it out the plate glass window into an alley below.

Bad news can make people very emotional.

When it's necessary for the good of the company to end a relationship (for reasons other than stealing, dishonest business practices, or immorality), there are humane steps.

(a) Set the stage, and give adequate warning.

This should be done before you have definitely made up your mind about continuing employment. At this one-to-one meeting review the job description, discuss areas in which you are pleased and displeased, and give the employee a prescribed period to get his act together. The meeting should end with your setting the date for the next meeting. You both know that the employee now is on review and that a change in performance is required.

(b) Schedule a second meeting to review progress.

At this point, one of three things will have happened:

After the announced time, (a) if there has been meas-
urable improvement, you so tell the employee but do not
take him off warning; you set a next meeting to see if
progress continues and if he comes all the way up to
expected standards. (b) If there is a turnaround situation,
you encourage the employee and tell him that you are
pleased to know that the concern you had was only tem-
porary. There should, however, be no special considerations for performing at the level expected; that is, there
should be no bonus, no increase in salary for performing
at the level demanded of others. (c) If there is no progress, you have the basis for terminating the employee.

Unfortunately not all firings can be handled in this way, a way
that permits the employee who is uncertain about his future to
begin to cast about for another situation.

If you find, for one reason or another, that you must fire
someone immediately, you learn through experience that the sooner
the better. In almost every office there is a thin thread of gossip
that links every eventuality with every person, and it is that water
cooler talk that ices the relationships within the office. So to keep
the temperature comfortable, talk as soon as possible.

Bring the person who is about to become your newest ex-
employee into your office. Over the years I have found that the
best opening line is the simplest opening line: "You've probably
guessed why I asked you to come to see me. I wish I had good
news for you, but I do not." That opening gives you the groundwork for stating the reason for the firing.

If you can, give a reference and/or the right to use your name
as a reference. If there are special arrangements for severance,
you may choose to discuss those or tell the person to deal directly
with your personnel director. Generally, the less the person who
is about to leave has to speak with you, the more comfortable you
will both be.

Reactions over the ending of any long-term employment are
emotional for the two of you.

Get out the handkerchiefs

Who says grown men don't cry?

When *Life* magazine died a few years ago (yes, the very same *Life* magazine that was resuscitated by its parent, Time, Inc.), Andrew Heiskell, then the publisher, wept in front of the staff.

When bad news comes, it does help to cry.

Women, particularly, have been afraid to shed tears in the workplace lest they be thought weaker than men.

I have had to fire men who wept at the news.

I have had to fire women who didn't.

I never thought more of people who remained tearless or less of those who wept. I do think, however, that the people who let their emotions show will recover faster.

It has been my experience that the person who gets rid of the emotional detritus will be healthy soon again.

After firing, what?

Pick yourself up, dust yourself off, and start all over again.

If, however, you feel compelled to write to your ex-boss, make sure that your letter has a tone that you will not regret were you to read the letter one year later.

Do people write to me after leaving?

Yes. Some of the people who have been most helpful to me have been those who wrote to me after leaving. I will confess that the helpful letters have all been signed and have been from people who were not fired but who went on to other jobs.

I consider helpful those letters that have told me about perceived office injustices (inability of creative people to get their work seen), possible infractions of office rules (drinking), and ways of improving office morale (retirement program).

What is the company manner in dealing with persons who have been fired and use you as a reference?

Honesty is always the best policy.

When you are called by the potential employer, tell the reason. Obviously if you are overstaffed, the reason is supportable.

If the person was fired for any infraction of office rules, that should be stated—and, if you think that the person was made stronger or more responsible as a result—tell the personnel director.

Under no circumstances should you paint a picture so rosy that it becomes difficult to know the person you're describing.

Honesty among peers is perhaps the important outside evidence of company manners.

Making a Move

Today we know that even founders of big public companies do not last forever (look at Steven Jobs of Apple); those who try to buy companies and have them bought from under them cannot be counted out because they can still come back and make it (look at Donald Kelley and Beatrice Foods).

We know that it is no longer shocking to change corporate presidents; titles are no longer automatically handed to executives for use until age 65. After a merger or takeover the bailout begins.

In late 1985 the *Wall Street Journal* reported that a recent survey of senior executives whose companies were acquired found that almost half sought other positions within one year; a similar study four years earlier showed that only 20 percent left in the first year. "The company's assets and franchise are primary, and the people are secondary," is the reason given by Windle Priem, a managing director at Korn/Ferry, the international executive search firm.

So we who observe the marketplace know that it is no longer a disgrace to be unemployed after 45; it is happening to some of the best and the brightest.

It is also not a disgrace—it is, in fact, downright intelligent—

to seek competent experts to help you find the job that fits your talents today.

Of course, there is more than one way to get a job today.

Stanley Pace was the president of TRW. He was a year away from retirement, and as part of his responsibility to the corporate community, he also assumed the presidency of the National Association of Manufacturers (NAM). In his NAM role, he called on General Dynamics, and in just a few meetings the people at General Dynamics decided that they liked what they saw. They dropped a few hints; Pace was pursued and offered the job of CEO at General Dynamics. He accepted.

That kind of business-to-business hiring is not unusual. All of us, whether hirers or hirees, whether we are looking for people to hire or want to make a change ourselves, become adept at dropping hints.

And we all know how to recognize the well-placed hint.

When a person who owns or runs a company asks if you can suggest someone for a particular job, he may indeed be asking if you are available for the assignment.

We also know that failing to pick up the hint is the silent rejection, which is the loudest "no" in business.

For years the *New York Times* ran ads that began, "I got my job through the *New York Times*." To this day many lower level jobs come through responses to box number ads on the financial pages of newspapers and business magazines.

It does not happen at higher levels.

People with polish, pizzazz, and performance credits are needed for the big jobs, and they are not the ones who answer the want ads.

So how does one find and qualify next year's stars?

By dropping hints in meetings, by calling friends in allied industries who have access to the kind of person you need to fill the bill, and by looking around at those involved in local power charities and/or those in the places of leisure-time activity—parties, tennis courts, golf courses, yacht clubs.

Getting the name is, of course, only the first step. The in-depth interview is the hard part.

What executive has not struggled through the rudiments in learning about a person who is cosmetically perfect only to find him or her intellectually lacking or inexperienced?

When he was the head of Monogram Industries, Marshall Karp hired executives only after he played tennis with them. He was convinced that he could learn everything he needed to know, from cheating to aggressiveness and graciousness, just watching someone play.

Not all people, however, are hired as a result of the chance meeting, the want ad or the tennis game.

Headhunters

Enter the executive search firm, popularly known as the head-hunter.

The term "executive search firm" has become popular during the past decade, although executive recruiters have been a part of the business scene for decades.

The executive search firm, the headhunter, is several notches above the personnel agency.

Personnel agencies generally function by seeking jobs for people who have registered with them. Executive recruiters, on the other hand, usually begin with a job description and seek the person who qualifies.

An unwritten rule in executive recruiting is that for two years following a search for a corporate client, the recruiter will consider all of that client's employees untouchable. Further, no search firm should place a candidate in one job only to replace him in another job situation.

Who needs a headhunter?

Any employer who believes that the qualifications for the job(s) to be filled exceed those of the candidates currently being presented for consideration and any employee at the executive level who (a) wants to explore the possibilities for changing jobs, or (b) wants to change jobs without anyone at his present place knowing that he wants to change jobs.

For many middle management people, the headhunter is the evaluator, the arbiter of one's true worth in the marketplace. Indeed there are people who are dissatisfied—until they talk to a headhunter, have an opportunity to see what's available, and then go back to their old jobs with renewed vigor.

But that is not the usual circumstance.

From a distance the grass is always greener and the perks always fresher.

The definition of a great headhunter is one who finds you the job (if you're looking) or the employee (if you're looking) you would not have found (if only you were looking).

There are hundreds of such executive search companies, and each industry has specialists.

Headhunting is a billion dollar industry in the United States.

The four largest search firms on retainer to employers are the following: Korn/Ferry International, Russell Reynolds Associates, Spencer Stuart (all New York), and Heidrick & Struggles (Chicago).

Headhunters are the seducers of the business world, and just as a good marriage cannot be rent asunder by an attempted seduction, neither can a good working relationship.

The job of the headhunter is to match prospective employee and prospective employer in such a way that corporate profits are increased and working conditions bettered.

Most bosses, however, talk about their working relationships but fail to work at it.

Obviously if each of us hired brilliantly, created constantly the precise program to stimulate and reward employees, patted them frequently, and had the next job in readiness at the moment employees needed it, there would be no need for headhunters.

In this less-than-perfect world, however, none of the above exists.

What does it cost to use a headhunter?

Nothing if you are the person seeking the job.

A percentage fee (it can be as little as 10 percent of the year one salary, but under some circumstances it can be as high as 35 percent) is arranged between the agency and the employer.

Headhunting is the computer dating of the corporate world.

Whether you are looking for a job or an employee, a headhunter is capable of helping you find your match in the marketplace.

How does a job hunter find the right headhunter?

The best way to begin is to find the names of the headhunters specializing in placements in your business.

If you are a job hunter who does not know the names of the executive search firms in your industry, call the industry trade association for names.

Or, if you are willing to share the confidence, ask others in your city who are in your industry.

And don't be above the obvious: check the Yellow Pages.

When you go to see a headhunter, be sure that you tell him or her exactly what you want in terms of challenge and compensation. Generally these are the things that make a difference, so think about them:

(a) Compensation

Be willing to disclose your current salary.

Be ready to name the kind of financial package that you want. Remember that salary is only one part of what you request; there should also be other financial perks including opportunities for increased earnings based on performance.

(b) Title

If you are hung up on titles (don't be ashamed; some of the best-known executives are), tell the headhunter.

If you long to be a vice president, don't whisper in your pillow. Say it out loud. The time to get what you want is before you meet the bride, not later.

(c) Challenge

If you're restless in your present job situation because there are no more mountains to climb, tell that to your recruiter. Don't play games, and don't be coy. If you really want someone special, then you had better open up and express your feelings about challenge.

On the other hand, if you don't want competition and heavy breathing on all sides during the workday, tell that to the recruiter. Every company is not looking for a next president tomorrow. Some industries need good senior and junior executives today.

If you don't want to travel, be sure to tell the recruiter.

More and more search firms are adding human resource consulting to the services proferred.

If it is your spouse's turn to make the career move in terms of where you'll live, tell that to your recruiter. Gilbert Tweed Associates in New York offers Spouse-Search to help the relocating spouse find work in a new area.

Spencer Stuart does compensation surveys for search clients to help them define the position and price the job in the market.

Handy Associates' executive compensation practice has a staff that plans, designs, and puts in place compensation and incentive programs that include such things as annual plans, long-term performance plans, stock plans, estate-building options, and a retirement income program.

Play fair with your recruiter, and you'll get the best job possible. Hold back, and you'll only cheat yourself.

(d) Training

Do you want to take one of the advance management courses offered by a college or university in your city?

Do you want your next employer to let you participate in courses at schools such as Wharton, Harvard, Stanford?

Then let your recruiter know that you are seeking that kind of growth in order to maximize your value to both yourself and the company that hires you.

Then, if you can take those four categories and put in the specifics for your lifestyle (in what parts of the world will you live, and where won't you live? do you need child care services? job for spouse?), you are on your way to honest communication with a headhunter, and that is the best way to find the job you want.

High-level job hunters seeking post-merger employment are often older, frequently feel that they have fewer job options, and are under greater emotional strain than a younger, lower-level job searcher.

For that reason there are significant *don'ts* for these job hunters:

(a) Don't be bitter

Don't look at everyone who is employed, think that you are better qualified, and develop a bitterness that will eventually come to the fore in every job interview.

(b) Don't sit back and wait for the world to come to you

It won't. When Morton Ehrlich left his $160,000 job as senior vice president at Eastern Airlines, he began his job search immediately. He contacted executive search firms and significant persons in business. He turned down several offers that he thought not right for him and finally—

after the recommendation of two partners in a Wall Street firm—ended up as the number two officer at TWA.

(c) Don't put on a phony "I-don't-really-give-a-damn" attitude

Nobody will believe you, and you soon learn the only person you are deluding is yourself.

View life realistically. If you are sad (and remember that job severance after many years is like death or divorce in terms of personal trauma), take time to be alone and express your own emotions. If you do this, you will make it easier not only on yourself but also on your family who are probably more confused and frightened than you.

(d) Don't procrastinate

After a decent mourning period, after a suitable planning period, get on with your life. Develop a plan—then follow it.

That is the only way your needs will be answered.

Employers have a different set of needs and wants. It all begins with one long moan and groan that sounds like this:

Find me an employee

Since a headhunter is more adept at doing what most employers cannot do—that is, find a gainfully employed person and persuade him or her to leave a job—it is important that bosses make sure headhunters understand their needs.

Maybe because I am an employer, I think it is more difficult for us to get what we want from headhunters. The job hunter knows his qualifications; we know what we want, but we also know that we will have to be flexible in certain areas.

Robert Neilsen, formerly with Handy, the major executive search firm, believes that executive recruiters and employers can work more effectively if employers take a strong hand. His advice to employers is:

(a) Choose your headhunter carefully

In order to find the company best for you, check associates in your business and ask for their recommendations. Get the names of three different firms, check their results with people you trust, and then go ahead and make a decision to choose one of them. In making the selection, be sure that the headhunter's success is rooted in your business. If it is, a lot of time will be saved; an experienced headhunter knows where to look in the forest.

Be sure that you meet the recruiter who will handle your assignment, and be certain that the recruiter understands you and your needs; it always helps to like the recruiter and to be secure in his knowledge of your business needs.

(b) Hire your headhunter promptly

If you narrow your choices to companies with a track record in filling similar jobs, you should not have to take a long time in making a decision concerning which firm to use.

You have a lot to lose if you wait.

Remember that no one is mistake-proof (aren't you hiring in order to replace your last mistake?). Delaying the decision, however, is always a mistake because the longer you wait to hire, the longer it will take to fill the job.

(c) Narrow the qualifications

Be specific. If you can spell out qualifications right down to blood type, much of the difficulty in finding the right person will be eliminated.

Don't be afraid that you are giving too much information concerning the candidate's qualifications. There is no such thing as too much.

The more time you spend on this part of the recruitment, the more time you will save. The tighter the profile, the faster you get good results.

(d) Ask to see three candidates within 30 days

Don't let a recruiter work at his own pace.
Set the parameters.

This is vital because (1) you will know early on if your executive search firm is on target, and (2) you will know if they have adequate time to spend on your project.

No recruiter should have more than four other major searches concurrent with yours.

This is particularly true if your search is at a high executive level. If your recruiter has bigger fish to fry, guess who'll get in the pan first.

If your company is running perfectly, sales are booming, and profits are good; if you love all the people you have in place and you trust them, then your concern with headhunters comes down to one nervous note:

Keep those headhunters out of here

If you want to keep employees headhunt-proof, take a page from Citicorp. When Citicorp was looking for a successor to CEO Walter Wriston, they brought three executives along in tandem. Each man was given responsibilities, compensation, and titles that were equal to the others. When a CEO was finally chosen, the other two executives stayed. Their roles were secure.

Chemical Bank, however, decided to deal with its three contenders differently. They divided the bank into three sectors and made the three contenders presidents, one of each sector.

The Higbee Company in Cleveland defied department store tradition and followed the Chemical Bank formula. When the president's chair became vacant, it was filled with presidents for each of the major areas of the store.

IBM keeps its people with intrapreneurialism, the newest kind of corporate challenge. It permits use of company funds to allow creative minds to function independently for the good of the company. It was just such a group, which IBM set up in Florida, that came up with their personal computer.

The key to intrapreneurialism is the ability to function with a small, manageable group to create a product or service that would not be possible to develop in the overlapping layers of the parent company.

One of the greatest talents of the headhunter is an ability to approach the unapproachable.

Headhunters can hire stars, and it isn't easy for any executive to approach, much less offer, a job to a heavy hitter.

But the headhunter is not the key to hiring stars.

Hiring on Your Own

Be as imaginative as you dare

Who says you can't look until the day you're ready to hire? When Warner Leroy, the owner of Maxwell's Plum and Tavern on the Green, was seeking a chef prior to opening one of his restaurants, he ran a newspaper ad offering the job at a salary of $75,000 a year. At that time the best chefs were making $50,000.

Mr. Leroy was several months ahead of his opening in seeking chefs, so he did nothing with the applications—except file them. And when the time came for him to hire, he had a long list of people to whom he could talk, good chefs whom he knew were willing to move to another opportunity.

To find superstars, ask someone who deals with them

Some of the top executives in our agency came to us because we asked people in our business, as well as people who know our kind of business, to help us find talent.

The best thing about being an executive is that you can create a network of people who are in allied businesses, people who will talk to you when you pick up the telephone.

The operating network out there works for both employers and employees.

The network is the first to commiserate when you're fired (when Ann Sutherland Fuchs lost her job as publisher of *Cuisine* because CBS sold the publication's mailing list—and scuttled the magazine—she was warmed by letters, phone calls, and offers).

And when a few months later she became publisher of *Women's Day,* they were the first to cheer.

In the advertising business the hot information network is made up of media people; they are in and out of agencies on a regular basis, so they know when accounts are shaky and people shakier.

Among the best of the media marvels who always has his eyes and ears turned to political, business, and civic matters is Pete Hlinka of WEWS in Cleveland. His trademark is the whispered phone call and the words, "Did you hear what's new on the Rialto?"

Assuming you've found your big gun, how can you learn what you need to know without sitting next to him or her on an airplane during an electrical storm?

Don't make any decisions after one meeting

Don't fall in love before the second date.

And don't make any promises until you have a witness.

Sometimes people with no talent for business and a large talent for tap dancing on the desk of life shine so bright in a first meeting that you are blinded into a job offer that you want to withdraw by the second meeting.

So go ahead.

Be impressed.

That's the fun of any business—discovering talent.

But don't declare your love until the third meeting.

Carl Spielvogel interviews three times before hiring a major person.

And the interviewing always takes place around mealtime.

"Much of the advertising business is done over meals," says Mr. Spielvogel, "and I want to see the way a person handles utensils and conversations and manages to keep both going. Besides, if I see a person who can't figure out what he or she wants for breakfast, I know I am dealing with someone who will have a difficult time making larger decisions. Further, you can pick up a lot of clues over meals. For example, I always wonder about the judgment of a person who salts and peppers food before tasting it."

If your interview should be kept confidential, then don't meet in a public place

The Bar Room at the Four Seasons is not the place to change jobs if you are in advertising or publishing—unless you want the entire communications industry to speculate on your future.

Similarly, don't head for an out-of-the-way restaurant where you just may be seen by someone who realizes that this is a corporate assignation.

Instead—if the meeting is after 5 P.M.—invite the candidate to your office.

If it must be a noontime meeting, then the best choice (in New York) is a hotel dining room. Business people don't use them.

If it's really hush-hush, suggest a Saturday or Sunday meeting in your home.

And if you want to avoid all possible suspicion, go to tea. Tea is the newest business hour of the day. In Chicago it's the Ritz for tea. In New York it's the Helmsley Plaza or the Mayfair Regent. And in other cities it's wherever the hotel is smart enough to take a page from European sisters and make teatime the new profit hour.

Try not to make the first offer

Charles Revson once thought he would hire me and named a sum less than I was making.

Instead of an offer, ask, "What will it take to move you?"

That gives you a little time to vamp, set the style for the offer. If the package sounds too rich, you can say so. If you want to think it over, you can say so.

If you're the superstar with the choices to make and the one who is giving the number, decide in advance what you'll ask. Best choice for the package is a number and a deal that the best company in the field would offer a person of your talent. Whatever you do, when you set the numbers, don't try to see how far you can go. Try to see how real you can be.

If you really want the job (or the person), act like it

In the Age of Computers there is very little honest passion emanating from business. So when anyone hears more than a carefully couched phrase like, "It just might work," it's a turn-on. A sportswear manufacturer who was looking at two people for a job as sales manager was having a difficult time making a decision. "The first person," he said, "has the right background, but he's so laid back I don't know if he'd be embarrassed by our enthusiasm. The second one doesn't have experience, but he wants the job."

The manufacturer played the percentages; he hired the experienced person.

One year later he fired him.

He looked around to see what had happened to the second candidate, but he didn't have to look very far. He was the sales manager of a competing company, the one that had just passed them.

Someone had been willing to bet on a person, not a résumé.

You have to be careful when you buy only a work history because people do not always match their résumés.

Always let your staff know when you're interviewing for a big job

It's part of your style, isn't it?

Tell your associates what's going on so they can be a part of the excitement. When you hire a star, it means you're doing well, and who cares more than the people who are right there with you every day?

Also, in case you can't remember what nervous really is, just watch the behavior of the people in your company when they think they may be replaced.

When we first computerized our offices, we had to sit down individually with accounting people to explain that the computer was there to help them and not to replace them.

Insecurity can cause more upset stomachs than bad oysters.

Tell it like it is

Honesty is not only the best policy, it is the only policy when it comes to hiring.

Be straightforward about everything.

If you are thinking about a benefits program, don't talk as if it's been in place for sixteen years.

If you are thinking of offering a car, don't say that you are.

If you fudge on the facts, you may end up hiring the right person for the wrong reason. That means you will have a disillusioned employee on your hands who will communicate that dissatisfaction to previously satisfied employees.

And no amount of style will help you then.

Introduce the person you want to hire to other employees as soon as possible

Always let somebody test-drive an old employee.

Show people the offices they will have.

Tell them about the people in their group.

Nothing gives a candidate more comfort and helps close a deal than a sense of security about a new place.

Remind the person you want to hire that real people live and work here. What's more, they like it.

We almost lost one of our most valued employees one day because she went to another office to interview at their request— when she was there, they were having a party.

She came back; she remembered that we have parties, too.

We also gave her a raise.

That seemed to work even better than someone else's parties.

But what some people seem to forget as they dream of greener grass is the difficulty of adjusting to a new environment.

For even if an executive moves up within the same company, he soon learns that the new job necessitates the learning of a whole new set of company manners.

The New Job

Remember the movie *The Candidate?* At the very end Robert Redford, who has just been elected to office, turned to his aide and said, "Now what do I do?"

That's the way most of us feel when we are promoted or move to a new job.

The people are new and different, and they all have a set of priorities that bedevils us—at least at the beginning. And if you go from a small- or medium-sized company to a corporate monolith, there is a whole new way of thinking to be embraced.

Not long ago one of the television producers at Wyse resigned to join a larger agency. After her first day on the job, she called her old boss, "I can't believe this place," she said. "The last job I did at Wyse was to produce a thirty-second TV spot for less than $14,000. Just now a creative director stuck his head in the door of my office and said, "Kid, you'll save my neck if you bring this job in for under $200,000."

Obviously her promotion is going to require some acculturation.

Even those who are promoted within the same organization often require acculturation. It comes as a rude awakening to learn one is loved as a worker in the ranks but not as a supervisor.

How much love can you afford to have from your associates when you move up to a new job?

Tom was one of a group of six product managers reporting to the hated divisional president of a major food company, a corporation that was famous for putting its managers on the fast track. The company was also known for its frequent top-level turnover.

Still, Tom and his five cohorts fantasized over lunch, over after-work drinks, over the telephone, over weekends about what each of them would do were he made president, for they all felt that it was simply a question of when—not if—the current, uncommunicative president would be terminated.

As time went on, it seemed fairly certain that Tom would get the nod. His leadership qualities were evident—he was a team player who was a star and a star who was a team player—and when indeed the hated president left, Tom was given the job.

Tom was thrilled. Not only was he getting the job he wanted, he would have "his guys," his team, working at his side. Communication would be their hallmark.

What could be better?

Instead of complaining about the company, these great team players would all be working together.

After the first flurry of excitement and congratulations, Tom began to notice some subtle differences in the way "his guys" were treating him.

It was hard to put his finger on the exact moment he realized he was no longer one of the boys, but the signs mounted. No one asked him for his football pool bets; no one asked when and where his lunch dates were; no one wondered whether he was taking the 5:11 or the 6:11 train to Connecticut.

Still he felt confident and enthusiastic.

He was sure that "his guys," the product managers, were going to make him look good. After all, hadn't they all hated the last president? (And, as every corporate person knows, doesn't hatred of a boss bind people even closer than love?)

Hadn't the guys dreamed of that president's downfall over after-work drinks for eighteen months? And now that it had come to pass—now that Tom was the president—wouldn't life be beautiful?

Deep down Tom knew the guys cared for him; still Tom was not going to take any chances. There was a new product report due for the chairman's review in two weeks. If the guys were feeling a little iffy, let them. He wouldn't bother any of them now. He would put the report together by himself. Besides, he knew how each of them felt. Hadn't they spent all those months telling one another how they'd do it if they ran the division?

The day of the meeting Tom and his managers met with the chairman. "The guys" were window dressing, just as they had been in the last president's regime. Tom stood to state the views of the product group.

Tom was doing well; he knew it. The chairman was smiling.

And then it happened.

One manager raised his hand, "Sir," he said to the chairman, "I don't think the product group sees this quite the way Tom does. In fact, if you follow Plan B, you could bankrupt the company."

Tom was stunned.

The chairman turned to Tom. "How could you make a mistake like that?"

After the meeting Tom went to his old friend. "Why did you do that?" He asked.

"What? What did I do?"

"You tried to sink me. Why?"

"Because, *pal*," said his friend with teeth clenched, "you didn't try to make us look good."

"But we're friends. We're all in it together."

"Wrong, *pal*," said his friend. "You're in it alone. You see, Tom, you really can't be a star without us."

Tom is now at another company, but he is still not certain that any action on his part at that time would have kept his guys as part of the team.

"If there's anything I learned from being made boss," Tom says, "it is simply this: when you start out, don't get too friendly with the people you expect to pass. They won't like you when you're on top, and they will find a way to do you in. For every Hamlet there are two Laertes."

Tom followed his own advice at his new job and did indeed keep an invisible wall between himself and his coworkers.

He lunched with them only when they had a business reason, and he listened to no complaints involving personalities. He did not get involved in discussions about their marriages, their concerns about tuition and car payments. And he did not ride the same commuter trains.

However, it need not take a disastrous experience to make a new executive aware of the pitfalls. There are stylish strategies for moving up.

Don't play Mr. Nice Guy

Tom took loyalty for granted, but you could go the opposite way and assume that you'll have to take extraordinary measures to build team spirit.

It might happen that you want this job so much that you sing to your mirror every morning, "If I get the job, here's what I'll do. . . . ," and you promise everything from a two-day work week to an office lottery that everybody will win. You will be the best boss in the history of bossdom.

You will make everyone love you.

That's the biggest mistake of the new boss. You cannot run a popularity contest. You simply cannot try to negotiate your new authority and assume old friendships. You cannot give the extra vacation days and look the other way when an old pal wants a new favor. If you do, you will have anarchy.

Everybody works best when the whole office understands who is boss. So the first thing you have to do when you start as boss is—unfortunately—stop acting like the same employee you used to be.

Don't give too much help

Why?

Because no good deed goes unpunished.

Larry, a Broadway producer, thought he had the perfect role to offer his old pal Cedric, who hadn't been in a play for four years. Larry called Cedric, told him he thought he had a part for him. Cedric was so grateful he almost dissolved in tears during the telephone call. "Have your agent call me," said Larry, "and we'll work out the details for you."

"Oh," said Cedric in a small voice, "I don't even have an agent now. I don't even know who I should call."

"I'll get you an agent," said Larry, and he promptly called an agent who needed clients. Larry felt good. He had done a favor for two people. Who said producers weren't really kind-hearted?

The next day the agent came to see Larry. "Here's the deal," Larry explained. He showed the agent the figures. "All you have to do is sign," Larry said.

"Sign?" snorted the agent. "We don't even walk around the block for that kind of money."

Larry no longer recommends agents to actors who have been out of work for a very long time.

Ask questions

Don't think you have to know all the answers the first week. Go to the old-timers in the department—and take a list of questions you want answered. Use your first weeks as a get-acquainted period. It's a time when you don't have to take any action (unless, of course, there is some kind of emergency).

Besides, no one trusts people who come up with answers too quickly.

But no one can survive bad timing.

If you want proof, just remember John Lindsay. When he was elected mayor of New York, the first weeks of his election he was confronted with a taxi strike, record snowfalls and no equipment to clear streets, and not long thereafter the city had a garbage strike. Ultimately citizens blamed him for everything bad that happened to New York.

Don't discuss your fears or concerns

Somebody thought you were good, and so you got the job. There is no need to be (a) humble or (b) insecure. Move with authority. When Jane Evans was only 30 years old, she was made president of Butterick, then the major pattern company. In her first meeting, Ms. Evans let everyone know who was boss. "Let's get a few things straight," she announced. "I don't have to cut it with you; you have to cut it with me."

Now, ten years later, Jane Evans has zigzagged through other corporate hierarchies and is today president of Monet Jewelry.

She knows only how to be boss!

Don't tell everyone how "we" always did it

"We" is now "they." You are part of a new team.

So learn everything that there is to learn—including all that you can about your predecessor in the job.

Was the ex-boss good?

You had better admit the strong points.

Was he or she weak?

Don't let anyone have false expectations that your talents alone can plug the gaps.

Permitting unreal anticipation to flower will only cause greater disillusionment later.

Stay out of the spotlight at the beginning

It's fine if you want to go in with a written agenda; don't make it a spoken agenda.

Keep a low profile.

Analyze your staff.

Study the style of the company or the division. But make no close friends, and open no doors to special individuals. If someone tries to extract a promise, learn how to smile enigmatically.

Above all, keep your face out of the company newspaper and far, far away from major media. A large beverage company had as the president of one of its divisions a particularly charismatic man. Handsome and articulate, he was persuaded to make a film of his activities for a bottlers' meeting. When the president of the company saw the film complete with the division head arriving at his office in a company limo, the division head's days were numbered. He is now bottling—and battling—elsewhere.

You have to learn to listen to the people above and below you.

How honest are they?

Who is a smiling, cooperative person in front of you but is an enemy with a knife once your back is turned?

Whom can you trust?

How honest are they about one another?

In my business I find that people are afraid of appearing "tattletale" and so become overly protective of one another.

Nobody wants to be the bad guy who tells about Sam who drinks too much. Or Gwen who's having an affair with a new man and taking three-hour lunch hours. Or Jim who takes home a year's supply of typewriter ribbons and paper.

It isn't that the people in the ranks don't want the misdemeanors discovered. They do want the wrongdoers found and punished. But *they* don't want to blow the whistle.

And until those who obey the rules get fed up with violators, the crime wave will continue—and promotions will go often to people who get away with more and not to people who do more.

The most difficult thing about running a company is the insulation it provides. You are wrapped in cotton and not allowed to hear about the problems, the bad news, and the fears that plague the business until, often, it is too late to do anything about them.

One of the tenets of business these days is to delegate, and in delegating many of us give up some rights we should keep. If a printer calls me and asks for a particular job, all I can do is check with a production person and ask to have that printer considered. I can't put him ahead of anyone else. Printing is not one of the fields where I consider myself expert.

However, many managers are abdicating areas in which they are expert in order to be democratic delegators.

One of the principals in a Fortune 500 company has a brilliance and kind of calculated prickliness that makes good advertising people do better work. But he no longer works with the corporation's ten agencies. Instead, with the wisdom born of years of business schooling, the company's advertising (which is just as much a company product as the stuff this company bottles and puts on supermarket shelves) is permitted to be supervised by a constantly changing series of executive mistakes.

Business is becoming a slave to the organizational chart.

Still, there must be organization; there must be capable individuals to carry out the goals of the company. And so all of us will continue to look at the people who work in our companies and wonder which ones should be moved—moved up, moved down, or moved out. But care and caution must be taken.

Before you promote another person to a new job, ask these questions:

1. Do I know enough about this person to trust him or her to supervise the business lives of the people who work here?

2. Does this person have enough strength to challenge me?

3. If the answer to question 2 is "yes," do I want to be challenged or do I want to be obeyed?

4. Am I preparing this person for a next step if I give this promotion now or will I be raising expectations I can never fulfill?

5. How will this promotion affect the rest of the office?

6. How will I announce this? Should I tell each person he is a candidate, then ask him to remain silent until I decide?

7. Am I giving this promotion for the right reason (because it will strengthen the company) and not for the wrong reason (because I think it is the only way to keep this employee)?

8. Does this promotion make me feel good?

If your answer to question 8 is "yes," then you probably know all the answers to the first seven.

Negotiating with Style

Suit the action to the word; the word to the action.

Shakespeare

CHAPTER 4

Leveraging: The Move-Up Movements

Nothing in business ever moves in exactly the direction you want with precisely the speed you want.

So, unless you are willing to leave your future in the hands of others, there will be many times when you will leverage what you are to gamble on what you can be.

Leveraging is the ability to apply pressure in one place in order to make something happen in another place. The gospel according to company manners defines leveraging as a complicated means to a simple end.

It is the fortuitous action you take so that someone will make the fortuitous change you want.

Leveraging is devious in that it requires departing from the direct course, but leveraging is not dishonest. Indeed, good leveraging requires the highest degree of honest appraisal in analyzing your business assets—and shortcomings. It is not always comfortable to inquire into one's own skills and deficits.

Executives who can evaluate a company down to its last paper clip are not always able to do the same kind of calculating in determining their own non-balance sheet assets.

It takes a smart, secure professional to leverage well.

The professional manager who is both smart and secure is one who considers himself still in the learning process. To recognize and analyze your strengths and weaknesses before attempting any leveraging in the executive suite, make sure you can answer "yes" to the following questions:

Are you receptive to new ideas?

Are you willing to try something no one has tried before?

Are you able to accept an idea if it originates with someone else, or from someone ranked below you?

Are you able to adapt emotionally to the ups and downs that accompany changes?

Can you accept criticism from your peers?

Are you willing to ask questions when you don't know the answers in advance?

If you have any "no" answers and leverage anyway, you may be headed for trouble.

Miller, the president of a candy company, liked to play his cards close to the vest. He communicated infrequently with his superiors, preferring instead to deal in endless meetings with his subordinates. In these meetings, which were akin to teacher-student relationships, he proclaimed his beliefs about the company, made the key decisions for his staff, and then assigned the subordinates' daily duties. Miller spent the rest of his time alone in his office dreaming of ways to promote and publicize the product line.

Although Miller was considered a corporate loner, he was also considered a very smart fellow. Since the tobacco conglomerate that owned the candy company was deeply involved with its bellweather divisions, Miller was left pretty much to his own devices year after year.

The candy company made only a small profit, but the executives at corporate considered it "a fun division that's good for the company image."

The continuing negative perceptions of the tobacco business, however, resulted in a corporate decision to strengthen and re-structure the candy company. Miller was upped to general man-ager of the division and given considerably more authority. Now he was responsible not just for the day-to-day operations, but was also put in charge of planning for the candy division.

Miller's first move was to hire an outside think tank. No one inside said a word. The subordinates in his executive group were too dulled by the teacher-student relationship to tell him that some of them had—or had ever had—ideas about where the company might go.

Miller, intoxicated with his new powers, not only hired an outside think tank but proceeded to hire researchers, equip a new test laboratory, and set up a special field-marketing group to test his new product concepts.

At the end of the first quarter, Miller's figures were not as good as the previous year's. Miller, anxious to keep his usual secrecy about his activities, told the executive vice president at corporate headquarters to whom he reported that the division was instituting some new procedures, and profits would be back on track the following quarter.

But the following quarter figures were even more dismal, and the shocked corporate staff immediately moved in one of their own managers to supervise and ask questions.

. Spencer was the manager assigned. It did not take Spencer a long time to analyze the situation. In Spencer's opinion Miller was guilty of a classic kind of corporate arrogance. He never let anyone know what was happening until it happened. He took his good record and leveraged it for a promotion. But when he got his promotion and got all the power that the corporation could give him, his weaknesses drowned his strengths.

In an informal conversation, Spencer said, "Miller could not take ideas from below. He could not tell those above what he was doing because he did not want criticism. When he asked for an opinion, he was not really seeking an opinion; he sought confirmation. Of course, this kind of behavior does not make Miller a corporate oddity. I have seen many like him. I describe Miller as just another amateur trying to learn to be head man."

Spencer wanted to clip Miller's wings, but he did not want to remove him completely. "What you have to remember when you deal with people," said Spencer, "is that they are rarely all good or all bad. What managers must do is save the good part and give the bad part to someone who will do it well. I had to remember in dealing with Miller that the people who sent me in to straighten things out were the very same people who had given Miller the authority to run the division. Therefore, I could not run the risk of telling them their judgment was bad. Further, I didn't really think their judgment was bad. It was just a little too good as far as Miller was concerned; they gave Miller credit for the talents they wished he had, not for the talents he truly had. Anyway, I knew we couldn't fire Miller. So I did what I think any good manager would do. I took a position and made a nonthreatening recommendation. I told corporate headquarters I thought we ought to take some of the financial responsibilities from Miller; they were too much for him to handle along with the day-to-day supervision. Corporate headquarters agreed. I know now what I will do next. I will leverage my successful recommendation to make my next recommendation. Step-by-step—it will take three steps— we will take Miller to a responsible position where his ideas can be monitored. But he won't lose face; the company won't lose face, and I will feel that I have done a good job for everyone involved.

"Corporations, you know, are about more than destruction. In the best of worlds, the corporation is as human as the people running it, and the people running this company really like Miller a lot. Why not? He made money for us for many years."

Positive leveraging includes those frequent, small actions that, when added to positive attitudes, increase the good feeling and result in a climate where change is possible.

What are some examples of positive leveraging?

- Canceling a vacation to attend a meeting.
- Hopping the red-eye to fly from one coast to another to be where someone wants you.
- Lending your secretary to someone in your office who is short-handed at the moment.

Positive leveraging is made up of attentive, interested company manners and is usable every day.

Leveraging your position to gain control of a situation

Annabel worked for an advertising agency as an account executive, and when her agency lost the business she had supervised—the account went to another agency in town—Annabel was offered a job on the client side.

She accepted with surprise and delight.

She hadn't realized that the client's feelings for her had been that strong.

Annabel met with the man designated as her immediate superior. He told her that she would be advertising director and that her staff would include the woman to whom she used to submit ad plans.

"What?" Annabel asked, unsure that she had heard right. "You mean that the woman who used to approve agency ads that I submitted will now be reporting to me? The woman who used to tell me what I did wrong must now take direction from me?"

He nodded. "That's the way it will be."

"I hope it will work, but I'm concerned," she said.

At first Annabel was so busy that she didn't have time to think about the arrangement.

However, the few times Annabel met with her staff she felt uncomfortable, and she sensed that her discomfort was coming from the attitude of her ex-client.

"Every time I looked at her I could see darts coming out of her eyes," Annabel recalled. "I am not good in confrontational situations. But what could I do? My authority in the department depended on her working with me and my sending the message out there.

"Finally one day I called her into my office. I told her that I had been spending time on organizational details. Now I was up to speed, and I felt that she was not keeping me informed. I swear I was shaking so inside that I wasn't sure I could get out all the words. I said that I knew she didn't need a superior, and I knew she didn't want a superior. But she had one. And I was the one, and she would have to work with me. I gave her total control of day-to-day operations. That was three weeks ago. Things are better now between us, but until I do a performance appraisal with her, I don't think it will hit home as to who's boss."

Leveraging to Advance

Leveraging to advance is possible only when you have a situation that combines fear with service. That is, you have to be an outstanding player for the company, one who has given extraordinary service. And someone has to be fearful that you may be lost to the competition.

Steve Florio was stuck in the corporate hierarchy.

As publisher of *GQ* magazine, he had risen fast and well at Condé Nast. Although he was not yet thirty-five, he had the feeling that his greatest challenges were behind him.

He had waltzed through *Esquire* in his twenties, arrived at *GQ* when he was barely thirty, whirled the magazine through a turnaround that saw it become viable both in terms of editorial quality and advertising dollars only to find that now—at 34—he was hemmed in by two old-guard executives who questioned every move he made.

He was itchy; he was restless; most of all, he was uncertain of his next move. Up until now it had been easy to figure where he wanted to go. He wanted to be a publisher and make a sick magazine well. Now he had done that. What was next, and how would he get his next next?

Steve Florio, a cagey player in the corporate game, understood that if he were to approach S. I. Newhouse, Jr., the head of the company that owns Condé Nast, Mr. Newhouse would be forced to defend the company's top echelon, and with that scenario, Mr. Florio would either be out or relegated to some publishing Siberia.

Steve Florio knew instinctively that attacking the top was never a way to reach it.

He began slowly. First, through a friendly third party, he called the publisher of a noncompetitive magazine in another corporation. The two men met at lunch. Said the noncompetitive publisher, "People in our business are all talking about the positive changes you've made at *GQ*. The word on the street is excellent. If I were you, I'd get a higher profile in the industry, work with other publishers in trying to do some things that benefit all magazines."

So he did.

Steve Florio became a spokesperson for magazines.

He made speeches, judged contests.

Then one evening at an industry dinner, he met the kingpin of a newspaper publishing empire, an owner who was in search of a chief executive officer for the company's magazine group.

He was so impressed that he called Steve Florio the next morning and offered him the top job in his company.

Mr. Florio was stunned. He hadn't expected anything this big this fast. "It's a dream job," he said, "and I want it, but first I must talk to Si Newhouse."

Mr. Florio called Mr. Newhouse and said he had to see him— immediately. They agreed to meet the following morning at 6 A.M. The hour was chosen because it was Mr. Newhouse's only free hour in the next twenty-four. Mr. Newhouse's usual arrival time at his office is 5 A.M.

At the meeting the next morning, Mr. Florio wasted no time. "Si, I came to tell you that I am leaving. I want to thank you for giving me the chance to work here for six wonderful years."

Mr. Florio made his speech and sat back. He felt great. He was not there to negotiate, not there to ask for any other job. He knew that there was no "other job" that Mr. Newhouse could offer.

Mr. Florio was wrong.

Mr. Newhouse did have the "other job," a job Mr. Florio did not know existed. Mr. Newhouse had bought a controlling interest in the *New Yorker* magazine, and now he outlined a package that included responsibility, authority, and compensation.

Mr. Florio was stunned, but he shook his head at the new magazine. "Thanks, Si," he said, "but I gave my word. I didn't come here for a better offer. I came here—gentleman to gentleman—to thank you for six wonderful years, but I don't think I can stay here now because what I want more than anything is to be in a situation where I can feel that I am still running things."

Mr. Newhouse took a deep breath. "But you will run things," he assured him.

Mr. Florio still was not convinced.

Mr. Newhouse looked at his watch. "I have another meeting," he said. "Come back in an hour and give me your answer."

Again Steve Florio extended his hand. "I can't change that fast. Let me thank you. . . ."

Mr. Newhouse shook his head. But he would not shake Mr. Florio's hand. He would not put an end to "six wonderful years." Instead he countered, "I'll give you 'til noon."

Mr. Florio went to the telephone and called his wife.

Hours later he called the CEO of the company that had made him the offer. "This is Steve Florio. . . ."

"And you're not taking the job," said the publisher.

"How do you know?"

"Because I can guess the offer Si Newhouse must have made to keep you. In his position that's what I would do."

And that is how, in a matter of six hours, Steve Florio became the president of the *New Yorker,* reporting directly to S. I. Newhouse, Jr.

"In the end it wasn't money that moved me," Mr. Florio said. "It was the chance to run something, and Si gave me that chance. If I make it work, I'll be rewarded. And if I don't. . . ."

You can get what you want if you give what they want

Florence Skelly, former president of Yankelovich, Skelly, and White and one of the smartest executives in the marketing and research business, is a firm believer in leveraging. "Leverage every day," she says. "Leverage the small things that you have. Our company used to be owned by Reliance, a public company headed by Saul Steinberg. I think I reminded Saul of his mother. Don't ask me why; I just felt that I did. So when Saul asked me about the business, I would respond just the way I figured his mother would respond. I leveraged those feelings I think he had. I was always nonhostile, and one time when we were discussing increased profits, I just turned to him and said in my best motherly tones—even though I am an owner of the business—'I don't need it, but, Saul dear, if you need it, I'll do it.'"

Be careful when you leverage; there's always next year

William Paley, the founder of CBS, used to set corporate style by telling his negotiators that he wanted them to go to meetings prepared to do the best for CBS, but he reminded them to leave a little on the table because they would have to return to negotiate another day.

Alan was the attorney who represented a baseball player in his negotiations with the GEFs, a major league ball club. At the final session, just before the contract signing, Alan requested an addition to the contract called "clause 29." It was a family medical benefit and not particularly costly to the club.

The attorney for the GEFs shook his head. "No way, Alan," he said. "This club has never done that for anyone."

"Are you sure?" Alan asked.

"Word of honor," came the answer.

The papers were signed, and the following season Alan found himself representing the hottest new player in the country. Just before his meeting with the owners, Alan met with another attorney who represented one of the other players. "This time," said Alan "I'm going to get the GEFs to change their contract and give us clause 29."

The attorney blinked. "What do you you mean by 'this time'?"

"I asked for it, but I didn't get it last time."

"I did," said his friend.

"You must be kidding," Alan said.

"Here it is in print." The lawyer opened his briefcase and showed Alan the signed contract, signed by the very person who had given his word of honor.

"Mind if I photocopy that?" Alan asked.

"No problem."

Alan went into the negotiations, and—because he had the player of the year—had his pick of clubs. At the end two offers were equal: the GEFs and one other. Alan picked the other club. After the papers were signed, the attorney for GEF asked Alan why—after their amicable deal the previous season—they had not been the club chosen.

Alan tossed the photocopy of clause 29 from his friend's contract on the table. "Any more questions?" he asked.

Home-Style Leveraging

Charles Peebler, the head of the advertising agency Bozell and Jacobs, wanted to be in New York to celebrate the birthday of his wife, Toni. His agency wanted him in the midwest for an 8 A.M. meeting the next morning with a prospective client, American

Stores. It was a big, hot piece of business, and Mr. Peebler wanted it desperately. So did J. Walter Thompson.

Then Mr. Peebler decided to leverage both his assets: his devotion as a husband, his dedication to his business.

He went to his wife's birthday party, and at 2 A.M. he boarded a chartered plane and flew out to his meeting. He arrived in time to shower and shave and greet the president of American Stores at 8 A.M.

Mr. Peebler never mentioned his activities during the preceding twelve hours, but the client realized that his business was so important not only to the agency but to Mr. Peebler personally that he was willing to charter a plane to be at the meeting on time. And Toni Peebler knew what spouses of busy executives learn along the way: you can't have it all, so smile when you get half a night because half is still better than nothing.

Leveraging Tips

Learn to take the temperature of the room before you get into a heated negotiation

Every day is not a day to buy, sell, or move a project to its next logical step.

It is important to trust your instincts and intuition in all deal making.

Just in case you think your antenna may not be operating at top level, take time to try to learn what is on peoples' minds before they begin to deal with you.

During a relaxed moment and before negotiations begin, ask some key questions that may indicate whether you are going to get the full attention of the other person. Types of comments-cum-questions to ask:

1. The weather has been so good. Is everyone in your family (name names when you know them) enjoying the summer?

2. A lot of our clients tell me business is slow these days. How are things in your industry?

3. If you have a lot going on today, don't be concerned about postponing our meeting. Tell me honestly if this is the best time for us to talk, or do you want to move this to a time when your calendar isn't quite so full?

You can tell when someone is not giving you complete concentration when you are in his office

a) If he eyes the telephone nervously as if waiting for it to ring.

b) If he glances toward his secretary's desk in anticipation of her interruption.

c) If he looks anxiously at his watch or desk clock.

d) If he stays behind his desk and does not offer to make you comfortable.

e) If he moves pencils around his desk and rearranges papers without ever looking at you or listening to you.

When this happens, act on the information at once.

Find a reason to suspend the conversation.

Remember a telephone call you have to make.

Ask if he will object if you convene again the next day. Let him off the hook gently—and don't make him feel guilty. Occasionally a white lie is part of the scenario in order to make someone comfortable. So do use one when necessary. Most people do. Anyone who says he has never lied in business is a liar.

Or a dummy.

Or both.

You can't survive the swirling eddies of the social swim, much less a business life, without a few well-chosen white lies now and then.

But you can always identify an executive by the kinds of lies he tells.

The executive is the one who says

"My valet forgot to unpack the bag from the country."

"I'm sorry, Bill. We would have held the plane for you, but weather was coming in pretty heavy, so I told the pilot to go ahead after we waited fifteen minutes."

"I would really like to go to your daughter Buffy's wedding, but that is the week-end that my daughter, Missy, is going to be at home with her roommate, Binky."

"I'm sorry I'm late, fellows, but the service was slow at the club today."

"I'm sorry I'm late, but the Concorde left seven hours late today."

"I'm sorry I'm late, but the seaplane from Southampton was canceled, and my driver hates the Expressway."

"I'm sorry I'm late, but the closing took longer than we expected."

"I'm sorry I'm late, but the partners from London were caught in crosstown traffic."

The ultimate executive lie is
"Gentlemen, why are all of you early?"
Ordinary everyday business lies sound like this:

"The bus was late."

"The alarm didn't go off."

"My child didn't feel well, and I didn't think I should leave."

"I called Mr. So-and-so, but he's out."

"Oh, I definitely made the call. They said to call back in two weeks." (In this particular lie, *they* is never identified).

"I never saw that memo; no one sent it to me."

"You were the one who wanted to launch the product in October, Jones. I always said it wouldn't fly."

Half-truths, however, are only half measures in terms of leveraging. The best leveraging is done from a base of honesty and self-respect. ·

The best advice about leveraging can be summed in a single sentence:

Know your priorities so you can leverage in a timely way

Ray was the sales manager of a large computer company, and one day one of his customers told him that she heard there was an opening at a smaller company.

"What's the job?" Ray asked.

"Marketing director," she said.

Ray repeated the words slowly. "Marketing director. Say, that sounds pretty good. Will you tell me who's hiring for the job?"

Ray dutifully noted the name and number of the company president, made the call, and went for his interview.

Ray got the job and he told the marketing director of his present employer that he would be leaving "because," he said with a smile, "I'm getting a job as good as yours."

The marketing director looked at him and asked quietly, "Are you sure? Do you know what you're trading for?"

"Sure," said Ray, "I'm taking my experience here and moving up."

"You're getting a title," said Ray's old boss, "but what else are you getting? What do you really want?"

Ray stopped cold.

He hadn't asked himself those questions. He was ready to move for a job and a title. Now his old boss was asking if that was enough reason.

When Ray went home that night, he borrowed a notebook and pencil from his eight-year-old daughter, and when she asked the reason he said, "Computers don't have the answers for everything."

Ray drove out to the country, parked his car, walked out and sat under a tree, took his paper and pencil, and listed his reasons for leaving the company—he wanted more money and a bigger title—and he listed reasons not to leave—staying and getting additional experience could mean a bigger job and more money. He had never thought about his future in this way before.

Was he smart to leverage his experience for a title?

Or was he smarter to leverage his experience for dollars?

When Ray got back in his car, he had a smile on his face. He was going to take the new job—but now he knew why.

His old boss had done him the greatest service any of us can do for another person in business—he had caused him to think in an orderly, logical way in order to make a decision that was comfortable for him.

Now Ray understands that leveraging is a powerful business tool—but only if you know why you are using it.

The Power Lunch: Getting What You Want on the Table

Business is a small seduction, and there is no better place to conduct the affairs of business than at a business breakfast, a power lunch, or a client dinner.

When I came to New York, the first thing I did was program my lunches. If I wasn't meeting with a client, then I went to a museum, walked through a bookstore or up and down the aisles of Bloomingdale's looking at faces. I knew that I had to get out of the office at noon. I had to reconnect myself to the outside world so that I could handle the inside office world with more grace.

It's depressing to stay in the office and have yogurt at your desk on a regular basis. There are, however, some people who pride themselves on never going to lunch. Helen Gurley Brown is one of them. The dynamic editor of *Cosmopolitan* magazine says that she never has lunch, but—what she fails to add—is that at least forty out of fifty-two weeks a year she hosts a luncheon in a private dining room at "21" for those people (mainly advertisers in the magazine and advertising people) who are important in her world.

Stockbrokers often forgo lunch; they think they can get a lot of work processed while the rest of the world is drinking its Perrier and eating its fish.

Professor Theodore Levitt, author of a number of books about marketing and the editor of the *Harvard Business Review,* once wrote, "The importance of things in business is inversely proportional to the frequency in which they are mentioned in business textbooks."

Not long ago Professor Levitt expanded that thought and said, "Since the business lunch is never mentioned in business textbooks, it must be very important."

A lot of eating out is done to be seen. And there's nothing wrong with that. Business life is all about connecting. And there are places where you can find the people who are never available on the telephone. In the Russian Tea Room you will find the movie and theater people who just happen to be in New York at the moment. In the dining room at the Algonquin are the truly literary. (The corner table at the Algonquin is held always for William Shawn, the editor of the *New Yorker,* and it is never assigned to anyone else.) The Four Seasons Bar Room is generally filled with people in communications: publishing, advertising, or broadcasting with a dollop of the real estate heavyweights, consultants, and various Seagram executives who work in that building. The fashion business goes to Le Grenouille; Europeans and South Americans gather at Le Cirque . . . and generally not before two o'clock. The ladies who lunch are also found at Le Cirque when they are not at Mortimer's, Woods, or nibbling at arugula and sipping Vichy water while being tended at Kenneth's or Elizabeth Arden.

But why not?

Despite its guises, lunch is still the time when you're good to yourself.

The more years you work, the more you realize that it's a lot easier to treat other people with kindness and consideration when you treat yourself that way first.

Of course, business eating is not just a business.

It is an art.

And the first thing to know is which meal to choose for your hosting.

Bagels, Brioche, and Croissants

Once popular only on Sunday, the bagel, the brioche, and the croissant have now achieved a weekday popularity with the advent of the Business Breakfast.

The Business Breakfast is the trademark of the financial community. Breakfast is an excellent time for buying and selling buildings, taking companies public, and arranging mergers and acquisitions. Generally the dining rooms in the best hotels in any city (regardless of how bad or indifferent their food may be) are the meeting places. In New York the Power Breakfast is hosted at the Regency Hotel (where you undoubtedly get the best service and the worst eggs), the Waldorf's Peacock Alley (a lot of out-of-town power sleeps overnight at the Waldorf-Towers), the Mayfair Regent (the best breakfast and the most subdued atmosphere), and the Carlyle (out-of-the-way location, tables far apart, food excellent). It is always appropriate to invite out-of-town visitors to breakfast. It adds profitably to their working day, and since almost all of us are powered by the Puritan Ethic, we are comfortable with the thought that we begin the day with a business breakfast. Breakfast, however, is a bad time for any arts meetings. People in creative businesses rarely like to make decisions involving taste (this includes decisions about programming, design, fine arts, food) before 10 A.M.

In Washington the power lunch has been replaced by the Breakfast Club; this is particularly true for suburban business people. Because Washington suburbs are so spread out with com-

panies strung all along the Capitol Beltway, many feel that going
to lunch takes too much time on crowded roads. And so restaurants in Bethesda, Rockville, and Silver Springs are filled with
those who cut the real estate deals and finance the growth of
suburbia. The suburban business breakfast (particularly for the
building trades) also takes place in other major metropolitan areas.
The usual meeting place for the business breakfast is in the dining
room or coffee shop of a major hotel in the area (Marriott, Sher-
aton, Stouffer), a neighborhood coffee shop or deli that serves
breakfast. The idea for the suburban business breakfast came
from the biggest suburban market of all: Los Angeles.

All people, however, do not use breakfast meetings for eating.
Barbaralee Diamonstein, the writer and lecturer, finds that while
she meets people for breakfast, rarely does anyone order anything
except coffee. "There never seems to be room on the restaurant
table for food," she explains. "Instead there are notes, charts, and
plans."

In New York literary agent Edward J. Acton had learned that
people are especially anxious to accept breakfast dates. "In my
business it's too difficult to get luncheon dates the week I ask for
them. People are traveling; they are booked for other dates; and
because our clients are in politics, entertainment, and sports, we
are also dealing with their other professional obligations. Besides,
there is an unspoken urgency to the breakfast date. It's hard to
say no when somebody wants to get up early in the morning just
to see you."

The president of a shipping company rechecks his calendar
for the upcoming week's luncheon dates each Friday afternoon.
If he sees fewer than three items to discuss with any of his luncheon partners, he switches to a breakfast date and frees those luncheon times for working at his desk, walking in the park, or finding
a more productive luncheon guest. "Lunch," he says, "is a semi-
languorous time. It's not as relaxed as dinner, but then it's not as
crisp and defined as breakfast. To be programmed properly, I
think you should always use luncheons for selling, not buying."

His rule of thumb for business eating is: If you have an hour, make it breakfast. If you have two hours, go to lunch. If you have all night, go to dinner.

In California Sherry Lansing, the independent producer, admits to eating five lunches and three dinners a week out, but she has given up the daily breakfast meeting for a 7:30 A.M. tennis game. This is done because of the increasing concern about health among her contemporaries—the over-forties.

And once California replaces breakfast with tennis, can America be far behind?

The concern with health is reflected in every business meal.

Where bacon and eggs were once urged on business breakfasters—in the belief that a big breakfast led to good health—now hosts urge guests to breakfast on bran muffins, whole wheat toast, and decaffeinated coffee, all foods which are current symbols of the health foods revolution.

The old two-martini steak-and-potatoes lunch has been replaced everywhere by Perrier, iced tea (with Sweet 'n Low, never sugar), grilled fish, and a salad with dressing on the side.

There is often more health than business at the luncheon table.

For some, luncheon is the first meal of the day, but whether they have been up since 5 A.M. or rise at 10, by noontime most people feel that their thought processes are in order, and they are willing to listen to tastemakers, dealmakers, and dream spinners. Michael Korda, the editor, knows this, and he conducts author-editor meetings almost every noon. S. I. Newhouse, who with his family owns Condé Nast, meets with the heads of his businesses (everything from Random House to *Vogue* and the *New Yorker*) over regular restaurant lunches.

There are some people who make a practice of eating in the office—and in their cases it's quite a treat. The best dining rooms in New York are the private dining rooms of the banks and Wall Street houses. The service is formal, and there is great emphasis on cuisine because the chefs come from France or famous American restaurants. Guests order from a menu just as they do in a club or restaurant, the chief difference being that no drinks are offered. Excellent wines, however, are served.

Other office dining can be less formal but just as effective. Avon has a comfortable executive dining room in its West 57th Street headquarters. American Express has a fine dining room. The J. Walter Thompson dining room overlooks a public atrium in its building on Park Avenue.

When David Mahoney was head of Norton Simon, he once invited me to lunch in his office. It wasn't exactly a cottage cheese and melon luncheon. His office was the size of Yankee Stadium. We sat at one end of a conference table that might comfortably seat twenty-four. At one point, Mr. Mahoney turned to me and asked, "Is everything satisfactory?" I looked around his vast office and said softly, "No. The people at the next table are too noisy."

Hosting a luncheon in your own office is the next best thing to inviting someone to your home.

It is not necessary to have maid service for an office luncheon. We rarely do at our office. Instead we serve luncheons to which people can help themselves easily. Most large cities today have excellent gourmet takeout. We serve our luncheons buffet-style in the conference room. Our luncheons are always quite simple: chicken salad (everybody seems to like chicken salad), a cold green vegetable like asparagus or green snap beans, a cold pasta dish, a variety of cheeses and breads. Dessert is equally simple and easy to serve: a fruit basket and cookies. We assume that luncheon in the office is done as a convenience. And we don't think anyone is going to pick our agency for the fancy lunches.

Indeed, fancy lunches for the sake of fancy are to be avoided. They have a way of backfiring. Besides, no one of any substance can be bought for a luncheon. Or a dinner.

On the subject of dinner, remember this: If you are considering extending a dinner invitation to someone you do not know well, think again.

The Client Dinner should never be a first invitation. Since dinner is open-ended (you can't look at your watch after ninety minutes and say, "I must get back to the office"), it's better to do business dinners only when you know someone, have a set agenda and a very good reason for meeting after 6 P.M. Besides, if you haven't done business with someone, it is presumptuous to assume that he or she will want to spend an evening with you. The only time a first invitation can be dinner is when the person you want to take is (a) from another city or (b) suggests that you have dinner.

The Power Lunch

The logical invitation is luncheon.

Indeed luncheon is so important that John Mack Carter, the editor of *Good Housekeeping*, announced that he was giving up the job of hosting a daily noontime show on radio station WOR because, "The job of an editor is to have lunch."

Setting up the power lunch

Don't be afraid to call.

No one was ever offended by an invitation.

But do be certain to make the call yourself.

No first invitation should ever be extended secretary to secretary.

A purpose should always be given for lunching, and the purpose should be stated when the invitation is extended. The purpose stated may not be the public purpose and not the true purpose of the luncheon—but no one should ever be asked to go to lunch without an agenda.

Invitations are extended and calls are made because, to the person calling, this is a matter of importance. It is incumbent upon the caller to communicate a sense of urgency to the person being invited. For some who are invited, simply saying, "I have admired you and want to know you better" is enough reason to accept.

Always know the location of your guest's office. And if you (or your guest) are not the bosses of your businesses, make sure you know where the boss(es) eat—and don't go there. Nothing will put a chill on a luncheon faster than to have to look across the room and see the person one of you works for.

When you extend the invitation, give your guest a choice of two places, both of which should be within easy reach of the guest's office. Since it is assumed you don't know your guest's preferences in food, the choice should be between a public restaurant and a luncheon club (if you have access to one) or between different food styles (a Japanese restaurant or a chop house).

Never ask (or have your secretary ask) a guest where he or she wants to eat. The burden of choice is not the guest's.

It is important for you to choose the restaurant because you will be more comfortable in a place where you're known and where you will feel more in control. Very few first-time guests will not agree to a place of your choice.

Only Phillip Johnson, the architect, who eats luncheon every day promptly at noon at the same corner table at the Four Seasons, has the right to be inflexible—he designed the room. But even he, with good cause, will eat elsewhere on occasion.

Never, never, never invite someone to a club that permits discrimination, sexual, religious, or racial. And if you don't know why you shouldn't do that, maybe you should just have yogurt at your desk.

Know the restaurant you are using

Before the day of a significant business luncheon, visit the restaurant if it's new to you. Meet with the proprietor (or maître d'), introduce yourself, and decide which table you want.

Make sure you don't have to wait for a table when you arrive.

I once lost a piece of business when a prospective client and I were kept waiting at the bar for twenty minutes while a maître d' who didn't know me seated everyone else in line. By the time we were seated, my one-time hot prospect said, "I think I just set the world's record for drinking Perrier. Do you always wait for tables here?"

Always offer a drink

Even if your mom is head of the Women's Christian Temperance Union, you belong to Alcoholics Anonymous, or your boss opposes drinking on religious grounds, it is still good manners to offer a drink to a guest. The best way to suggest something—and make it easy for people to refuse alcohol—is to say, "Would you like something to drink—wine, Perrier, juice?" Never make someone feel he isn't one of the real people if he doesn't drink.

And while you may feel that you have to keep someone company while he drinks, you don't have to do it with an aperitif. You can order juice, iced tea, mineral water, or even—guess what?— plain iced water. Don't explain your reasons. Nobody really cares. Just do what you want to do. After all, did you invite your guest so you might tell the story about the time you drank at lunch and fell asleep at the big presentation?

Don't preorder wine

Even if your guest is a little old winemaker, don't have wine preordered. Many companies have rules against any of their people drinking at luncheon. Woodward & Lothrop, the Washington department store, does not permit anyone—from the chairman on down—to drink at lunch whether dining in the store cafeteria or the Jockey Club.

But if you know you're with an oenophile, ask if he or she cares to order some wine. If he orders a bottle, rather than a glass, he should offer to pay for it—or give you his business at that moment.

If, however, you're going to have to take the plunge and order a bottle of wine because you've been backed into position, Paul Kovi of the Four Seasons says that the way to keep the cost down is to say to the waiter, "I'd like to order a nice little country wine." Those code words, he says, tell the restaurateur that you want something inexpensive.

Pick your table

Get a table that gives you maximum privacy when you're lunching with profit in mind. You should also have an idea of where your guest will sit and where you plan to sit.

Things to avoid: a table facing a mirror, a table next to the rest rooms, and a table near the kitchen.

If you can't pronounce it, don't order it

Ordering should be simple.

If you see something on a menu you don't recognize, ask for a description.

Lee Stevens, the head of William Morris talent agency, tells about the first time he was taken to 21. His host ordered steak tartare. Eager to please, Mr. Stevens said, "I'll have the same— and make mine well-done."

Always think in advance and plan your menu choice. You look silly and indecisive when you take five minutes to look at a menu trying to make up your mind about luncheon. Can you expect someone to trust you with his business when the head waiter can't even trust you with an order?

Never order food that is difficult to eat, requires your full-time attention, or squirts, slurps, and makes a mess. Best foods to order at luncheon: any grilled fish, salad, omelet, or grilled meat. What not to order: anything out of season (you look too chichi), lobster (it's too expensive and takes too much attention), snails (same reasons), foods with a lot of garlic or onion (obvious reasons).

Try to eat like a native

As you move from place to place, try to adapt to the local foods and the local lunching customs.

In New York don't look around for sandwiches on the menu. They are difficult to find. What you will see is a variety of fresh fish, nouvelle pastas and pizzas, and very good greens for salads. You will be expected to eat Tex Mex (but only if your host is youngish and only if you are taking someone who wants to go to "a real New York kind of place").

The newer, more interesting New York restaurants are downtown in Soho and along Park Avenue South. Decor is New York new; instead of the Italian restaurant's old-fashioned little red-checkered table-clothed table with wine bottles or the country French restaurants with pickled pine and lovely flowers, the new restaurants are high-ceilinged, spacious, and noisy. They have style and energy, are definitely not the place to take the solid, stolid chairman of the board who wants to discuss the reasons the stock is not moving. If you do go to one of the new restaurants, the best seats are not the secluded ones but those in the middle of the action. In New York the theory is that space is at a premium, and since so many New Yorkers are forced to live in small, overcrowded apartments, they want their restaurants to be arena-sized.

In Los Angeles the restaurants are clubs unto themselves. Morton's and the Ivy are two trendy restaurants with simple menus. Jimmy's is a favorite, as is Spago's, the pizza place with pizzazz where Irving and Mary Lazar hosted their last two Oscar Night Parties. There are those who go to the Bistro, where the Lazars used to host their annual Oscar party and where attorney Sidney Korshack lunches daily at the Number One Table.

Trumps is another popular spot. Yet despite the popularity of the new restaurants, the Beverly Hills Hotel Polo Lounge at breakfast or luncheon, particularly for older deal-makers, is still without peer for deal making. Since its recent renovations, the Bel Air Hotel is a good, open-air meeting place. The Beverly Wilshire Hotel gets fewer of the business lunchers, even though many people prefer staying there because it is within walking distance to Rodeo Drive.

Most frequently ordered California lunch: the salad in thousands of different guises.

When you go to lunch in London, expect the English to eat

heartily, the Americans lightly. For the English the midday meal is their dinner, and they frequently have four or five courses. The favorite luncheon places are Langan's, any good pub, a gentleman's club, the Savoy Grill, and my personal favorite, the restaurant at the Connaught.

In New Zealand the business lunch is going out of business. In view of the country's economic downturn, companies are looking closely at all expenses. Instead of the restaurant lunch, businesses are more likely to provide buffet lunches at the office. Regardless of where luncheon is served, however, you can be sure that you will be offered tea by a resident tea lady.

No matter where you lunch, the preferred way to handle cutlery is European style. None of that American hand-switching eating. Instead the preferred way is with the fork in the left hand, knife in the right—and no switching en route to the mouth.

Make sure you get to the point before you get to the dessert

Virginia wanted to sell her company, and her lawyer set up a luncheon date for her with Kingsley, the head of a holding company. "Let me do this alone," Virginia said. "I think it makes more sense to talk directly with him."

The attorney agreed.

They met at a favorite luncheon place of Virginia's; she knew half the room when she entered. Kingsley joined her, and it seemed he knew the other half. They each spent fifteen minutes saying their hellos around the room.

Virginia was smart enough not to begin the conversation with "Want to buy my company?" Instead she began with small talk, moved to the headlines of the day, and by the time she was ready to take the plunge and do her selling, Kingsley looked at his watch. "I'm due back at the office in fifteen minutes," he said. "Sorry to be so rushed, but it's nice to know you better."

She met the next prospect for luncheon in her office—and she sold before the main dish cooled.

Handle the check the way you handle all your bills—privately

Arrange to have your credit card stamped and signed in advance with taxes and tips added. Any restaurant where you are known will arrange to have the receipt either mailed to your office or picked up later in the day.

The very best way to pay is to establish charge accounts at the few restaurants you use with frequency, determine a standard percentage for service, and never have a check brought to the table. Regulars at the Four Seasons Bar Room, men like Ned Doyle, a founder of Doyle Dane Bernbach, never see or sign checks at table.

This practice is particularly valuable for women in business who find that some men are still nervous when a female picks up a check.

And it's gracious. Business guests, always pressed for time, appreciate it because you're not waiting for the check when everyone is ready to leave. And then, once the check arrives, you're not counting on your fingers and toes to figure tips and items (did he order two coffees and one ginger ale or two ginger ales and one coffee?).

Don't keep a luncheon companion waiting

Of course, that doesn't mean someone won't keep you waiting.

The best way to keep your cool while waiting for a hot lunch and late guest is to have something else to occupy your mind.

Arthur Hettich, the president of *Family Circle*, always takes a magazine with him when he goes to lunch. He assumes he will be kept waiting. And he says he's usually right.

If you are waiting for a guest (or even the times when you are a guest) and the captain or waiter asks if you want a drink, it is proper and sensible to go ahead and order anything you feel like drinking. Doing this puts the other person at ease because most people are concerned when they are late, and they feel less need to apologize when you have indicated you can care for yourself.

It is, however, thoughtless to keep anyone waiting when a telephone call might save the waiting time.

If someone is more than fifteen minutes late, no excuse except death en route to the appointment should be tolerated.

Fifteen minutes is the maximum waiting time.

If, after fifteen minutes, your luncheon companion has not called, sent word by carrier pigeon, or caused his next of kin to appear and explain his absence, you are free to leave or to place your luncheon order and to invite everyone in the place to have a drink—at what's-his-name's expense.

Handle early birds

Much as you dislike the latecomer, the early bird is equally annoying. Worse, early birds make you feel guilty because you are on time.

The only solution: schedule luncheon with the early bird fifteen minutes later than you want it to start. In that perverse way, you will both be on time.

Don't play Escoffier

Nobody came to lunch to learn what you know about foods and wine (unless, of course, you're in that business). So don't act like the French chef and start correcting your guest's pronunciation. And don't tell about the great meal you had at another restaurant with someone else.

Even if food is your hobby, don't stop and ask the chef for the recipe. Always remember why you are lunching together.

Be a firm police officer

If the service is annoyingly slow, try to find your waiter and hurry things along. If it's impossible to find a waiter—I once had one who quit in the middle of luncheon and left my companion and me stranded between the vichyssoise and the cold salmon—try to find the owner or the captain. Literally try to find that person. Get up from the table, and look. If I hadn't on that ill-fated day, I'd still be in the same restaurant with my friend because when a restaurant is crowded during the noon hour, the people who run the place seldom know what's happening at individual tables.

On the other hand, don't hurry a waiter in order to show your power.

The best rule for dealing with waiters and captains is: be businesslike and make all requests in a normal tone of voice prefaced by the word "please."

If hot food is served cold, send it back.

If any food does not taste fresh, send it back.

And if you reorder, never reorder the same dish. I don't know why this is so, but it is—it just won't taste good, no matter how many times the chef tries.

I forgot my wallet, my credit card, my allowance, etc.

When you are a luncheon guest and someone forgets to take money, sometimes (the first time) it is excusable.

The second time it is possible.

The third time it is reprehensible.

The fourth time you get the invitation, say gently, "No, no, I insist. This is my turn."

Then forget to take your credit card.

Call for Mr. Important

Since any restaurant other than McDonald's will inform you if you receive a telephone call and thereby permit you to excuse yourself and take that call, it is both pretentious and unnecessary to have a telephone at the luncheon table.

It also announces that anyone who calls is more important than the luncheon companion of the moment.

If your friend (this is no friend, friend) insists on a phone at the table, then ask if the phone also eats and drinks and needs a place set for it.

Remember, This is only lunch. The show doesn't have to go on.

If you feel ill, don't be afraid to say so. The worst thing in the world is to feel faint, upset, or weak and think that you must stay at a luncheon table.

Everyone understands.

Everyone wants to understand.

If you are the host, act like a CEO

Take charge from the moment the luncheon begins.

If the restaurant is one with which you are familiar, you will be able to order quickly from the menu and make two suggestions to your guest. If you do not know the restaurant, arrive in enough time to preview the menu, make your own choice, and find the suggestions. Suggestions should always include one of the most expensive dishes on the menu (so your guest will not feel you have money hang-ups where he is concerned), and one suggestion should be (a) a food you have tried there and enjoyed or (b) a house specialty.

If there are six or more persons attending, preorder for the table. If you do not, it will take longer to order than it will to eat.

Six ways to lose an order over lunch

1. Table-hop while your guest sits looking at his soup growing colder by the moment.

2. Talk about yourself.

3. Indulge in too much small talk before getting to the reason for the luncheon.

4. Eat so fast that your guest hasn't had two mouthfuls before you're finished, or

5. Eat so slowly that your guest is wondering if he'll make his afternoon appointments.

6. Arrive at (a) the wrong day, (b) the wrong time, (c) the wrong restaurant.

Dealing with Dinner

The most difficult meal for deal making is dinner.

There is always the danger of drinking too much, eating too much, and—ultimately—talking too much.

As most businesspersons know, too much often results in too little.

There are some basics to keep in mind should your business dealings require that you dine with an associate:

Don't assume your guest's dinner hour is yours

Americans do not all eat at the same hour.

Smaller cities consider 12 noon the luncheon hour; in many larger cities 1 P.M. is considered more fashionable; in all cities 12:30 is the best compromise.

Dinner, however, is another matter.

Vincent L. invited to dinner three out-of-town auditors who were in New York to negotiate the sale of a health care company Vincent wanted to buy. "Meet me at 8 at Christ Cella's," Vincent said, thinking that a steak and lobster restaurant landmark would be a good choice.

At 8 promptly the men showed up.

Vincent was already there waiting for them.

"Great steaks and lobsters," Vincent promised as they prepared to join him.

The men looked at one another, said nothing, and were handed menus.

"We'll just have coffee," said one of the guests shifting uneasily in his chair.

Vincent was floored. "Why?" he asked. "The food here is fantastic."

The man blushed. "Well, you said 8 o'clock so we figured it was for coffee. We had dinner at the hotel. You see, we get hungry. Back home we eat at 6."

Vincent ended up drinking instead of eating, apologizing instead of negotiating. The deal never did go through.

Had Vincent asked, when he extended the invitation, "What time do you want to have dinner?" instead of making assumptions, no one would have felt too awkward to make a deal.

Keep the dinner one-to-one

Lester was a jewelry importer, and a very important retailer was coming to town. Lester wanted to show him a proper good time—the definition of a proper good time, in this case, meaning dinner at a staid restaurant with no words like "nouvelle" and "radicchio" on the menu.

An hour before dinner, Lester received a call. "May I bring someone along?" the guest asked.

Lester was the seller, not the buyer. "Of course," he said, assuming the retailer would bring one of his business associates. Instead the retailer brought a young lady, currently the object of his out-of-town affections. Lester figured it was a wasted evening, since he was unable to talk business. He did assume, however, that the retailer would be appreciative of his hospitality and remember it in the days to come.

The following month Lester went to the retailer's city. Instead of a warm reception, he was told the retailer could not see him. It was many weeks later that Lester learned that the retailer was now in the middle of a publicized and ugly divorce suit in which the young woman who had accompanied them to dinner was named.

"That taught me something," Lester says. "Under no circumstances do I permit customers to bring anyone who has nothing to do with the business to a business dinner. I feel that so long as I pick up the check, I have the right to ask in advance, 'Is this someone who will work with us?'

"Even if the person is an employee, if he's not going to be working with my company, I don't feel I have to entertain him. In the long run, I feel that the business attitude toward the business dinner pays off.

"Maybe I hurt a few feelings along the way, but nobody can say that I'm not professional. And I've learned that I never want to get mixed up in anybody's private life in the course of pursuing business."

Get to the business at hand before the second drink

The first drink is to relax your guest.

But by the time he is ready to order another drink, you'd better be certain he's not too relaxed to do business.

Although moderation is certainly in vogue today, there are still many businesspersons who will not drink during the day but find they feel more convivial in the evening.

As the host you can bring the conversation to the point of the dinner by saying, "I am very glad to know that we can see one another away from the ringing telephones and pressures of business. There is something I want to discuss with you. Let me tell you what it is."

Only a person who has no company manners—or who plans to pick up the check—will say, "Not now."

When You Are the Guest

Just because he invited you doesn't mean that you don't have an agenda of your own.

Indeed, the invitation extended can be the best opportunity for you to present ideas that you want to air, to get off-the-record opinions, or to suggest something that could be more easily dismissed in a memo but will get considered judgment across a table.

Remember always tha the table is like a football field. You can be offsides, out of bounds, and penalized for unnecessary roughness. You can also score big.

Don't tip your hand too soon

Roger was pleased when his boss poked his head in the doorway of his office one noon and extended an impromptu invitation to lunch.

A super opportunity, thought Roger. He wanted three new computer stations added to the department, and this would be an excellent opportunity to make the request and give the supporting reasons. Further, luncheon was at the boss's suggestion, so Roger wouldn't appear opportunistic or pushy.

They met at a nearby Italian restaurant. Roger was careful to order a salad (pasta required too much concentration), no wine (although his boss had a glass), and waited for his boss to give his opinions of the weather, the headlines in the daily paper, and his child's progress with her tap dancing lessons.

Now they were six minutes into the luncheon.

As they began to look at the menu, Roger said quickly, "We need more computer stations in order to be competitive and get more work from present staff."

His boss looked at him disbelievingly. "What did you say?"

Roger repeated his request.

"Look," said his boss. "I asked you to lunch because I wanted to get out of the office and just have a nice, friendly lunch. I know what you need. I wasn't asking you for your next budget."

Roger, somewhat abashed, ate the rest of his lunch in nervous silence. It has been four months since that luncheon, and Roger still does not have the relationship back on a good footing.

Roger realizes now that had he waited until he was asked—rather than plunging with his own agenda—he would have had a better chance to know his boss and to get what he wanted.

It was a case of too much too soon.

Watch your host for clues

If your host seems uneasy (the body language of uneasiness is communicated through constant looking around the room, the need to have everything you say repeated because the host doesn't seem to hear it the first time, continual wetting of the lips, twitching in the chair, brow-mopping), chuck your agenda.

Nervous people can't buy anything.

Don't sell your brains for a ham on rye

There will be times when people think they can harness your creative energy and talent for the price of a lunch.

You can tell if someone is getting beyond genuine interest in your abilities and reasoning powers when

1. You are asked for specific recommendations.
2. You are asked to put those ideas in writing.
3. You are asked for original concepts.

When this happens, you must remember that you sell your talents and those of your company for a price. At such times it is necessary to remind your host that you are part of a profit-making organization.

It is entirely appropriate at this time to say

"Do I understand that you are asking us to go to work for you?"

"I am sure you realize that this is the kind of work we do for a fee for our clients."

"What you are asking requires a lot more thought than I am giving over lunch. Do you want us to pursue this?"

"If this is what you really want to know, maybe we need a business relationship that is more formal than an occasional lunch."

And that is the kind of conversation that leads out of the restaurant and directly into a meeting.

Meetings: The Work of Working

Meetings are the show business of business.

Often a meeting is where you learn how good or bad people really are.

A meeting can tell you

Who is honest in appraising goods and services

Who accepts responsibility

Who tries to talk too much

Who has ideas but lacks the confidence to present them

Who offers emotion and rhetoric in place of solutions

Who advances through shrewd handling of others

Who can say no without destroying people

The most exciting meetings result in management adopting an idea or taking an action never before considered.

In order for that to happen, an open atmosphere must be

created, one in which people who speak do not think they will be punished for suggesting an idea that someone else may consider foolhardy.

If you are the person who is going to make the suggestion that someone may consider off the wall, couch the suggestion in careful language.

Instead of saying, "I think we should . . . ." ask "What if . . . ."

Instead of saying, "I have an idea . . . ." ask "Would it make sense if we . . . ."

Instead of saying "I want . . . ." ask "What would you think if . . . ."

Whether you run the meeting or are there as an attendee, there are two things that you can do to make the meeting more successful:

(a) Probe for the answers

When you don't have the solutions—and most people do not—ask the quesions that will lead to the answers you must have in order to make an intelligent decision. Ask direct questions: Why can you really do? Do we need more staff for that? What are the costs?

The faster you get to the guts of the question, the quicker you will reach a solution.

(b) Permit people to challenge your ideas

Answer with directness and authority.

If you think you are wrong after hearing new information, say so.

If, however, you intend to hold your ground, say so with conviction. Give your reasons based on experience. Do it with dignity—no shouting, no loss of temper. And remember that your associates will not respect you if you simply cave in every time an obstacle is put in your path.

*   *   *

In advertising, we have many meetings for new business presentations.

These are particularly hard to program.

For me each new pitch is like my first day in the business.

And each time I think I have the right format, someone comes along and challenges my thinking.

I had always thought that looking at published agency work done for other clients was the only way that a prospective client could buy a new agency. Then Edward J. Piszek came to see us.

Mr. Piszek, an authentic original, founded Mrs. Paul's Seafood Products, sold his company, and now—in his sixties—was starting a food conglomerate.

We told him of our experience, chatted a bit, and then I said, "Mr. Piszek, would you like to see our work?" In my mind I was already halfway to the place where the lights went out and our TV reel came on screen.

"No," said Mr. Piszek, "I really don't want to look at your work. I figure you wouldn't have been in business this long if you didn't know how to make ads. Let's talk about me instead."

With that incident fresh in my mind, the next client presentation was done with emphasis on the client's need. And an hour later the advertising manager asked, "Don't you people ever show your reel?"

In a meeting that you run, you have to watch for signs of boredom (looking at a watch, doodling, note passing, heavy sighing). Each of those is an indication that it's time to close.

If you are attending a meeting, remember that you communicate a great deal by your body language.

Characters at the Meeting

The sprawler

All arms and legs, the sprawler becomes at one with the furniture.

The sprawler is more at home in the meeting room than the

person who called the meeting. Everyone half expects him to take off his jacket, roll up his sleeves, and put his feet on the table. And, if he should be among the early arrivals at the meeting, he never stands to shake hands or otherwise acknowledge the presence of new persons.

Maybe every sprawler should be told about Andrés Segovia, the nonagenarian preeminent cellist. Segovia often begins his evening with a rehearsal, plays a concert, and after concertizing welcomes guests in his dressing room—springing to his feet to greet each new arrival.

The street-smart person

Male or female, the street-smart person is the one who answers everything in the meeting with references to being "street-smart."

This is the person who attacks ideas by saying, "It sounds good, but the street-smart guys will laugh you out of business with that."

What street-smarters forget is that a true street-smart person makes decisions tempered with knowledge, common sense, and an instinctual regard for others.

A true street-smart person may have little formal education or—on the other hand—may have a fistful of advanced degrees. Often those who pride themselves on being street-smart are those with limited formal education who wear the label "street-smart" the way some others wear a Phi Beta Kappa key.

But watch the professional street-smart guy because in a meeting he's the one with a chip on his shoulder, and instead of trying to work with a positive agenda, he is more concerned with besting everyone.

The street-smart person is the one who frequently confuses toughness with bullying (his target is anyone weaker, and that to him often means women).

The best way to control a street-smart person in a meeting (you do, after all, want his positive contributions) is to say, "Even if you're right, you wouldn't have any respect for me if I didn't investigate further."

Mr. Clean

It began in the 1960s, the use of the four-letter word by people who knew longer—and shorter—words. It is now a kind of short-hand that is used to let others know that you're not as old as you look nor as stuffy as you seem.

Primordial language, however, is not the only way to become one of the crowd.

If you object to the language being used in the meeting, say something privately afterward to the offender. Chances are that if you protest publicly in a meeting you become too much a Goody Two-Shoes unless you treat this particular deviation with humor.

While I think that tough language generally indicates an inability to communicate, I concede that there are times when the language has to match the occasion—and some business happenings are worth rough language.

Also, I have learned that language doesn't indicate one's personal value system. Charles Revson, who was certainly the toughest boss I ever saw in my life, would attack ideas and executives passionately and in so doing he would explode with an occasional "damn" or "hell." Each time he did, he stopped cold, turned, and said, "Excuse me, Lois."

But Mr. Revson never apologized for his verbal steamrolling and flattening of the egos and self-respect of grown men.

The maven

This is the person in the meeting who will tell you how it was done forty-seven years ago.

This is the person in the meeting who never heard a new idea because he tried it before George Washington crossed the Delaware.

This is the person who knows it before you say it.

This is the person who will drive everyone mad.

Make sure this person is not you.

Meetings Are Held for a Thousand Different Reasons

There are meetings held out of habit. ("We meet every Tuesday morning because that's the way we've always done it.")

There are meetings held because executives don't have anything to do. ("Harry, I've got an hour before lunch. Why don't you get everybody together and bring me up to date on the XYZ project?")

And there are meetings held because a decision that is needed either cannot be reached or has been reached and cannot be made official until some group gets together ("Let's have a meeting so they'll think they're part of it.")

Most meetings are too long, too dull, too unproductive—and too much a part of corporate life to be abandoned.

But that does not mean that efforts should not be made to streamline, update, and—wherever possible—get rid of unnecessary meetings and unneeded participants.

If you run the meeting, then you can set the style. And the most effective style rule is: keep it short. Keep the list of attendees short; keep the agenda short; keep the time allotted for each subject short.

As the presiding person, consider carefully the hour of the day or evening you convene. The best way to follow the "keep it short" rule is to schedule your meeting during nonbusiness hours. The head of Kaynee, the children's-wear company, scheduled every one of his meetings at 5 P.M. each day so that no sales representative would miss a telephoned order, but he also realized that by starting at 5 P.M. he would eliminate a lot of conversation from people talking for the sake of being heard in a meeting. Who wants to talk himself right through the 6:20 bar car?

Meetings that begin an hour before the office opens are almost forced to end when the whistle blows and work begins. At Wyse we schedule many of our internal meetings an hour before opening time; it puts a closing time on the meeting.

*   *   *

A meeting is where a star is born or ships are sunk.

I have been in both kinds of meetings.

I was once in one of those corned-beef-on-rye meetings (an emergency meeting that began at 6 P.M. and went until midnight with time out for nothing but corned beef on rye), and after that meeting there was a special bonding between all of us on the agency side and all of the client people. As someone said when we left, "I feel like singing 'Nearer My God to Thee.' "

Not all meetings have such a salubrious effect. At another meeting I saw an executive ask one of his staff for information that had been disclosed in an office memo distributed the week prior to the meeting.

The staff man didn't have the answer.

He was not there at the next meeting.

Public humiliation is the downside risk of any meeting.

Therefore, every precaution should be taken to protect oneself from the vicissitudes of corporate dart throwing.

If, however, the meeting covers one's field of expertise, all ways to allow one's own light to shine should be explored.

Do's and Don'ts of Style

Prepare! rehearse!

This is not the Sophomore Speech Contest; you don't have to write your speech and declaim. But if this is a meeting where you are going to be selling yourself, make sure that the real you can come through. The only way that can happen is if you have prepared in advance.

Preview the agenda, and decide which key words and phrases will communicate your most important thoughts, and then rehearse a few times. It is always better to use key words on cards instead of a written text. Anything you believe deeply will never be said precisely the same way two times in a row. Some significant phrases will always be there; still the emotion of the moment will charge the speech differently each time. And that emotional punch is what will make your thoughts as memorable as your words.

It is always a good idea to rehearse before a meeting, particularly if you are making a presentation, or you may find yourself in an embarrassing position as one advertising agency once did.

The agency was asked to name a new brand of Kent cigarettes. Not only were they to name the new longer Kent, the agency was also to position the brand and give it an exquisite package. In instructing the agency, the client repeated over and over the need for a "noble" feeling.

The cigarette needed a noble name.

It needed a noble package.

It needed a noble position.

A special crack creative team was assigned the project. This was one of those hush-hush projects that, in terms borrowed from the CIA, requires all those involved to refer to their work by a code name.

For months the team labored.

For months they reviewed consumer data.

They tested possible positions.

They researched names.

Finally the pieces came together. There was tension and excitement throughout the agency.

Twenty-four hours before the presentation was to be made to the client, the agency president met with the creative team to see the results. And because the job was so important to the agency, other inside executives were invited to see the results.

The group assembled in an agency conference room.

The lights were lowered, and the project supervisor rose proudly to speak.

"We have chosen a noble name," he intoned.

Around the room heads nodded. They all knew that was what was needed.

"A noble name for the new Kent," he repeated. "A name that is a logical extension of the name we know, a name that holds a promise. A noble name indeed. The name is *Kent Sirs.*"

A gasp went around the table.

The president left the room.

In the pressure for secrecy, no one had ever said the noble name aloud.

And Kent Sirs sounded exactly like cancers.

The creative team learned the hard way that nothing ever takes the place of rehearsing in front of a mirror.

Don't resort to the star-studded conversation

You do not always have to validate your presence at a meeting.

But, if you feel you must, remember that one significant reference will do.

The producer of a Broadway show assembled some of the most famous names in the theater to discuss a new project. Among the attendees was a man who was a good and loyal worker—but he was less well-known that the others in the room.

As the morning wore on, the attendees were worn down by the man's constant references to "When I worked with This Big Star," and "When That Famous Composer told me . . . ."

Finally the producer looked at the man and said, "Pardon me, but don't you know anyone who isn't famous?"

The meeting proceeded productively.

Don't overprop a meeting

If you can find ways to make your words more interesting, use them. I have a particular aversion to those transparent floppy slides laid over projectors and shown on a screen. Generally the slides are filled with blurred, tiny numbers which some researcher invariably writes over with a grease pencil during a presentation. These pages then pile up next to a machine like so many spent shells. Presenters can become so attached to their own use of the grease pencil, their own swoops and flourishes, that they fail to notice the audible yawns in the room. And when the meeting ends, participants remember nothing except that they were bored.

The best-prepared presentation in a meeting is one that uses visuals which communicate something the person cannot. Florence Skelly presents market information, the kind of information most people like to show on screens, but she does it with so much imagery that she never needs a visual prop. She is in constant demand as a speaker. Maybe there's a lesson in that.

Look for the pot of gold

Decide in advance whether this will be a meeting that will move your marker past *go*.

It will not be your meeting if you know in advance that you have certain people in the room who are openly hostile to you and/or your ideas.

It will not be your meeting if the subject is not one in which you are expected to be expert. For, even if you should have the answers in this alien field, the people who are the experts will both hate and hurt you publicly for displaying knowledge that is not within your province to discuss.

Don't despair. Most meetings with more than two people will not be your meeting. A rule of thumb: meetings belong to the person(s) calling them.

Required conduct during a meeting where you cannot make points: don't lose points by talking, coughing, smoking, and otherwise calling attention to yourself; don't ask questions; join in group laughter even when you see no reason for laughing.

If, however, this is a meeting where you do have a contribution, make your point at an appropriate time in the meeting.

If an agenda is supplied in advance, consult with the presiding person so that you will be added to the agenda and have, in effect, a supporter in the room, someone who knows in advance what you want to say and is predisposed to your saying it.

Keep your remarks brief, and try to avoid controversy in a large meeting. If someone at your level tries to make you look like Howdy Doody revisited, chances are that you will fare better by not responding at the level you are questioned.

If somebody beats up on you verbally, don't try the snappy comeback. Just sit and listen, and you'll feel the waves of understanding come washing over you. The rest of the room will gravitate to you.

We all tend to have sympathy for the underdog, and no one likes to see another person victimized in a meeting.

Put every decision in writing, and inform participants

After a number of client-agency meetings and intraagency meetings, an advertising agency was given the job of creating a campaign for Amaretto di Saronno.

It was scheduled as a two-week shoot in Italy, and it was considered one of the agency's choice creative assignments.

As often happens, some of the shooting took longer than expected, and the whole trip wound up as a three-week assignment in Italy instead of a two-week job.

The agency people, however, knew the client would find the results worth the additional cost and effort.

The creative people had discovered wondrous sites, had shot special and distinctive photos—the locations were highly identifiable and would, they were sure, be well known by the Italian client.

The slides were sorted lovingly by the group upon their return, and the client was called to see the results.

Proudly the agency people assembled.

The lights were lowered, and the first slide was shown.

Beautiful sea shot. Click. Next shot. Another beauty shot.

Click. Still another beautiful shot, this time with bottle against location background.

Click. Another.

Click. And. . . .

The client shouted, "Stop."

The lights went up.

"Where is this?" the client snapped. "Where did you take these pictures?"

"In Italy," the agency spokesman replied.

"Of course, Italy," said the client. "But where in Italy?"

"Sorrento," said the agency people.

The client put his head in his hands. "Didn't you even read the label? It's Saronno. Saronno, not Sorrento."

The agency paid for the reshoot.

It was a costly lesson in the importance of not only listening, but sending minutes of meetings to all participants.

Presenting New Ideas

New ideas are what make instant stars.

But new ideas are not easy to introduce, so the key in presenting something unfamiliar is to make sure you go slow.

Send up a trial balloon twenty-four hours in advance of the meeting. Take your idea, clean and press it, and try it on somebody you trust.

If your friend advises you not to proceed—and you go ahead anyway—well, don't say you weren't warned.

If your trustworthy pal gives you a green light, take the idea to the meeting, and, at the appropriate time, see if it can stay aloft by itself.

Don't try to present something which is complete; most attendees will resent the idea. It is always better to offer an embryo and let everyone in the room help nurture it. Even if you are the only person with the ability to do it, you will have trouble selling an idea to which others do not feel they can make a contribution.

Laugh, Clown, Laugh

We once handled the advertising for a financial institution whose president, Bill, was an unusually witty man. Hal, the account executive running the business, was also a quick wit. The meetings with the client were hilarious, I was told by the account executive. Then one day when I had one of my regular client-agency luncheons with Bill, I saw that he was uncomfortable; he was trying to tell me something. In business, as we all know, napkin fumbling is body language.

"Is there a problem somewhere, Bill?" I asked.

"Now that you mention it . . . ," he began, and then he went on to ask if he might have a new account person.

"I thought you two fellows hit it off so well," I said. "What's the problem? Please tell me so I can correct it."

Bill got right to the point, "I'm tired of playing 'Can You Top This?' No matter what I say, Hal tries to top it. I'm at the point now that I freeze when he walks into the office."

A surfeit of wit wins no friends.

Generally we all do better when we let the people in charge tell the jokes and set the level of levity.

Ladies and Gentlemen of the Industry . . .

There are many times that you will find yourself in a meeting with your contemporaries (also known as competition) in the marketplace. You are all working together on an industry program or a charity function, and you want them to think well of you. After all, you never know who will be on which side next year.

This is one of the times for situation humor, and if you do indeed have one of those kinds of minds that is able to see the laughs in the moment at hand, go ahead and share the mirth.

We once handled an automobile dealer association. Certainly

no people are more competitive than those who are selling the same cars for different prices. Nonetheless, they had all banded together in order to have an advertising program, a part of which was shared by the manufacturer—but only if each dealer made a contribution. Under those kinds of circumstances the dealers agreed it made sense to band together and pool their resources.

Every week we met at luncheon, this hardy band of fairly rough-and-tumble men and me. They watched their language, never insulted one another openly, and generally were gentlemen. They did not pretend to be disciples of David Ogilvy, but they were giving the advertising more attention than just a tire kick. The dealers discussed the advertising each week; we went around the luncheon table, each man deliberating carefully. All were articulate, voicing their opinions loudly and regularly—all except Max. Finally one week the chairman looked quizzically at Max. "Max," he said, "we've just looked at final copy for the ads. Don't you want to say anything?"

"Yes," said Max. "Pass the rolls."

The Telephone at the Meeting

Once a meeting begins you show your style and company manners by the kind of attention and courtesy extended.

Interrupting a meeting for a telephone call—unless it is of equal importance to the others in the meeting—is a basic discourtesy. Still, it is a discourtesy of which almost all executives are guilty.

If you leave a meeting to answer the telephone, try to do so unobtrusively. If the meeting is being held for your benefit, ask those making the presentation to excuse you for the number of minutes you will require. If the time you need is unfairly long, either tell the rest of the participants to continue without you or, if it involves people within your organization, reschedule the meeting for later in the day.

It's a Conference Call

Telecommunications will change all our meeting habits within the next few years.

Even now we all have more conference calls than we did five years ago. Participants are plugged in from all over the world.

The teleconference meeting requires a new style.

Even though you may be taking this call on your lanai in Hawaii, do not remind the others who are freezing in Kansas City and Chicago that you are giving up your tennis game in order to accept this call.

Once the teleconference call begins, it is best not to speak unless you are addressed directly. It is difficult for the person running the meeting to know who is speaking when disembodied voices suddenly come rushing through the wires.

When your name is read and the presiding person asks if you are present, a simple "present" or "here" will do. Don't go through the horror story of your trip there or the delights of arriving.

When the call is declared finished, don't hang on the wire with a few extra words for the chairman. That is more appropriately handled by a separate call when you can speak one-on-one.

Since the meeting is where people reveal themselves in many ways, take great care before you speak out. Consider not only the words and thoughts you want to express but also the group effect of what you are about to say.

A jocular observation made in the privacy of a peer's office may be greeted with icy silence when delivered in a roomful of people. When told to more than one person, an inside bit of information may make you look and sound like a snoop—instead of an aware executive.

The *New York Times* executive William Kerr believes that the question facing all of us in business is

To whom do I give my trust, and when do I take that trust away?

Keep that in mind next time you are tempted to give an off-the-cuff answer in a big meeting.

No one really trusts an answer that comes too quickly. Never mind that you really do think fast and can come up with solutions.

There are many executives who believe that quick answers are glib and glossy, not at all trustworthy.

As an attendee you will maintain your associates' trust if you don't introduce anything too new, too explosive, too daring.

Company manners often calls for campaigning for your causes outside the meeting. Plead your cause one-on-one or in small groups, and do not expect group dynamics to result in anything beyond the chairman's agenda.

And when you are in charge of the meeting, remember that an idea may be attacked viciously because it is presented by an unacceptable parent.

Be certain that people who say "no" with ease are negating the idea and not the idea's originator.

Just as criticism should be handled gently in a roomful of people, so should praise. There are a lot of thin-skinned people who can't understand why the chair is recognizing a quasi-accomplishment by someone the troops regard with disdain. Before you pat the back, you'd better check with the others.

Of course, you will treat each speaker with equal courtesy, and play no favorites. But should a speaker go on too long, you might suggest a subgroup to consider further points.

As you run the meeting, do not forget that you are on display every minute. You will raise your trust level if you are patient but not patronizing, fast but not feckless.

After all, what you really want to do in a meeting—whether you are the no. 1 chairman or vice president no. 62—is to assure your contemporaries that you are smart enough to be trusted with the company, its present and future.

Surviving: Living through Mergers, Acquisitions, Reorganizations, Shakeouts, and Corporate Warfare

The best-loved politicians, the ones we reelect, are those who somehow manage to disassociate themselves from unpleasant things like taxes, crime, and graft.

These wise politicos cluck in horror at the headlines and ask, "How could they?" By the time we also finish clucking, we know that our elected officials are really a part of "they," but by then we are convinced that their hearts are really with us.

That political attitude toward survival works in the corporate world, too.

If you want to become a part of a new team, convince the new owners that you think and feel as they do.

This is not easy for everyone to do.

There are those whose pride is more important than their jobs. They will have difficulty if they do not subscribe to the new corporate catechism.

When Karen, the cosmetics buyer of a large department store, found that her store was to be taken over by another chain, she realized that the new owners had back-up talent so it would be easy for them to replace her. She was, however, determined to have management notice her and let her stay.

At her first meeting with the general merchandise manager who was brought in to consolidate the store efforts, Karen was told what was expected of her. As she listened, she realized she would be on trial with the new people. She also realized that their approach was thoroughly professional. Typical of the questions asked were

What are your relationships with this vendor?

How do you promote the spring events with that vendor?

Which of your ads did you approve? What were you forced to run?

As she answered, she kept several things in mind. She never disparaged the management for whom she had worked. She realized that if she did, she would not automatically become a part of the new team. Instead the new owners would assume she was an antimanagement person. So she quickly put herself on the side of store versus the vendor.

Instead of criticizing her old management, she criticized the vendors' lack of respect for that management. "Some of the things 'they' expect of the store," she clucked. "I'm sure that you have real power with them. We'll be able to do a first-rate job together. I do have some ideas. . . ."

As the conversation with the new management continued, Karen was questioned further about her willingness to cooperate. As she listened to the questions, she realized her chances of staying were excellent. Now she had to convince them that she also had some backbone.

She listened to more and more questions:

Will you add these lines?

Will you take out those lines?

Will you add demonstrators?

Karen was impressèd by the new management's desire for excellence; the questions were good, the attitudes constructive. Still, she had to show her own spirit. She did not disagree with their recommendations, but how would they know that despite her acquiescence, she was a woman of independent thought?

Finally the answer came to her. She waited. Then, as she was leaving, she said, "I am sure that someday I will have the courage to say no to you. But not now, not when your ideas are positive and constructive and helpful to me. I like what you are saying, and I think you will make *our* store better."

Karen not only kept her job; she is now a merchandiser.

That does not happen to all people following all mergers.

Living through Mergers and Acquisitions

After Chevron and Gulf merged in 1984, many Gulf executives spent more than a year wondering if they would fit in—and found at the end of the year that the answer was—they wouldn't.

The newest approach to the "who's in/who's not" game is called the Club Sandwich approach. In these cases management takes one level of staff from the acquirer, puts it on another level from the acquired, and tops it with a level from the acquirer.

Most merger survivors are familiar with the Chinese Menu approach whereby the manager takes one staff person from column A, another from column B.

Good company manners would dictate that early on a face-to-face meeting should be held with all executives of an acquired company. Even if the only word is, "We don't yet know," it adds a humanizing step to the dehumanizing process of merger.

When CBS hit its bumps in the rocky road to finances after battling the attempted takeover by Ted Turner, senior executives were offered inducements to take early retirement. Many did.

When an acquired company is in an expansion mode, that can be good news for executives of the acquired company. It is tougher to find top executives and middle management than it is to find lower-positioned persons, and many new jobs may be opened.

The most difficult merger is that of two clashing corporate cultures—when a conservative and slower-paced company joins forces with an aggressive marketeer. Only a willingness to spend time together, to share and interpret company policy, to seek sanguine solutions to complex concerns will help the oil and water mix.

Mergers are like forest fires, floods, and volcanic eruptions. You don't cause them, but you do have to cope with them.

And, like those natural disasters, mergers begin in unnoticed and unexpected ways. Perhaps there is a casual conversation between two men who serve on the same board. It may be a chance remark made by a social friend. It can begin when two people happen to sit next to one another on the dais of yet another charity dinner.

Regardless of how casual both claim their interest to be, you can be certain that there is—standing in the background—a vast army of lawyers, accountants, and bankers rubbing their hands gleefully as they get ready to discuss feemail, greenmail, interest-rate swaps, junk bonds, mortgage-backed securities, poison pills, shark repellents, and white knights.

For in this scary new world of the merged and submerged, the big profits do not go to the stockholders, the middle executives, or the loyal employees who carried lunch buckets and built the business for thirty years. No, the big winners are people who never even thought of the two companies as one until the fateful calls from the CEOs alerted them.

The big winners in the merger games are lawyers, accountants, and bankers.

In mergers—as in all deals—there are three hurdles before the papers are signed and stationery is redesigned.

Before a merger is a merger, the principals must agree on

1. Price
2. The new merged name
3. The no. 1 officer and the no. 2 officer

Once those three points are resolved, every deal is as good as made.

CEOs, as we all know, parachute happily to a next cushy job or become "consultants," in case they choose not to remain with the newly formed company.

But what of the rest of the players?

What is to become of the others?

What of the middle managers in Beatrice after its latest $6.2 billion sale? What of the executives at General Foods who are supposedly duplicated by executives in the buying company Philip Morris? And when R. J. Reynolds acquired Nabisco Brands for $4.9 billion, what of the $75,000-a-year managers? The $150,000-a-year executives? Where do they go? Who educates their children and fills their refrigerators?

In some cases they will be absorbed into the new structure.

In others people will free-float for long periods of time.

In others like Lehman Brothers, which was merged into Shearson American Express, the investment bankers will find the character of the merged company so changed that they will leave for jobs in other companies.

In only a few, like the Higbee Company department store, which was bought by Industrial Equity, an Australian off-shore company, the parent company will keep hands off and permit acquired management to stay in place and manage its affairs as it always has. Gimbels, on the other hand, was sold by Batus, and the Gimbel name will disappear in this latest sale.

If you are below the rank of CEO in a newly merged company, one of two things will happen to you. You will either patty-cake your way to the best job you ever had, or you will scramble madly in an attempt to find the best job you ever had.

The time between the first rumor of merger and the day

the ink dries on the final papers can be a terrible time for anyone who depends on the company for a livelihood. You are
caught up in the drama of "Dallas" being played right there in
the office. It is big bucks time, and you are fascinated by the
interplay.

Will your boss stay?

Will you stay?

It's a fearful-exciting time, not a joyous-exciting time.

It is during this period in limbo, the days spent between guessing and knowing, that you can set the style that will keep you at
the new company.

There are attitudes—styles—that will keep you in place despite mergers. Remember always that the new owners cannot possibly fire everyone. This is advice of how to survive at all costs.
Only you can decide if the prize is worth the price.

Hanging in there at all costs

Will they be comfortable with you?

Not necessarily, for sometimes, just when you think all is going
well, it all falls apart.

Why?

No one really knows. There you are—minding your own business and doing your very best—and still someone up there decides
you are expendable. Don't make yourself crazy looking for reasons. Sometimes there are no reasons. Sometimes management is
willful, capricious, and out to get you. No matter how many home-
made fudge brownies you bring to the office, no matter how many
times you salute the company flag, you will not survive.

Could you have done anything differently?

Perhaps.

But some positions cannot be protected in business.

Some situations are without opportunity.

There is no way to protect or expand your job, or even to
hang in there, when you are forced to overcome an immediate
superior, a CEO, or a corporate board that is interested either in

advancing or protecting an old school pal, paying an unknown debt with your job, or securing a beachhead for a relative.

But hanging in there is sometimes possible with preplanning.

Don't go too high in the hierarchy

If someone wants to make you captain, and you know the *Lusitania* is about to collide with an iceberg, decline the offer. Contrary to what you may have heard, it is not easier to get a new job if you were the president at a company that was merged into another.

We are all familiar with LIFO (last in, first out) and FIFO (First in, first out) accounting methods. To that you can add a new corporate term: WIPO. It stands for "we're in, president's out."

The higher you are in the corporation, the more likely you are to lose your job, to go WIPO. Lopping starts with the biggest titles and the biggest salaries.

So eschew the corner office and the well-rounded perks.

They won't last.

Spot the players on the other team

Before the merger ever takes place, check out the players on the new team.

Where are the strengths?

What are the weaknesses?

If you find that the company is very strong where you are very strong, your chances of staying are somewhere between slim and zero. If there is adequate time before the merger takes place, make every effort to strengthen yourself in their weak areas.

Don't have any answers immediately

When you are interviewed by new management, always answer, "That's something we'll have to check. The company never did find out about that. Oh, I know they should have, but they didn't."

If you are asked to get the information, take a lot of time.

If you are asked for an opinion—don't give it. Just explain that it takes time to answer that.

Keep your department weak, and never hire your replacement

Nothing keeps you there longer than the inability of management to replace you.

If, however, you drag your feet too long—you will indeed be hanging. But you will not be hanging in there. You will be hanging around the unemployment and/or headhunter offices.

There are, however, some more savory solutions for survival.

Be action-oriented, not reaction-oriented

Van was not the company gossip, but it did happen that his wife had a friend who had a friend—and so Van was among the first to hear that there was a good chance that the company where he had worked for eighteen years was about to be sold.

Van did not go screaming through the corridors, but he did approach his boss and ask whether he thought the rumors were true. His boss committed the unforgivable sin; he knew the rumors were true, but he denied them.

Van, being of sound mind, did not believe his boss.

And so the groundwork was laid for constant guessing, whispering, and covert conversation. Needless to say, Van did not get much work done during this period. He spent all his thinking time thinking about himself. Would he be kept? Would he be let go?

One evening at a party Van was discussing the possible merger with a friend, a business consultant. As Van went on—and on and on—his friend cleared his throat and said quietly, "Van, what good does all this conversation do? Why don't you stop talking about what your company is going to do and think about what you are going to do? You can't have any effect on their decision. The only decision you can affect is your own. What do you want to do?"

Van had never really thought about his choices in the matter. He had been so excited about the daily drama that he had neglected to realize that there was only one script he was capable of writing—his.

The consultant gave Van sound advice.

Van hired a headhunter, sent out letters, and—as a result—felt more relaxed about the company than he had in weeks. He was actually able to think about the job he still had.

When the company finally was sold, Van had another job offer. But the new owners, in talking with Van, were impressed with his relaxed attitude toward them. He was the first of the executive group who did not seem nervous, anxious, and fearful. The new president said, "Van is our kind of man."

Van now has a better job that he had before the merger, and he is sure that the confident manner, his survival technique, is what kept him going.

Learn from Penelope

Remember Penelope, the wife of Ulysses?

When Ulysses went to war, she spun yarn in his absence. Each day she wove; each night she raveled her day's work, and so she made her work continue year after year.

The moral of the lesson is: When word is out about a merger, find yourself a never-ending job.

When the new people come into power, the first thing they will do is get rid of those who seem not to be working at something. The second thing they will do is fire people (they will call it "consolidating jobs") who do things the new bosses understand.

The people who never get fired or replaced or let out are those who get lost in projects that the new people cannot quite figure out.

So find yourself a complex job, preferably a project that requires constant travel. Be away when new management comes into town; be at the office when they are not.

Don't be underfoot; don't let anyone find you, and you will be there for a long, long time.

Don't stand out

In their first days on the new job, no one is interested in the maverick, the loner, the person who is the office individualist.

Don't make waves.

Don't try to be a star before you know how the new people define "star." Keep in mind the immortal words of Simon Ramo of TRW, "If you're going to act like a prima donna, you'd better make sure you can sing like one."

Betsy wanted to stay with the new company, so when the group vice president came to town and interviewed the old staff, Betsy appeared in a low-cut white dress.

The group vice president took one look at her, fired her—and then asked her out to dinner.

That was not what she expected.

Be very careful because the wrong attention is always worse than no attention.

Take time to evaluate the company style before you send a memo, request a meeting, or move a picture on your wall

After you get their first memo, go to their first meeting and see whose pictures (children, wife) or what pictures (a photograph of his boat, a museum print, an oil painting of a horse) so you have an idea of what your new bosses are about.

If they are casual and friendly, then you know what you can do without attracting too much attention.

If they are reserved and standoffish, you'd better keep the wild ties and the story about the guys on Fire Island under wraps for a while.

Do your best

Nothing beats your doing a good job when it comes to impressing a new owner.

As you do your job well, however, be sure that the rules haven't changed with the owners.

Your old boss's idea of excellence may not coincide with this regime's evaluation.

But no matter what the rules or what the people demand, you will be comfortable with the new people so long as you feel you are treating them courteously.

All you can do is hope that they are equally comfortable with you.

Living Through Shakeouts and Shakeups

There are ways to grow old gracefully in one's job, but only if you first learn to fight with pistols, swords, and words.

Before a full-scale corporate war breaks out, there will be many skirmishes. No one, of course, is certain just when a skirmish will develop into a full-blown war, which is why a skirmish must be fought with the same intensity and planning as a full-scale war.

The usual antagonisms which cause people to choose up sides in the turf wars are antagonisms bred by differences in discipline.

In a publishing house the natural enmity or rivalry is between the editorial and the business sides. Somerset Maugham once said of his publisher, "The reason I am unhappy is that the auditor in chief is more important than the editor in chief."

In a conglomerate the division from which the CEO came is the division that gets the greatest attention. When William Howlett was the president of Consolidated Foods, he always had a warm spot for the Lawson Milk Company, the convenience food chain he once headed, despite the fact that Sara Lee was certainly Consolidated's most prestigious division.

It is predictable; it is human nature. We all like what we know best.

The turf wars

Turf wars take place wherever power collides.

In some companies it may be marketing versus finance; in others, old boys versus new boys or Harvard MBAs versus the world.

The turf war does not have to result in a toppling of an empire; it can be fought with dignity and grace.

Think of the turf war as fencing, not the dropping of the atom bomb.

Think of the turf war as an intellectual war, one where you have the freedom to decide which battles you will fight to win and which you will choose not to enter.

Think of the turf war as a two-part situation, one part offense and one part defense.

And, if you think first, always think first, you will be able to wage this most intellectual of wars with great politesse.

Defensive Manners

When you are aware that your very own department is harboring the person who wants to create the sequel to "All about Eve" and that you are the person whose job is in jeopardy:

Speak up immediately

Sean was in charge of European sales for a manufacturer of western wear. His wife, an art dealer, loved his job, too, because it gave them continuing and mutual reasons to keep a foot on two continents.

Then one day Sean came home and told his wife that there

would be a third person on their trip to London the following week, the third person being a newly hired MBA. Sean's wife later recalled that the words "newly hired MBA" made her nose twitch.

But the only question she asked her husband was, "Why is he going with us?"

Sean smiled proudly, "The big boss called me in and told me there are very big things ahead for me. The European cities are mature markets, and they don't need my kind of talent to keep going back to them. . . ."

"But what could be more important than London and Paris?" she asked.

"Just wait and see," Sean said mysteriously. "The office just wants to be sure that my old territory is covered before I get the big new assignment."

Sean's wife remained unconvinced. "Why don't you tell them that you don't need help? Why don't you tell them to give you the promotion first and let you decide if you want it? Who says every promotion is a good one? Why don't you ask where the expansion is? Why don't you see if they are trying to get rid of you, after making sure that somebody else has all your contacts?"

Sean laughed. "You don't trust anybody do you? Honey, I think you're getting nervous over nothing. Besides, what do you know? You're an art dealer. This is business."

And so Sean took the new MBA to Europe, introduced him as his associate.

Two trips later the "associate" covered the London market alone.

Now Sean, his wife's words ringing in his ears, was nervous. Still he said nothing.

When the "associate" shared Sean's secretary and office, and when two months later Sean found all his old contacts in Europe calling "the associate," he was too afraid to say anything. He was afraid he'd be fired.

"Something will happen," he said to his wife. "This associate isn't that good. Wait. You'll see. He'll make a mistake."

The only mistake was Sean's.

From the beginning he had been paralyzed by fear.

Fear of consequences kept him from talking early. In the beginning he truly had power; he had the contacts. It was then that he should have confronted his bosses and asked for a contract assuring his job and salary level.

The big mistake many people make in the turf war is the mistake of not defending the turf when the turf is most defensible.

Defense must begin when you have weapons, not when you have the sword knocked out of your hand.

Be certain your department's organizational structure is in writing, and be certain it has been approved by management

Debbie, the overworked brand manager for a foods company, asked for an assistant.

The director of her department agreed that she needed help and decided to give a secretary a promotion.

"Fine with me," said Debbie. "If she can read and write, I have work for her."

And so, in best of corporate tradition, a move was made from the inside and the secretary not only became an assistant, she even had cards made with her new title.

In the days that followed the assistant not only showed that she could read and write, but she offered suggestions—good suggestions.

Then one day Debbie saw a note that her sweet little assistant sent to the president asking for more information on a new project.

Debbie sizzled.

The president?

She, Debbie, didn't even say hello to the president, much less send him memos.

Debbie called her assistant into her office, sat down with her, and said calmly, "I guess you never saw the organizational chart for this department. Either you don't know to whom you report or you don't want to know. But look now, look at the organization of this department, and look at it in writing. Then make sure you never forget it."

Debbie handed her assistant the chart. "You are on notice with me," she said. "You are not to go over my head. You are not to go behind my back. And if you do, you will not only be out of my department, you will be out of this company."

The assistant, somewhat chastened, is still working for Debbie.

"In an office," said Debbie, "everybody knows everything. The story about that assistant got around very fast. What it did was make everyone understand that no one will walk over me. All in all, I'd say the incident did me a lot of good. My vice president, in my last review, told me that I had improved in management skills."

Cry wolf

Everyone knows the old fable of the boy who cried "Wolf" every time he thought he saw a wolf. Finally, when he really saw one and cried out, no one believed him.

So make sure that you have a highly identifiable wolf before you alert the world.

Stuart, the manager of a women's sportswear shop, part of a national chain, sent reports back to the home office every time he heard of a store to be opened in the shopping center where the store he was assigned was located. Not only did he report news of the competition, but he even identified the competitor's resources, analyzed the consumer appeal, and recommended ways his store might stock, not only to defend their position, but to gain a share in the marketplace.

By increasing the company's awareness of the wolves and concentrating on ways to fight them, Stuart moved up to district manager.

His turf is increasing, thanks to an offensive strategy taken for a defensive position.

Deal from strength

Stuart dealt from strength.

He was an uncomplaining realist.

He did not spend his time thinking of excuses he would use when his sales began slipping.

Instead he considered his value to the store.

He knew that his best talents were analytical.

Real estate was not his specialty.

He did not tell management to move the store, nor did he suggest other locations.

He considered the way to take what was there and make it better.

In all turf wars, the best way to defend one's turf is to deal from strength—take a marketable talent and find the best way to extend it in the company manner.

Offensive Manners

You do not have to evict little old ladies from their apartment houses, or rob, cheat, or steal in order to make offensive moves in the spirit of the company that employs you. Turf wars are not all defensive. You can strike out on your own.

Cover your job

Gaining turf can be as simple as moving up.

The best way to move up and get more turf is to do your job and to do it so well that you will be given another job, a bigger job, and a better job.

The world is full of receptionists who have become account assistants, sales representatives who have become marketing directors, and mail-room boys who have become chairmen of boards.

In our office we hire fresh-from-art-school trainees, call them "puppies," and put them in our art department doing pasteup and working with senior art directors. Many of them have gone on to become senior art directors and television producers.

It comes down to what most of us were always taught: work hard and someone will recognize your fine work and reward you.

To that there is but one word to add.

Sometimes.

Take someone's wrong turn, and make it a right turn for you

Corporations, being only human, make mistakes.

Sometimes you may end up working for one of those mistakes.

When that happens, you have an unusual opportunity.

Your boss, known hereafter as "the corporate mistake," will one day drop the ball.

If you are alert, you will pick up the pieces—and keep them.

When this happens, you will really win if you do your act with both tact and humor so that you do not come off showboating.

Bobby was the son of the owner of a radio station, and when Bobby was made president of the station, everyone groaned.

But Kelly did not groan.

Kelly went to Bobby and said, "I think it's great, but I really think I can help you. I've been here two years longer than you, and I could be your eyes and ears."

Soon everyone was calling Kelly "eyes and ears."

Less than a year later Bobby's father bought another property, a sporting goods store, and Bobby went off to run that.

Kelly who, after all, was "the eyes and ears of the station" became president.

Sometimes the turf wars are easier than other times.

Hire well

Treachery and deceit sometimes come in on little cat's feet of love and loyalty.

If you want to prevent invasions of the body snatchers, if you want to keep moving up in your company, then show your ability to hire good people and have a loyal staff.

There is, however, a difference between a loyal staff and a staff that insulates you.

Try to be certain that among your loyal staff you have people who are smart enough and secure enough to tell you what's really going on in the office world around you.

Reorganize for power

If you are brought into a new position, assert your authority and organize in a way that protects your turf.

This can be tricky.

Pitt wanted to be president of the motorbike division; he had languished in the executive vice president (EVP) position long enough.

Corporate told Pitt that he could not move up to president until he found a solid sales person to succeed him as EVP.

Pitt contacted four headhunters and saw thirteen likely candidates before he met Neil. In Neil he saw a worthy successor. Never mind that Neil had worked with cars, not motorbikes. Pitt reasoned that if you knew wheels, you knew wheels.

Management was equally impressed.

They made Neil EVP and moved Pitt up to president.

Pitt loved his new job. He loved the fun of the company plane and the thrill of being president of the company he'd worked for and loved for many years.

Neil reveled in his job.

The first week—while Pitt was out visiting dealers—Neil moved the director of sales over to production.

Then he took the head of production and made him director of sales.

"A little switching will freshen the company," Neil promised.

What Neil did not add is that by moving two experienced men to areas where they had no knowledge, he was creating a situation in which he could not be second-guessed.

Without firing one executive, Neil became the supreme authority.

He had kept two company people, but he had them in roles where they had no background.

Pitt never cried, "Stop."

And so Neil changed the organizational chart until the company was so crippled that no one could move.

No one, that is, except corporate—who ultimately did away with both Pitt and Neil.

Warped and twisted though he may have been, Neil did understand the principles of turf.

Analyze possible responses to your actions carefully and realistically

Even though Neil acted in an aggressive, motivated manner, he failed to realize that his power play would be halted by people far above him.

The inability to think far enough ahead is the greatest danger for those who would move from a small pond into the open sea.

I once asked a corporate director of research how the president of the company's consumer goods division had become chief executive officer.

The research director smiled enigmatically. "Aaaah," he said, "that man has an uncanny ability to swim between battleships."

Company Relationships: Love on the 44th Floor and Other Special Situations

My friend leaned across the luncheon table. "It's terrible being single after so many years of marriage," she sighed. "I don't know what to tell all those men who want to come home with me. I used to be able to say, 'My husband is waiting. Now what do I do?' "

But women today are not the only ones looking for answers to would-be office lovers. Said one man, "Sometimes I feel as if my office is a walking singles bar. I get propositioned just going for coffee."

It really is not very surprising to know that sex is alive and well in corporate America.

The office is a warm, nurturing environment where close personal relationships can blossom into—well, into close personal relationships.

Are sexual liaisons all bad?

And can anything that starts out so good turn out bad, providing you are both adultlike in your attitude and resolve together that you "will not hurt anyone?"

Certainly there have been office romances that have gone un-
discovered—but, so far as I know, only in the minds of the principals. For even when nothing is happening, there is office talk.
And office talk is something to be reckoned with.

Can you handle that kind of gossip?

The Equal Opportunity Lover

The workplace, according to many sociologists, has become the
new mecca for singles. Bars and health clubs were the places for
swinging singles just a few years ago, but the scene has shifted.
The reason, of course, is that it is a lot easier to know the personality, assume the intelligence, and guess the salary level and
potential growth of someone at the next desk than it is to evaluate
someone at the next barstool. You can judge a heavyweight in
business better than one who lifts weights at a health club.

The change of scene in romance is causing both employees
and employers to reevaluate their attitudes towards business love
and sex.

Psychologist Srully Blotnick claims that 82 percent of all single
women are involved in office romances as compared with only 18
percent just a few years ago. If this is true, then there ought to
be a code of company manners to guide both employees and
employers in their intramural romances.

For Employees
Never complain, never explain

If you are involved in an office romance, not only should you
refrain from discussing it with anyone in the office—you should
deny it if asked.

The person who admits an office romance is inviting conversation about his or her private life. Conversation and concern
about one's private life during business hours infringes on both
time and energy owed the company and is a way of devaluing an

employee's contribution. Certainly the employee who permits himself or herself to become a topic of conversation and thereby causes numbers of people to focus on something other than the corporation's work is cheating the company.

And cheating the company is not part of company manners.

Make a move before you make a mistake

If you find that you are romantically involved—and both of you are single and working at the same corporate level—promise yourself to take ninety days, and then make a move.

If you are going to continue the romance, one of you should ask to move to another part of the corporation or one of you should leave the company's employ.

If you are going to end the romance, aren't you glad you never discussed this with anyone?

Under no circumstances should you continue a departmental romance that you know is going to increase in intensity. If you do, you will soon learn that working side by side will not help the romance. It is difficult enough to be judged during a romance— but to be judged on the job *and* as the object of another's affections makes any employee self-conscious. As a result one makes decisions that are self-serving instead of decisions that benefit the company.

For Employers
Don't make any accusations

Even if you see them holding hands in the hall, make no accusations about their relationship.

However, if you notice that two people who are assumed to be romantically involved are doing less than their usual level of satisfactory work, it is part of company manners (and your responsibility as an executive) to call each one to your office and communicate your dissatisfaction with his or her present performance.

This conversation will serve as a first warning.

If you choose later to fire either person, you will not be sued because you will have communicated your dissatisfaction with that person's performance. Just be sure that you are judging performance on the job and not commenting on his or her love life.

Don't get involved in someone else's love affair

If a married person in your workplace is involved in an affair with another employee, do not become an advisor to either or both parties.

Under no circumstances permit the married person's spouse to call you, confide in you or seek your guidance.

Do not permit yourself to be used in any manner. If, for example, you are called by an irate spouse and asked if you kept someone at the office, the answer always is, "She (or he) operates with a great deal of independence, and I cannot answer for his (or her) whereabouts."

Don't play Dear Abby and don't be Dr. Ruth

You're not supposed to have the answers to romantic questions.

You're supposed to be the best boss you can be, not the best dispenser of free advice on love and its consequences.

You cannot fire people simply because they fall in love, but it is incumbent upon you to remind employees that you can fire people who are so preoccupied with their personal lives that they fail to fulfill the job responsibilities.

You cannot expect people to sign pledges assuring you of noninvolvement, but you do have the right to expect the people you hire to think about the job during work hours. You do have the right to expect people not to distract others because of the intensity of their personal affairs. And you do have the right to keep your office from becoming the Dating Game.

Remember that the people you meet in business are in various stages of marriage. Some are perfect spouses and parents; others are less than perfect. Some commute to their marriages; others fly from theirs. Some are first-time marriages; others are four-time repeaters.

There are CEOs who fall in both categories. Still, regardless of the way they themselves may live, most CEOs cannot cope with sex in the office.

Could you?

Test yourself with the case history that follows:

Case Study of a Lover-President

Andrew was graduated from the State University with a degree in engineering. Twenty-three years later he was proud to say that his first job was his only job. At the age of forty-six he was in line to succeed Percival Brown, the seventy-two-year-old founder of the privately held company, manufacturers of airplane parts.

Mr. Brown, a gentleman with very firm views about ethics and morals among his staff, was convinced by an outside personnel consultant that Andrew, while he was brash and bold, was a good choice for the company. And so Andrew was made president.

The first year life was good, and Mr. Brown made plans to announce his retirement at the annual company picnic in June.

Then in April, just weeks before the announcement, Mr. Brown had a telephone call from Andrew's secretary. "I am suing the company," she said, "and I want to tell you why."

It was a stunned Percival Brown who, with counsel on both sides present, heard Andrew's secretary of four years tell of her affair with her married boss. She explained that when she tried to end the love affair, Andrew not only protested, he wrote letters telling her that if she did, he would fire her.

The young woman, with the law firmly on her side, was suing the company for sexual harassment. Mr. Brown was horrified by the story. Every employee had been notified of the company's firm stand concerning human rights and equality. What could they do to make amends? The young woman explained that she truly liked working at the company, and—if she could be given another job in another area—she would stay and drop her suit. She understood that it was one man and not an entire company that was at fault. Mr. Brown promised her she would be reassigned.

Immediately after she left, Mr. Brown called Andrew into his office. Contrite and abashed, Andrew admitted that indeed he had been involved with the woman but swore that he had learned his lesson and hoped he could still stay and run the company.

When Andrew left the room, Mr. Brown's attorney said, "You are going to fire him, I assume."

"It's a bigger problem than you think," said Mr. Brown. "We are in the midst of very delicate negotiations concerning patents owned by another company. If we can get these patents, we can change the course of this business for twenty-five years and dramatically affect the future of the one thousand people who work here. I abhor his actions, but what am I to do?"

What would you do?

What Mr. Brown did ultimately was to postpone his retirement and divide the operating responsibilities of the president among two other executives. The three were named to Office of the President. At the end of eighteen months, Mr. Brown will follow his original plan to retire and expects to make one of the three "presidents" the chairman.

Andrew's former secretary has been assigned to a research job in new products. The office grapevine thinks that, after the smoke settles in eighteen months, she will still be with the company— and Andrew won't.

However, not all adulterers do as well as Andrew and his ex-secretary.

Will was the personnel director of a small bank who was involved romantically with his secretary. The whispering had been going on for months. No one had actually seen them together. Still, everyone suspected.

Too smart for hotels, Will managed to have Connie work late each evening, and they picked as their trysting place the bank's boardroom and, more specifically, the conference table in the boardroom.

One morning Will came to work, and one of the vice presidents came up to him. "I think you ought to know something, Will. Somebody left the video on in the boardroom last night, and you know how we are at banks—we tape everything. Well, it seems there are some pretty interesting tapes starring you and. . . ."

Will resigned later that morning.

So did his secretary.

Office romances do not always lead to one or the other partners leaving. If the romance is not at the executive level, most of the office staff can handle it easily because you will not have sex mixed with power.

A few years ago I had a chrome, glass, and white office with a white fur rug in the middle of the room. We all knew that two of our young assistants in the art department were seeing one another, but I didn't realize that my office played a key role until the woman came in to see me one day and told me she and Hank were getting married. "Yes," she said, "we got engaged on the white rug in your office."

I later gave the rug to the Goodwill Industries, which seemed an appropriately named charity considering the emotions it fostered.

When the man is boss and the woman a striver, it is flattering to be selected for the Great Man's attention. Both feel validated by the relationship, she because a person in a power position recognizes her worth in the business world, and he because a younger person is smart enough to see how valuable he truly is.

The William Agee–Mary Cunningham story is the one that was played out in the business pages of the daily press. The disastrous results were a combination of his inability to understand the harm that speculative gossip can do to a man's executive posture and her unwillingness to recognize that even if there were no relationship between them, both permitted a climate for conjecture to flourish.

The president of a steel company was having an affair with the secretary of the chairman. It was a long-time relationship and was well-known by everyone who did business with the company. The secretary, however, acted as if there were nothing between them except her great respect for his judgment. When the president's last child left home, he got the divorce he wanted and married the secretary. She promptly left the company and went to work for another firm. The story (remember there's always a story whether it's true or not) was that she was finally willing to work someplace else now that she was married to him. But before the marriage, she wasn't sure she'd be able to keep his interest until the last child left home. She stayed at that job in order to keep an eye on him.

The new situation in office romance is the ascension of the woman and the new kind of affair: the woman executive and her male assistant.

Cheryl, the product manager for a soap company, found herself attracted to a man who worked with her. Her marriage had hit the ten-year mark, and she was ready for the intrigue, the spark, the excitement of love again. As she and her assistant became more and more involved in a research project, she found herself working nights—all night—with Phillip. Some months later they found an apartment together and, telling her husband and officemates that she would be out of the city, she traveled instead to the other side of town. Cheryl felt herself doing her best work ever. The excitement of a new love, a man who found her both sexy and smart and wasn't threatened or made jealous by her position, gave her additional potency in her job.

But Cheryl found power—hers and that of other men—more seductive than any romance. In time her enthusiasm for Phillip waned, and she became involved with the client for whom she was doing the research job.

"I work better when I have a strong sexual relationship," Cheryl said. "I don't want to hurt anybody, but I love the thrill, the danger of it all. If my husband knows, he's not saying anything. Maybe he doesn't want to know. As far as the people in my office are concerned, I feel that what I do is my business, and it doesn't matter what they say."

Paula and Gene were investment bankers actively involved in the merger of two major corporations. They ended up spending a lot of time out of town putting their heads—and eventually their beds—together.

But Paula knew that as soon as the corporate merger was effected, their merging would end. And when they returned to Chicago, she told Gene that was it. It had been fun and probably good for the company for them to be as together as they had been, but now they were, as business equals, back to being just that.

Gene was furious with Paula and kept her out of the next major merger activity. She went to the managing partner and explained that she felt Gene's resentment of her was standing in her way, and she explained that his resentment was based on her unwillingness to continue a road affair. The managing partner, for all his talk about equal rights, was both embarrassed and uncomfortable with her confession. Because he could no longer treat Paula with the same emotional detachment he once had, she left the company.

Said Paula later, "Don't ever expect a man who hears about a woman rejecting a man to have compassion for the woman."

Sometimes, as a manager, you get into a Cupid role in a most unwitting way. It happened to me when the product manager for a beverage company suggested that we hire his assistant. She was bright and attractive, and after consultation with the people at the agency, we felt she would be an excellent addition to our staff. She was leaving the beverage company because her opportunities were limited; she wanted a marketing job, and none were available there.

When Christina came to work for us, she was a delight, did her work well and on time. But I did hear that she took very long lunch hours. It wasn't until I mentioned this to her old boss that I found the reason. He nodded and said soberly, "If her late lunches are on Wednesdays, they're mine. But you tell me if there are other days, and I'll kill those bastards."

The ultimate sexual courtesy in the office is not to get involved in the first place.

Over the years I have developed a list of "nevers" for never getting involved:

- Never go to an office party that lasts beyond 6 P.M. If everybody wants to go on to the newest disco, sneak out and go home, and do not answer your phone.

- Never tell a person of the opposite sex your troubles with (a) your spouse, (b) your lover, or (c) both.

- Never tell a dirty story to a person of the opposite sex.

- Never tell anyone what your doctor said about your body.

- Never tell anyone which part of your body needs reduction or expansion.

- Never bar hop with a person of the opposite sex. If you decide you want to have a drink in the office, ask if you may open a bottle of wine with four other people at the end of the work day in your office.

- Never discuss any sexual experience with anyone in your office—male or female.

- Never tell a person of the opposite sex that you could really go for him or her if only. . . .

And if you think in your heart of hearts that you really could go for him or her if only—do not go to lunch alone with that person.

Because, as we all know, lunches for two inevitably lead to sex on the 44th floor.

And sex in most offices is the end of company manners and the beginning of company politics.

The romantic involvement is affection carried outside the limits of acceptable behavior.

Yet affection, that attached—rather than detached—goodwill that is both given and received, is sought in the corporation in much the same way that it is in the family.

For in this impersonal world of the nine-digit zip code, credit cards, and numbered bank accounts, in this world of no marriage, late marriage, and remarriage, the operative word in office relationships is "family."

We work like a "family." We think like a "family."

Never mind that the family has fallen on hard times for several decades. Still the dream of family remains a viable business concept.

For some executives employees are the children they never had—or the kind of children they wish they had had.

That sense of family is seen in both small and large companies.

Helen Gurley Brown plays big sister to her staff, and their experiences frequently fill the pages of *Cosmopolitan*.

William S. Paley, who created and ran CBS for thirty-seven years, said when he announced his resignation, "I'm like a father with a child."

Comparisons between family structure and business are heard often.

Staying many years with one company has been compared to a long marriage.

Changing jobs has been likened to the trauma of divorce.

Partnerships are compared to sibling relationships, and like sibling relationships, they must often withstand intrafamily squabbles. However, should anyone from the outside criticize, everyone links arms to fight the enemy.

And, like brothers and sisters, partners must sometimes go their own ways because of different values.

When Meshulam Riklis, head of Rapid-American (and a sometime moviemaker who is also the husband of Pia Zadora), and Carl Lindner, head of American Financial, were involved in a deal together, Mr. Lindner eventually wanted out. Mr. Lindner confessed that he could not understand the thinking of a partner who could spend $20 million a year on his lifestyle.

All rich people do not think alike, nor do all entrepreneurs function with the same parental style.

Acting out the role of Stern Parent is the company head who is formal with employees, precise about duties and rewards. On the other hand, the Fun-Loving Parent–Pal is the one who is called by his first name, may see his employees socially, accepts office pranks as a part of the daily life, and tells jokes with the best of them.

Some executives are always father figures, even when they are with other father figures.

Charles Allen, the head of Allen & Co. investment bankers, was in "21" one day along with D. K. Ludwig, the shipping magnate, and Mrs. Ludwig. Mrs. Ludwig choked momentarily on a piece of food and an alert "21" employee immediately applied the Heimlich maneuver, a method for helping a victim release the blocking food. The next day, in appreciation, Charles Allen—not D. K. Ludwig—sent the employee $500. Charles Allen is always the man in charge, the acting father.

Family Ties

The modern, professionally run public corporation is almost devoid of any kind of obvious nepotism, and rarely is there any non-obvious nepotism, such as a relative getting a contract.

Professor Theodore Levitt,
Harvard Business School

So where is all the nepotism?

Professor Levitt pinpoints it, "The small, privately held companies are awash with it. Very often it (the small, privately held company) is an institution to achieve certain styles of life and extend the family. The purpose of such a business," he concludes "is not to make money, but rather to be a vehicle for the family."

As a principal in a closely held family business for practically all of my business life, I know what Professor Levitt means.

Over the years both my son and my daughter have worked at Wyse Advertising. I know one thing—children don't always agree with their parents in the office. My daughter, for example, doesn't even agree with me on how she came to work at Wyse.

As she remembers it, I asked her to leave her job at a publishing house and come to work for us as a writer. As I remember, I asked her to recommend a writer, and she asked if she might be the writer.

No matter how we think it began, we both agree that at the end of the first week she told me she wanted to leave, and I remember the tearful scene—both of us in tears—as I told her no. No, she could not leave. No, she had a responsibility to me that was unlike the responsibility of others who came to work there. She couldn't casually walk in and walk out.

She understood what I said, agreed to recognize her responsibility to both herself and me and stay for at least three months. The three months became eight years, and she eventually left because she married and moved to Philadelphia where she was hired by another advertising agency and moved to an even higher level than she had been at Wyse.

Rob Wyse went to work in our Cleveland office starting as a media buyer, worked his way through account services, and, realizing that he would not have an immediate opportunity to develop his entrepreneurial talents in advertising started a public relations division of the agency. The success of the division reaffirmed his self-confidence and earned him the respect of others in the agency.

So my experience in a family business has been both joyous and rocky.

I know now that the child who enters a parent's business brings more than his or her formal education; the child also brings a lifetime of dinner-table conversation, a lifetime of postponed vacations, a lifetime of business-related sacrifices. Real estate developer Peter Friedman (a friend of Andy Tishman, son of one of the premier real estate families in New York) once said, "If my name were Tishman, I'd be smart about stock options and diversified splits, too."

A lot of learning in a family business takes place by osmosis.

When my son was twenty years old, he said that he had been in the advertising business for twenty years. He had been lullabied by singing jingles, and he grew up in front of a TV screen watching not the children's shows but the commercials of Wyse clients.

Still, when Rob went to work at Wyse at his first media job, he described himself to outsiders and coworkers as Wyse's s.o.b. "Which means," he would explain with a smile, "son of boss."

Humor with a twist of wry is helpful when the rest of the office staff tries to adjust to the son or daughter entering the business.

If you are the son or daughter of the person running the business:

Don't remake the business the moment you arrive

The first three months are the critical ones for both parent and child.

Will the kid get it?

Will the parents forget they are parents and not nag the same way they did when Junior came in late after a date?

Will the office not be paralyzed with fright at the sight of a relative in residence?

When they come into an office, children sometimes forget that their parents have a difficult time dispelling the notion of "my child" and substituting recognition as "my associate" or "my employee." And, in their eagerness to remind parents of their new grown-up state, children can become infuriatingly authoritative and all-knowing.

Connie's mother had a sportswear boutique; the shop provided a comfortable enough living so that the single mother was able to send her two children to private schools and eventually to good colleges.

During her junior year, Connie decided that she would like to leave school and join her mother. At first Mama was ecstatic; even when the three sales persons, the auditor, and her attorney were less enthusiastic, Mama maintained her cheery outlook toward her daughter's entrance into the business.

The first week in the shop Connie looked at current inventory, reviewed orders, and sat in with her mother on a budget meeting. Then, with four days' experience under her belt, she listened as her mother gathered all the employees and presented merchandise ideas for the fall season. In the midst of the presentation, Connie turned to her mother. "What is your percentage of returns?" she snapped. Without waiting for an answer she plunged on. "What are you budgeting for shop improvements? Expansion? The way you're running this business it's incredible there is a business. The first thing I learned in college. . . ."

Mama felt her temperature soar. "Wait a minute," she said. "I don't know my percentage of returns, and I don't think we need improvements. Besides, this shop has given you a very nice living. Who wants to expand?"

"I do," said Connie.

Mama controlled her desire to scream at her child. Instead she knew they were at a crossroads. Connie's questions were sharp, but they were early. Mama took a deep breath, counted to ten, and as she did she knew what she had to say. "Connie, why not wait a few months and raise those questions again?"

There was an embarrassed silence. No one knew what to say. Mama realized it was up to her to add something, to soften the blow. But what?

Mama looked at her desk and saw a large yellow pad. "Oh yes, one more thing, Connie. Get yourself a yellow pad like this one and a pencil, one with a very large eraser. Then go through this store and just observe our practices and talk to our customers. After ninety days you are free to come to me, and only me, and tell me what I'm doing wrong. But until then, my darling daughter, shut up and work."

Connie smiled. "I hear you."

Mama reached for Connie's hand and squeezed it.

Mama had gambled. Connie could have left at that moment. But Connie didn't, and what Mama realized was that her child was indeed made of her parent's fiber, and the tough talk Mama had endured to make the business happen could be endured by Connie, too, so long as she felt it would make the business grow.

After that conversation, Connie made no suggestions aloud. Instead of speaking she wrote, and at the end of her ninety-day observation period, she sat down with her mother and calmly and dispassionately gave her a list of ideas she thought might help the store.

"I'm amazed," said Mama in relating the incident. "Two of the ideas were really original; some of the others were extensions of thoughts I had had but not followed through. Only one or two suggestions were totally impractical and not worth considering. I'm glad I had the nerve to be tough when I had to be at that meeting, and I'm glad that Connie stayed. But if I hadn't happened to notice that yellow pad on my desk, I don't know what would have become of us."

The meeting had a salutary effect on the staff. They loved Mama for asserting herself and not putting up with her daughter's bad manners. It also put them on warning, for Mama's actions informed them that if she were not going to put up with Connie's peccadilloes, she certainly wouldn't put up with theirs.

Don't become the worker's tool

Skip always brought home stray dogs and stray kids. He was the kind of boy who listened, the kind of young man who protested everything from school injustice to world hunger.

When he joined his father's machine tool company, the word was out. "Skip is a softie."

His first job on the production line brought him in contact with people who had been trying to get his father's ear for years. Skip was sympathetic; it was true that the lunchroom was dingy, and it was true that many of them worked for salaries much smaller than that of Skip's father, and it was true that the workers were telling their stories to Skip in the hope that they might get the word to the old man through Skip.

But Skip saw no ulterior motive; he saw only the workers' plight as they described it. He personally promised his coworkers that he would do something for all of them. He would get them what they wanted.

The first time that Skip told his father about the lunchroom conditions his father was in the midst of labor negotiations and barely heard his son's account. The second time Skip relayed the grievances, his father half-listened. The third time he sat back astounded, and then he spoke.

"Skip, if I hear you correctly, you told these people that you would do something for them."

"Yes, sir."

"Skip, do you know that I am in the midst of labor negotiations, and you are going behind my back making deals with employees?"

"I'm not making deals," Skip explained.

"You think you're not making deals," his father continued, "but *they* think you are. You are undermining the business. You have to understand something about working here and having my name. You can't be just another fellow. You are a weapon. You can be used to shoot off a lot of stuff that people feel. But no matter what they think and no matter what you feel in your

heart, you are management so long as you work here. If you want
to play Robin Hood, that's fine with me, but don't do it at work."

The company is doing fine these days.

So is Skip. He is working as a paralegal among the city's poor.
All children are not meant to be in the family business.

Don't pretend to be what you're not

Tony owned three furniture stores, and when his son came home
from college the summer after his freshman year, he asked his
dad if he might have a job for three months.

Tony Jr. used his mother's maiden name among the employees
so that no one would know who he really was. He wanted no
favoritism, and he knew he'd never be respected by his fellow
workers if anyone knew he was the boss's son.

Tony Jr. did admit to himself that it was tough to listen to
outsiders berate your dad. Oh sure, Tony Jr. himself thought his
dad was wrong about a lot of stuff, but still it wasn't easy to stand
around and listen to outsiders attack your family and then expect
you to join in.

One day when the fellows were having a beer after work, one
of them said, "I hear Tony Sr. has a son working in one of the
stores."

One of the other fellows laughed. "If he's one of you guys,
I'll kill you all."

Tony didn't drink the rest of his beer. He left and went home,
and when he went into work the next morning, he said to one of
his coworkers, "I think you ought to know that I am Tony Jr."

By the end of the day Tony Jr. knew he had made a grave
mistake in concealing his identity earlier.

No one spoke to him.

None of the employees with whom he worked could remember
exactly what had been said in those after-hours beer-drinking
sessions. Had Tony Jr. been there or was that a day when he
hadn't gone along with them?

The faith of the employees in both Tony Sr. and Tony Jr. was shaken. No one was ever convinced that the summer employment was not an elaborate scheme by Tony Sr. to spy on the troops.

Tony Jr. never worked another summer in the stores, but after graduation he joined the company.

To this day people in the company, with the imagination always displayed by those not in the know, tell about the time Tony Sr. had his son spying on everyone until the employees found out, and two of them cornered Tony Jr. and beat him up.

Don't bypass the system

You really cannot mouth a lot of platitudes about equality when your family owns the business.

The boss's son is not equal.

You are not necessarily the one he would pick to run the business.

But you are the one he is getting.

So if you really think you are going to run the business one day, then start now to live under the system over which you expect to preside eventually.

- Don't go to Pop with your skinned knees. Go instead to your immediate superior.
- Don't tattle.
- Don't overreact.
- Don't abuse your expense account privileges.
- If everybody at your salary level pays for his own compact car, don't drive to work in your company-owned Maserati.
- Don't become Daddy's police officer standing there to laugh gleefully each time he makes a mistake you learned during your first year in business school.
- Occasionally find something that can make you proud to be part of the company and your family—and say so. Nothing will please your parents more than praise. If you ap-

preciate what has been done for you, tell those who did it. Don't wait for the testimonial dinner or the funeral.

- Make no idle threats.
- Don't threaten to move—unless you have already packed the china and called for the vans.
- Don't threaten to leave—unless you know where you are going and what you will do.

Remember always that an entrepreneur created the company, but it takes a manager to grow it.

If your dad (and/or mom) is an entrepreneur, be grateful but not superior. It will take a lot of intelligent work to keep the company in good health today.

And it takes a lot of respect for what has been done to make growth possible.

If you are running the business:

Don't talk baby talk

They are not your babies any more.

If they are old enough to work, then they are old enough to be treated like other adults in your employ.

So don't talk down to your children. It belittles them in the eyes of their associates, and it makes them feel inadequate. The only way to make your children feel like responsible adults is to treat them like responsible adults.

Forget the cute little baby names. "Brother" is fine when used in the family circle, but in business be sure that you call him "Perry."

Sheldon went to work in his father's auto parts business. His first job was as a sales representative. He sent his orders to his district manager, and two weeks later the district manager quit.

Sheldon was assigned another district manager.

Again, in time, the district manager quit.

The regional manager went to the sales manager. "I have a problem, and I don't know how to solve it because my problem is with the boss's son. He's doing an okay job with his territory, but I'm losing district managers over him. It seems the old man doesn't want to call his son and ask how he's doing. So every night the old man calls the district manager to find out what the kid did that day. If the kid had a good day, then the sales manager is congratulated, and if the kid had a bad day, the sales manager is asked, "Why? What's wrong?""

The sales manager knew that this kind of parental overkill could ruin the company as well as the boss's son.

The next day the sales manager went into the president's office. "Sir," he said, "there is a district manager I want to hire, but I have an unusual problem. This man knows our business well, and I can get him to leave our competitor because where he is now, he has the president calling him to find out how all his relatives are doing with the company. Now this man says he'll come to work here if we leave him alone. So I want to ask you, sir, would any of our vice presidents do a thing like that? Because if they would, then this fellow won't work here."

"What are you really asking me?" the president demanded.

"I want to know if you will send a memo asking all home office staff to filter their requests about the performance of any individual sales representative through the sales manager."

The memo was sent.

And both district managers were eventually rehired, never to be bothered with calls from the president again.

Program a child for success

Just because he or she is your own flesh and blood does not mean that he or she possesses all your skills and talents.

However, even if this remarkable child does possess your identical traits, do not assume that you can bring him or her in over the heads of veterans and continue to have the organization function smoothly.

When Brad Jr. got his MBA, his proud dad made him the marketing vice president.

Never mind that Brad Jr. had never written a market plan for the company.

Never mind that Brad Jr. didn't know the talents of the people he had to position.

He was the boss's son and heir apparent.

The first year of Brad Jr.'s tenure, the company showed its first loss in seventeen years.

Even Brad Sr. knew something was wrong.

After the third quarter of losses, Brad Sr. had to admit that the problem was his son.

The father and son sat down together, and Brad Jr. readily admitted that the job was beyond his experience. "Why not let me out, Dad?" he asked. "Let me work someplace else until I feel ready to come back here."

Now, six years later, Brad Jr. is returning as advertising director.

"I don't know if it will work this time or not," Brad Jr. said as he began his new job. "My father still wanted me to come in as marketing director, but if there is one thing that I have learned working outside my family business it is that the greatest danger is to come in too close to the top. Even if you are the boss's son, people want to think you've earned the job."

More important than what others think is the importance in giving a child confidence in himself. If you bring someone in at a level where he or she cannot be successful, you will shake that self-belief which is vital to success.

Don't report to Mom and/or Pop

Relationships are weakened, even destroyed, if you criticize every action of your child.

It is easier for everyone in the organization—and family— when someone else points out the mistakes and gives praise.

No matter how small the company, be certain that the parent is not the one to whom the child reports.

For the person who will have the direct reporting relationship with your child, choose someone who is very good at his job and is

1. Secure enough not to be threatened by the relationship— generally this means someone who is (a) older and/or (b) more than adequately compensated with both title and salary.

2. A good teacher.

3. Loyal to the company and has company spirit.

4. Able to serve as a role model and mentor.

5. Able to evaluate your child's skills and shortcomings honestly for you so that you can be guided in determining the future course for your child.

Don't be sensitive about family relationships

The president of a candy company came in to see us with three of his staff: two women and another male.

The man was the marketing director; one woman was presented as the advertising director and the other woman "a consultant."

Halfway through the meeting, we noticed that the consultant, instead of using her notebook, was writing notes in the president's notebook. There was something overly familiar about the gesture, and I was immediately suspicious as was the rest of my staff. The people on our side of the table looked at one another. I knew they were waiting for me to say something.

"Pardon me," I said as I turned to the consultant, "but may I ask you a personal question?"

She nodded.

"Are you the president's wife?"

"Yes," she said, "but how did you know? I never use my married name in business because I don't want people to realize that I'm his wife. They won't respect me. But this way I can go along and give my opinion."

"But why would you do that with me?" I asked. "I think I invented nepotism. I was part of a family business, and while I don't think you have to fight or coo in front of associates, I do think you have to be honest."

Our relationship with the company was short-lived and unhappy. I hope the president and his consultant did better with their marriage.

Fire when necessary

Jasper runs a small bank in the midwest, and when his daughter—a graduate economist—married Duncan, also a graduate economist, Jasper knew he had found the line of succession he so desperately wanted.

"My son-in-law," said Jasper, "was educated at one of the three best universities in the United States, and with his background, I knew it would be easy to make him president of the company.

"But from the first day Duncan just didn't know how to handle people. Duncan and my daughter were both o the Dean's lists of the schools they attended, and while I knew my daughter didn't have the people skills necessary for banking, I thought Duncan did. But he simply was not one of those fellows who knew how to bring our staff together to function as a team.

"One day I called Duncan into my office, and I said to him, 'Duncan, I think you can make money as a broker, but we have a problem with you in this business. You weren't raised in this business, and you believe that emphasis must be placed on textbook management. But that simply is not what my bank is about.' "

Duncan left and became a very successful broker.

Muses Jasper, "Strange thing, but Duncan wasn't even that good as a theorist. His economics were no better than his people skills. I asked him one day about Gresham's law, and he didn't even know what it was about. My daughter didn't either. By the way, she teaches economics now."

Washburn owned a small gas and oil exploration company, and in 1961 he was approached by Pete, an old Navy buddy who wanted him to invest in offshore drilling in the Gulf of Mexico.

Washburn liked the idea. "Let me handle this job with you, Pete," he said. "I'll put some of my people down there, and let's see where we go with it."

Washburn picked his best man for the job and sent him to New Orleans.

A week later Washburn's son came to see him. "Will you have lunch with me today, Dad?" he asked.

Washburn had a sense of something amiss, so he broke the lunch date he had scheduled. What could be bothering his son? Over lunch the son broke bread—and some news. "Dad, I am going to leave the company. I want to go someplace where I have authority."

"That's not a bad idea; every man should try to make more of himself," Washburn said. "But tell me, son, what will you do if you flop?"

"Oh," said his son, "if it doesn't go well, I'll come back."

Washburn looked his son in the eye. "You can't come back. You're my son, and you can't have it both ways. You can't have the privileges of ownership and then think that you can act like an employee and leave—only to come back. That sends up the wrong signals around here."

"I'll take my chances then," said the son.

"Why?" asked Washburn. "Why leave a good job where you do well to go out in an uncertain economic period?"

"Because," said his son with more than a little anger, "you picked another man for the job in New Orleans that I wanted. You humiliated me; I can't stay."

Washburn shrugged. "I didn't set out to humiliate you. I made a business decision. This is business, not a personal choice. I picked the person I thought was best for that job. I'm sorry to see you go, and I wish you well."

Washburn's son eventually became successful as a small driller; his father went on to become one of the largest in the country.

But despite the business success of each, their personal relationship is cold and distant.

In business, as in life, there are happy families—and there are unhappy families.

The Age Factor

Ever since the social revolution of the 1960s there has been less emphasis on age as a requirement for advancement and more concern about moving up with people of talent.

Some companies call for retirement at 55; other firms will not promote a chairman unless he is 55.

In Los Angeles a woman can be too old at 25, an age that is too young for Milwaukee.

What, then, is the right age?

The answer, like most answers, depends on company manners.

In the entertainment and computer industries, a premium has been put on being young.

In more mature businesses (particularly in the financial community) there is a tendency to seek older executives because there is an assumption that the older person inspires confidence.

Sometimes the older person is amazed to find how young the rest of the world has become. Dr. Caroline Zinsser joined the Center for Public Advocacy Research, and one of her coworkers said, "I had a classmate named Zinsser—Joyce Zinsser."

"Yes," said Dr. Zinsser, "she is my niece."

There is no age that is right for all business, particularly in a society where emphasis has been placed on looking and feeling young. As Satchel Paige, the veteran ballplayer once asked, "How old would you be if you didn't know how old you was?"

Companies do not ask that question.

What we need now is to find a company manner in dealing with the question of age, particularly as we deal with males working for younger persons who have passed them by and as we adjust to women reentering the job market.

The reentering woman will often find herself reporting to someone who once reported to her, and it is sometimes with unrepressed hostility that women learn that their years at home count for nothing in the business world.

Each of these male/female age relationships is a special situation that calls for special kinds of handling.

Older woman versus younger woman boss

Gretchen felt she had been pushed aside for years, a victim of the time warp; she was born thirty years too late. When she was deciding what to be when she grew up, women were not admitted to business schools, nice girls minded their p's and q's, not their p and l's.

When she went to work for a Boston computer company, she knew that chances were she might have a female boss, and she welcomed the idea. Nowadays the chances of the older woman having a younger female boss are increasing; today more than 1.3 million women under the age of thirty-five hold managerial or administrative posts, a million more than in the 1970s.

The first day that Gretchen met Millicent, her boss, Gretchen's heart sank. How could she be an assistant to a woman so different from herself, a woman who seemed to have computer dots where everybody else had a heart. Millicent was neat, hard-working, and noncommunicative. She expected her coffee to be brought to her, her calendar to be updated, and her assistant to be quiet except when spoken to. At the end of the third week, Gretchen could not stand it any longer. She brought in the opened mail, laid it on her boss's desk, was greeted with a muffled thank you. Gretchen stood silent for a minute or two, and when Millicent took no further notice of her, Gretchen said sadly, "There's something I want to say to you."

Millicent continued her work and did not look up. "What is it?"

"I thought it would be wonderful not to work for a man. I thought that you would get me involved in a lot of interesting projects and see that I really moved ahead here. I guess," she concluded with in a soft voice, "I expected more of a woman."

Millicent looked up from her work, a quizzical expression on her face. "Why should you?" she asked. "You have every right to expect equality but not difference."

Gretchen has been transferred; she still has a younger woman boss, but she has learned not to tell a woman boss what she expects her to be.

"I think that in the last two years I've learned a lot about having a younger boss, and I've learned a lot about how the world has changed since I was in an office twenty years ago," Gretchen said. "You can't become bitter and resentful if you don't move up as fast as some of the younger people. At the same time you have to try to stay as young as the people around you. Read what they read; see the movies they see; watch your boss for clues so that your counsel will be sought because you are more valuable; you have to prove that you are contemporary and have the experience that comes with years."

Millicent regards this advice with a wry smile. "Gretchen was one of those women who is back at work thinking that having a job is going to make her hot stuff in the 'burbs. She doesn't want the tough stuff that goes with working. I want somebody to make my coffee, but I don't want somebody to listen to stories about where I went last night or who I'm dating. I don't want comments on my letters and my conversations. I don't need a girl friend; I need an assistant. The trouble with these women who come in here is that they think they're special because they're women, too.

Well, look, ladies, I don't think I'm special, so why should you think you are?"

Older man versus younger woman boss

At Wyse, the first time that I had an older male employee, I found myself doing things he should have been doing. I was writing his reports, making his calls. I couldn't *ask* him to do things for me, could I?

After he'd been with us for a month, he stopped by my office at the end of the day. "You're not satisfied with me, are you?" he asked.

"I don't know if I am or not," I said, "but I'll tell you that I feel funny asking you to do things for me. I always feel you're judging me and thinking how you'd do it. I sense that you're sure you'd do my job better. I'm not comfortable around you."

"Look," he answered, "I've had jobs as good as yours, and I don't know why I don't now, but I have to make a living. So will you let me or won't you?"

He stayed with us for a few years and did a good job, but by the time I had my second, third—and who knows how many since—older male employees, I understood what I had to do to make things work for all of us.

I had to act like a boss and give orders and not worry about winning popularity contests or wounding feelings. The welfare of the entire office must always precede the feelings of an individual.

Besides, age is subjective. There are old young people and young old people.

Sharon, who runs an electrical supply company, says that the biggest problem with the older male employee is sexism. He assumes that he can flirt his way around the boss. Sharon is pragmatic when she says, "I don't want to wake up ugly tomorrow, but I don't want men working for me to comment on my hair, my makeup or anything else."

Patricia M. Carrigan, a clinical psychologist, was named the first woman to manage an assembly plant for General Motors. One man, hearing she would be his boss, spit on the floor. Another called her "Miss Boss."

How did she win them over?

With time and example. Says Dr. Carrigan, "It's important to give people an opportunity to see how you operate. I said, 'I'm here to support a very competitive organization that does its job well.' "

Older woman versus younger male boss

It isn't easy for an older woman to change; she already has an ingrained style. There are older women workers who admit that they treat younger coworkers like the Boy Scouts in the troops, and they treat their bosses like their children. Said one thirty-two-year-old male boss, "I already have a mother. If Personnel sends me another yenta to mother me, I'm going to send them chicken soup."

But not everyone feels that way. A publisher with a secretary who thinks she's his mother says, "I love it. She cares for me. I need that. Besides, my wife won't admit it, but she's relieved that I don't have some hot, young, gorgeous woman working next to me all day."

Older male versus younger male boss

"You know what freaks me out?" asked the general manager of a television station. "It's when the sales manager, who works for me and is ten years older than I am, tells me how it's supposed to be done and how they did it back in the golden days of television.

"The worst part though is that he resists my authority. No matter what I want, he knows a reason it shouldn't be done. He just can't take criticism, and he won't act as if I'm the boss.

"I know that sometimes he's right, but I wish the damned fool would say things so that I can accept them. He's smart, and he's still got mileage, but it's all uphill between us. I've been in business long enough to know that you give raises and promotions to people who can do the whole job. Now here's a fellow who, I think, can do parts of the job, but he's so angry at all of us younger guys who are making it that I can't totally trust him.

"And in business, some things are real simple. Don't promote a guy you don't trust to a position where he can really knife you."

Whom Can You Trust?

It begins with a telephone call, and you hear the magic words, "Tax shelter." They are immediately followed by a collection of four-star corporate names. And, almost before you hear the details, you say, "Why not?" And, indeed, why not? Most deals are presented by authenticated tax consultants or attorneys, and most of the deals do what they are supposed to do: they shelter a percentage of otherwise taxable income. A particularly good shelter will also be a sensible investment.

Not all shelters, however, are protective.

Some are defective.

And others, like the J. David financial scam, are swindles that gather into the net both the financial sophisticates and the numbers novices. The J. David operation, headed by a glamorous San Diego woman and a meek-mannered man, attracted investors who were often smarter than they—and just as greedy.

Fueled by a public with an insatiable appetite for more, J. David (Jerry) Dominelli and Nancy Hoover used a variety of financial instruments that few persons understood, and the two created a scheme around offshore currency trading. Captain Money and the Golden Girl, they were called, and their real trading was on ambition and greed.

But where is the line between ambition and greed?

Who draws it?

Henry J. is the chairman of a company whose stock is traded

publicly. Six weeks ago it was announced that a conglomerate acquired 5 percent of Henry J.'s stock and would make a run for the company. It was a friendly takeover. Henry J.'s family who owned much of the stock urged Henry to sell. So did his board. It was a good fit. Everybody liked everybody. And so the major stockholders sat back, relieved and relaxed. Henry J. could continue to run the company; the family would have their inheritance problems solved.

But what no one reckoned with totally was Henry J.

Henry J. fancied himself a fine negotiator. And indeed he had been when the company was buying other companies. But this time Henry was selling. And while his strategy for buying—to stop short of his top figure—had worked because he knew the top figure, he was having more difficulty selling. He didn't know the acquirer's top figure. And so Henry J. kept demanding more. When one figure was met, he asked for more.

And even on the day the acquisition was to be confirmed, Henry J. went back to the well for more.

The acquired company said no. And Henry J. was left with egg on his face and stock on his hands.

Said one board member, "The problem was greed. He wanted to get the most. More would have been just fine with everybody."

Greed trips the ambitious on every level.

More is sometimes less in the business world.

When you run a company, you can't outlaw greed.

But you can set standards.

And it is those standards that form the basis of company manners.

John Lonergan, the president of In Transit, a San Francisco travel agency, believes that if people must work with constant, stressful deadlines, it is incumbent upon those who run the business to have as happy a workplace as possible. So this San Francisco agency invites a concert pianist to play for its employees every Wednesday and serves dim sum to the employees on Thursday.

In addition to its customary travel services, In Transit sells MUNI passes (San Francisco surface transportation fares) at its office, and Lonergan uses the proceeds to buy extras for the staff. The last purchase was a microwave oven.

Says the ebullient John Lonergan, "Spontaneity is the key to style."

George Lang, a creator of restaurants and now the owner and operator of Café des Artistes in New York, takes the change in his pockets each night and dumps it into a big wooden bowl. When the bowl is full, he converts the change to bills, gives the bills to his office manager, and all the staff has a lobster dinner served in the garden. "Even the office cats are made happy," says Lang. "We feed them the scraps."

Lang believes that company manners start early.

"When he was new to the United States and working at the Waldorf-Astoria on Park Avenue, he thought it would be a good idea to bring a group of his contemporaries, young and struggling businessmen of the 1950s, together in a luncheon group. The group, although no longer the brash young men of New York— and certainly not exactly struggling for their places in the sun— included Lang himself, James Rosenfield (a TV producer), Ed Bleier (a Warner Communications executive), Mort Janklow (attorney and agent for many important authors), Bill Adler (head of Bill Adler Books), John Diebold (head of his own company), Ed Meyer (head of Grey Advertising), Marshall Loeb (head of *Money* magazine), Judge Irving Young, Robert Menchel (executive with Goldman Sachs), and Father Paul Chan.

"We learned a lot together," says Lang.

The rest of the members agree.

Star Power: Dealing Under Bright Lights

The computer is not the only new presence in corporate America.

Stars shine brightly in every business from the airlines (where ex-astronaut Frank Borman headed Eastern) to the White House (where an ex-movie star makes a powerful media personality the norm).

Business executives now flock to classes in television technique. Few, if any, executives appear on CBS's "Sixty Minutes" or other news shows without professional coaching beforehand.

We all know that the entertainment business has no lock on Star Wars; all business today is one part talent and two parts star power, a star power that is fueled by careful use of the media.

Major corporations are an amalgamation of Wall Street–Washington–Hollywood and the sports circuit.

Big business had an early taste of the star business when Mark H. McCormack founded International Management Group and hired real celebrities to lend their names to sporting equipment. Arnold Palmer and Jack Nicklaus were the first guns in the corporate star wars.

Now companies look for the stars who will sell their products, liven their corporate boards, head their companies, and front their deals.

Use of star names can mean business. The Kaufman-Astoria studios in New York got off the ground by announcing such show business names as Alan King, Neil Simon, Johnny Carson, and Jimmy Nederlander as stockholders. Wall Street stock deals, tax shelters, and oil and gas deals have for years been sold on star names.

Business and entertainment stars regularly sell their names and faces for products that range from mink coats to newspapers to countries.

Even once-sacrosanct corporate boards have been given a glamour nudge with the addition of movie star power.

Cary Grant served on the board of Fabergé; Polly Bergen was on the Singer board; Dina Merrill was put on Continental Telephone's board.

And corporations have real live stars as their heads. Bill Cosby owns television stations; Gene Autry for many years has been both a sports team owner and a TV–radio station owner.

Merv Griffin, the syndicated talk show host, has made a fortune that extends to radio stations, music publishing, and television production. He has created and produced the highest-rated game show of all time ("Wheel of Fortune") as well as the highest-rated syndicated show of all time ("Jeopardy"). When he was developing the new show "Headline Chasers," Griffin suggested to his associate, Wink Martindale, that contestants be couples rather than individuals.

"What a good idea!" said Martindale. "Now why didn't I think of that?"

Replied Griffin, "Wink, that's why I own this building and desk."

The primary purpose of many star entertainers who switch to business seems to be to make life more interesting for chief executives. Only when the star is used to sell a product on television (as Ronald Reagan was with General Electric and Brooke Shields in Calvin Klein jeans spots), or when a star name is used on merchandise (the golf and tennis stars on sports equipment; Cheryl Tiegs for her own Sears Roebuck sportswear line), or when the star is used as a ploy in order to get an order (tennis and golf stars are hired with regularity to be the fourth in a friendly, corporate game) is star usage both fun and deductible.

Businessmen made show business kinds of headlines early in the 1970s when Revlon hired Michael Bergerac from ITT and gave him an employment package that included a seven-figure bonus for signing—a practice until then confined to sports stars. Upon leaving Revlon, however, Mr. Bergerac had an eight-figure Platinum Parachute.

Stars of business today are those who travel the professional route from government to both Wall Street and corporate boardrooms (former president Gerald Ford is a director of American Express; former senator Howard Baker serves as a director of the good-news newspaper *USA Today*).

After serving as president of the City Council in New York, Carol Bellamy took herself down to Wall Street and became a vice president of Morgan Guaranty.

Lee Iacocca parlayed his business stardom by attaching his name to patriotic projects beginning with the Statue of Liberty and continuing as one of the spokespersons for the "Crafted with Pride" advertising campaign by American manufacturers. In one of those commercials, however, Mr. Iacocca was guilty of indefensible company manners—he appeared in the commercial touting American-made clothing while wearing a Burberry raincoat. When the gaffe was called to his attention, the commercial was reshot.

Peter Ueberroth, the businessman who gave us the Olympics, now captures headlines as the commissioner of baseball.

Messrs. Iacocca and Ueberroth understand that making money is a new kind of sexy stardom that translates to more headlines, more power and more stardom.

Peter M. Dawkins went from football hero to Army general

to Wall Street tycoon and is now flirting with a political future, the unique promise here of a sports star turned Army hero turned financier moving to politics.

Moving between spheres of influence is not new. It has been going on for years between Wall Street and Pennsylvania Avenue. Back in the 1930s Franklin D. Roosevelt selected financier Joseph Kennedy to clean up the Securities and Exchange Commission. Before the Depression the Washington alliance with business was centered on the men who built the railroads, developed shipping, and made the steel, the Harrimans and Hannas and Carnegies.

Today Wall Street has a large share of former government officials. Peter Peterson was once Commerce secretary; William Simon was Treasury secretary. C. Douglas Dillon served as undersecretary of state in the 1950s and was Treasury secretary in the early 1960s. Henry Kissinger and James Schlesinger get impressive fees for consulting to major companies.

While you may not have these kinds of Washington stars in your business life, chances are increasing that somewhere along the way a star will come into your life.

It may be a corporate star, someone who's a hotshot in another company. It may even be a home-grown star maturing under your own eyes.

It also may happen that the new star is you.

If you now have high-voltage star power, treat your new status with respect, remembering always the old adage that one meets the same people going down the ladder of success as one does going up.

More important, don't act more important.

There is a show business story about the famous musical comedy star who was being considered for a Rodgers and Hammerstein musical. He went to see the producers with twelve other scripts in his briefcase. He wanted the new part, but he was a star, and he didn't want to seem too anxious, to eager. So he said, "I'm trying to make my mind up. I'm not sure what to do next."

The producers looked nervously at one another. If this actor were that popular, then his demands would be outrageous. They sighed. "Let's go ahead and hire an unknown," they decided.

So they did.

The show was "The King and I," and the unknown actor they hired was Yul Brynner.

But supposing you are not the star.

In that case what do you do when a star gets aboard your particular spacecraft to the top?

The Star and You

Talk to management—fast

Now is the time to have a heart-to-heart talk with the person who is responsible for your employment package.

When a new star comes on board, you must remember—no matter what anyone says—that someone on top is committed to that new person's success.

You are never going to be more important to management than you are today; they cannot afford to let you go (hopefully)— at least not until they see how the new celebrity works out in the job. So now is the time to cut a new deal.

Best way to approach management: "With Mr. X coming to us, I think I can be very helpful. I want to be sure, of course, that you agree. Here's what I can do. . . ."

Never approach from fear. Never ask for assurances from management, assurances sought because you are insecure. Ask for assurances and promises because of what you promise; you are the hope for the celebrity.

Management, in its slow-footed, slow-witted way, suspects and hates anyone who is frightened. That is because management itself is so frightened that it certainly doesn't need another frightened executive. So look everyone in the eye, and be strong, tough, and sure. Tell them what you need in order to make the star look good.

Meet with the new person as soon as possible

Be on the welcoming committee.

Don't be a sycophant, but get on the new person's dance program fast.

Schedule a lunch. Ask for breakfast. Sit down for coffee. Be ready, willing, and able to tell him how to do things the company way.

Be honestly helpful. Chances are that the new star is no dummy; if you're doing all this with a phony smile pasted over your grumpy face, he'll know.

Harry was a major art director at an advertising agency and was named creative director at another agency. The art directors at the new agency got together and decided they'd make life hell for Harry and get him out fast.

Their plan worked. They did make his life miserable, and they did get him out. But along the way one or two of the rebels lost his job (in advertising you don't have to be a bad art director to lose a job; if your agency loses a major piece of business, you have to take your book and your reel and go job hunting). Harry, meanwhile, found himself another big job at another big agency. And guess which three unemployed art directors can't even leave their books and reels for Harry to see!

Don't lose your head and your heart to the new star

Keep your feet on the ground.

Don't fawn and act overly impressed.

Joyce came into the new products group in the plastics division of a major conglomerate. Preceding Joyce was her press. The word was that she had done a great job everywhere, was a real star, and was definitely on her way to corporate.

This was just what Cary had been waiting for. For two years he had been a departmental assistant to a corporate nerd. At last! A way to move up.

Two days later Cary introduced himself to Joyce. "I want to work with you," he said. "How can I help?"

"I need help with some reports," she said the first week.

So Cary wrote two reports that Joyce presented—without him.

The second week Joyce said, "Why don't you go to the midwest meeting for me, Cary?"

And so Cary went, leaving Joyce free to politic with corporate.

It went on this way for months. Whatever Joyce wanted, Cary did. Somehow corporate never knew Cary's name, just Joyce's.

Six months later no one was surprised when Joyce went up for review and came back to her office with a bottle of champagne to celebrate her promotion to corporate. As the team poured the champagne and shouted congratulations, Joyce paused to say how happy she was. "But with good news, there is bad news, too," she told the staff as she touched a tear in the corner of her eye. It seemed Cary would have to leave the company.

When the initial shock subsided, what the people in the division learned was that while management thought that Joyce had excellent qualifications, she had made a few errors. There was that new products report. "But," explained Joyce, "I was so new that I just listened to the people around me."

And what about the midwest meeting? "Oh yes," said Joyce, "I couldn't make it so I sent a representative. I guess he just couldn't handle it."

Joyce never mentioned Cary by name when she explained her lapses; in fact, one of the reasons management promoted her was that she didn't go around naming names and pinpointing staff errors. But she did understand when and how they happened, and after all, isn't that the kind of person everybody wants in corporate?

When Cary heard what happened, he said, "I know Joyce would have taken me with her if she could because Joyce is a star, and she is kind and thoughtful and good."

What Cary did not understand is that star mentality requires thinking of one's own star power first. Everyone else comes later. No one protects himself better than a star.

So, when it comes to manners and stars, treat a star with all the respect and courtesy due any rich and powerful person who has a right to shape your life.

But don't fall so deeply in love with your star that you fail to see the star's real motives and the ways you are being used.

Sooner or later a star will leave for a dream, a promise, or a bigger deal that's just around the corner.

All star packages are not made in the heavens.

The onerous task of firing a star may one day be yours.

How to fire a star

Some stars need no help getting fired.

When Orson Welles was doing commercials for Paul Masson wine, he was interviewed on a television talk show. The host asked how Mr. Welles had managed to lose so much weight recently, and he promptly replied that he had stopped drinking wine.

So ended Orson Welles's association with Paul Masson.

For most companies, however, it is far more difficult to find a satisfactory explanation for firing a star. One reason, of course, is that the star has been brought in with so much fanfare and so much investment on both sides. The star has invested his reputation, the company its dollars, and both want to make sure the investment pays off.

Under such circumstances, there is only one courteous way to fire a person and that is to promote him to Never Never Land, a job at corporate level far removed from any place where the star can do harm—or good. Then keep the job boring but respectable.

In time the star will quit, for the cardinal rule in firing a high-level person is simply to elevate him to a place where he can quit without a loss of face.

If, however, you cannot avoid firing the star, make sure that you let him go with as much dignity and as few headlines as possible. Once the deed is done, communicate the news first to your office family.

Always be certain that they, your office family—the people with the most to gain and the most to lose because of your actions—hear about the firing from you.

Handle the official release to the media with care.

Check with your star and see how he or she wants the separation handled.

Sometimes in this age of merger-acquisitionitis, ex-executives are angry enough to send their own releases and announce bluntly that they have been fired.

Other times executives who honestly have plans they cannot yet announce say simply that they will make an announcement about future plans within a few weeks. Those with no plans use those code words that sound like plans—"pursue personal interests," "consultant," "join a family venture."

Star Qualities

The stars of business develop their company manners early in life.

It has been my experience that the stars who endure—both corporate and entertainment—are those who listen to others, have innate courtesy, are loyal, give credit where it is due, and don't worry about the media manipulation of others in their business.

In other words, the stars really are stars.

*   *   *

Loyalty is characteristic of many stars.

Bob Hope, for example, keeps the same people around him for years. Many years ago he named as his agent an old pal, Eddie Rio, who was a vaudevillian and ex-hoofer on the circuit with him.

And who eventually replaced Eddie Rio?

Frank Rio—son of Eddie Rio.

While manipulation of the media is part of the star game for many, nobody violates the media rules more often than George Steinbrenner.

But there is a lot about George Steinbrenner that never gets into print. Once, when the wife of a good friend of his died suddenly, Mr. Steinbrenner chartered a plane and flew her husband and young children five hundred miles to her hometown where she had wanted to be buried.

That wasn't in any newspapers, and George Steinbrenner never told anybody.

The best company manners go to dinner nightly.

Several years ago Vidal Sassoon, a friend of my husband, came to town and asked us to join him for dinner. We met at a restaurant, and I found myself at the table next to Dave, a soft-spoken, intelligent man. On the way home I told my husband about Dave, the nice man who worked for the Yankees.

My husband stopped and looked at me. "You mean you don't know who that was?"

"No."

"That was Dave Winfield," he said.

There is a postscript to that story.

When our agency went to work for Ambat, the baseball bat toothbrush, Rob Wyse told me he was thinking of asking Dave Winfield to become involved on behalf of children's dental health and the Winfield Foundation. "What do you think?" Rob asked.

"I think he's one of the nicest people you'll ever meet," I assured him. "If I were you, I'd ask him."

He did ask, and Mr. Winfield did accept.

Mr. Winfield doesn't remember the dinner partner who never heard of him, but I never forgot the star who was secure enough not to tell me who he was.

When Shirley MacLaine opened her one-woman show at the Gershwin Theater in New York, there was a preopening night benefit for the Literacy Volunteers. The entire theater was sold out, and afterward there was a dinner at a restaurant for the real workers, those day-to-day volunteers who were the real backbone of the group.

The glitterati, the chairmen and co-chairmen, were off at a Fashionable After-Theater Supper.

Miss MacLaine, of course, was invited to that celebrity party.

But after the show, she did what none of the fashionable committee people did. She went to the real workers' dinner. And she did more than make a simple ceremonial stop. Although she had just done her show and was tired, she went from table to table, talked to everyone and let each worker know that she was pleased to be able to help them raise money for a cause she thought worthy.

Bill Cosby is a giver, too.

Although he earns millions of dollars from commercials, he once did a commercial for East Ohio Gas Co. to teach viewers how to conserve their usage of gas and save money, and he did the spot for scale (he's not allowed to do it for less than scale) because he knew that those who would benefit most from learning the ways to conserve were the poor.

When you run a company, you can't always be certain you'll deal with first-class stars. You can't limit their demands, but you can define the star limits of acceptable behavior. You can set standards.

And it is those standards that form the basis of company manners.

Style Makers

Style is the dress of thoughts.

Earl of Chesterfield

=======

CHAPTER 10

Power People

=======

Power is what people say they want—until they get it.

What most people truly want is the aura of power because the burdens of power are overwhelming, and few can handle them with both style and grace.

When business booms, and raises and perks such as titles, bonuses, trips, credit cards, and cars are given readily, Power becomes infatuated with its own largesse. Most Power enjoys being the good guy.

But when business falters, Power is the first to be second-guessed. These are the times when middle managers often say, "When I run this place. . . ."

Yet few middle managers are capable of running the place.

A significant difference between middle management and the power level is that middle management is often self-satisfied while remaining critical of others while Power is frequently self-critical and more tolerant of others.

The moment Power becomes self-satisfied is the moment the company and the person both lose momentum.

And the moment that Aspiring Power forgets where Real Power lies is the moment that aspiration ends and reality sets in.

Franco and Albert went to work for Horatio immediately after college. Horatio, a crotchety bachelor, enjoyed having two young men in his employ. He put Franco, a fun-loving bachelor, in charge of advertising and marketing.

Albert, a sober-sided chap, was made an understudy to the chief financial officer.

Before he realized he might find two young men to succeed him, Horatio had, over the years, shared his confidences and given his trust to Willard, an executive who started as a shipping clerk, rose to product manager, then vice president in charge of production and finally senior vice president.

But as Horatio entered his last illness, he knew he would have to make a decision regarding succession. He opted in favor of strong management, made Willard the president and both younger men executive vice presidents. The stock, however, was left to a charitable foundation Horatio established with several members of his family and friends as trustees. During his years as Horatio's fair-haired boy, Willard was properly deferential. But upon Horatio's death, Willard felt he had finally come into his own.

He laughed privately at the ineptness of Franco and the fussiness of Albert as he personally took over the reins of the company and commanded the trappings of Horatio's power: private planes, hotel suites, chichi entertaining. Willard spent less time than ever on the company's business. Instead, each month he accepted another industry honor—he was "Man of the Year" one time, keynote speaker at the industry convention another time.

Franco and Albert attended each event and seemed to be in harmony with their president.

Under the smooth surface, however, all was not calm. Albert did not like Willard's ignoring him. Still, what could he do? As one executive vice president, he could not move mountains. He could not even move Willard.

The more he thought about his corporate impotence, the more he resolved to do something about it.

He called Franco for a luncheon date, and somewhere between the chilled asparagus appetizer and the cappucino, he told Franco what *they* had to do.

"We?" asked Franco.

"We," repeated Albert.

It was simple, Albert explained. By combining forces, the two of them would have the power to squeeze Willard out of position. "Power," explained Albert, "is a matter of numbers. The two of us against the one of him—plus the fact that Willard has failed to lure the troops to his side—will make it possible for you and me to take control of the company."

"What about the trustees?" Franco asked.

"The trustees will understand when we start showing them the bills for Willard's lifestyle. What you have to understand, Franco, is that when you really go out to get someone, all you have to do is begin to look at the books. It is always amazing how many good people do very bad things."

Together Franco and Albert left the luncheon.

Together Franco and Albert went to see the trustees.

And together they were told that the trustees would rely on them to do whatever had to be done to get the company in proper shape.

"Will you back us?" Albert asked the trustees.

"You have our authority."

"Even with Willard?" Franco asked.

"Especially with Willard," they were told.

The next day Willard was called into Franco's office. Albert was also there. "Sit down," said Franco magnanimously.

Willard sat on a small sofa for two.

Albert squeezed in on one side.

. Franco squeezed next to Willard on the other.

"Uncomfortable, isn't it?" asked Franco.

"Not enough room for three," sighed Albert. "And that," he said with a soft smile, "is the story of our company."

Willard left the room with not a golden but a silver parachute. And, like many other ex-CEOs, he is now an independent consultant.

Willard was seduced by the trappings of power, and he chose to overlook the real responsibilities.

It is the understanding and acceptance of responsibilities that make up the character of power and give it its peculiar style.

The responsibilities sound old-fashioned and prissy.

At the core of power is a genuine desire to create change that one perceives to be for the betterment of others. Willard's love affair with Willard is a constant danger for all executives.

Instead of self, power must concentrate on corporate talent— it must be sought after, nurtured, and rewarded.

Exterior toughness does not mean that one does not care for employees. Often that toughness indicates Power's high standards, Power's ability to challenge, and Power's innate desire to make himself and others better than they ever dreamed they would be.

Power has a commitment to excellence, a code of ethics, and an ability to communicate a sense of the business to the people depended upon to achieve goals.

All of this is what power is about, for power is about the inner person.

Real power is rare.

The perception of power is not.

It extends into every area of life from offices to clothes, outside activities to charities and time off.

Today, unlike the old days when nouveau riche was a denigrating term, nouveau power is not.

So let us take a closer look at the trappings of power, the so-called power style.

The Offices of Power

Power always works from the corner office.

Generally it is the biggest office.

It is always the best-decorated because office decor is a mark of power.

Ed Kolodny, the head of U.S. Air, eschews fancy offices, frills, and fluff. For him the company style is expressed with offices in the old hangars at National Airport in Washington, D.C., and simple, functional headquarters offices in Pittsburgh.

The only thing about Mr. Kolodny that is not low-key is his profit statement. U.S. Air profits are consistently among the best in the airline industry.

When Howard Hardesty became chief executive officer of Purolator, he decided that the best way to impress his staff with his commitment to orderly business and profit was for the new regime to abandon old, wasteful ways.

The first week Mr. Hardesty sold the company plane.

The second week he took away all staff cars.

By the third week, everyone got the message.

Big city offices tend to remind visitors that they are now in the presence of Power. Even San Francisco, traditionally more relaxed in its approach to business, now has company offices that look as uptight and corporate as those of any in New York.

Only in Denver and Los Angeles are offices still eclectic. Los Angeles offices are usually open to the sun (despite the fact that the sun may be blotted out by smog). Denver offices are frequently western, rugged in feeling with photography on the wall that repeats the sense of mountains and cactus just outside.

Formal, traditional corporate style offices do not all look alike, however.

An office may be furnished with Louis Quinze–styled desk and desk chairs (as is the New York office of Ralph Destino, the chairman of Cartier), or it may have an unparalleled view of the

Statue of Liberty (as does the office of James D. Robinson III, chairman of American Express), or it may, like the office of Arthur Rubloff (who created Chicago's Magnificent Mile on North Michigan Avenue) house Remington bronzes and Chinese ivories in a room with a rosewood floor and a rosewood and marble desk.

Regardless of the furnishings, however, almost all power style has certain similarities.

Today Power rarely has anyone sit across the desk from him. It would seem that all power persons have read the same how-to books which advise that the desk creates a barrier between the office owner and the guest, and in a constant effort to remove barriers in business, Power runs from behind its desk to greet guests and sits side-by-side on sofas or on comfortable facing chairs. However, when Power is firing, Power never leaves its desk. Then Power likes the barrier, the protection, the psychological distance of the desk.

When Power powwows in its office, Power never sits at a lower level than the guest. Therefore, if Power is a short person, Power is careful not to sit on a sofa (it makes one sink too far down).

House Power

While Power offices are usually decorated by professionals (in some cases the CEO's wife assumes this responsibility, gets herself a decorator card, and uses this occasion to put herself in business), the Old Guard of Power often lives in shabby homes with elegant addresses. Fortunes have been made by New York interior designers during the past twenty years as Old Guard has given up its wonderful old Fifth Avenue, Park Avenue, and East Side brownstone residences to make way for New Power Money.

New Power is a voracious consumer with emphasis on such words as *chic, style, lifestyle,* and *quality of life.* To New Power the right interior designer is just as important as the right address.

Since the death of Billy Baldwin, the status designer is Sister Parish who, with her partner Albert Hadley, has created livable backdrops for people with names like Paley, Astor, Whitney, Mellon, Rockefeller, and Getty. The mark of a Parish interior is the homelike look, a combination of excellent patterns and bibelots that is always pleasing to the eye, never attracts attention because of a single flamboyant or outrageous piece of furniture or accessory.

Mark Hampton (with his wife Duane, they are a prize party catch for the New York hostess) is preferred by many of the younger rich including the Basses of Texas.

Mario Buatta, who spans the power generations, designs for both older and younger persons and for a number of years has chaired the prestigious Antiques Show at the New York Armory.

Annelle Warwick spans the ocean and decorates everything from North Shore country homes to Parisian apartments.

For some power persons a decorator becomes a member of the family because the family is constantly refurbishing one of its many bases—the house in Malibu is finished only to be sold for the ski lodge in Idaho which will be sold when the apartment in New York is bought, and by then it is time to refurbish the palazzo in Palm Springs.

Dress for Success

Only a third assistant vice president would believe that one must dress for success. The uniform approach to clothes does not work at the top level.

Still, who but the chairman of a Fortune 500 company would feel secure teaching a class at the University of Chicago reportedly with dandruff all over his lapels?

Somewhere between the studied and the sloppy is the power look.

Theater agents, who used to dress in whatever kind of sports attire suited their mood, changed to black suits and dark ties when Dr. Jules Stein became the president of MCA. Today, for the most part, they still dress like sober businessmen so no one will take show business too lightly. And, considering that they are negotiating multimillion dollar deals for individuals every day, that seems appropriate.

The exception is superagent Sam Cohn, the ICM executive who manages the careers of many brilliant actors including Meryl Streep. Cohn appears publicly, everywhere from the Laundry (the stylish restaurant he owns in East Hampton) to the Russian Tea Room (the restaurant where he "owns" a booth up front) to the opera and opening nights in the same attire: a pair of rumpled trousers, a shirt, and over it a sweater with rolled sleeves.

Howard Hughes always appeared in tennis shoes at tennis matches, as well as at black-tie events.

In order to dress that way, however, one needs the confidence that comes with recognized importance.

The best-known American look is the Wall Street Look.

The Wall Street Look has no fashion, but it does have style. It has evolved into both a young look and an old look. Surprisingly, it is the older men who wear the relaxed and looser look of double-breasted suits and were the first to bring back hats. Younger men favor a more rigid look. Young Wall Streeters in their Brooks Brothers and Paul Stuart suits (characterized by the basic natural shoulder in gray, navy, or striped wool) are free to worry about business; they know their clothing is safer than their stock recommendations.

These men consider positively racy such accessories as pocket handkerchiefs, bow ties, suspenders, and tasseled shell cordovan loafers.

Power has many options in dressing but takes only a few. Jeans and sandals are out, of course. They have had their day, but now even aging hippies like Jerry Rubin dress up to go downtown. If you had any questions about business being the center of the contemporary life, note that Jerry Rubin, ever anxious to be part of a current scene, now dresses like a Wall Streeter and holds weekly business networking cocktail parties every Tuesday after business hours at a New York disco.

The business look is the most important look in America. In

almost every city in the United States are pin-striped clones of both sexes with button-down white shirts, rep ties, and shoes made to match briefcases.

The best-looking clothes for a man are generally those made for him.

A Saville Row tailor is worth his weight in cuffs. Once a man has had his clothes made, he understands those things that are the immediate giveaways in the way a male dresses: details like hand stitching, bone buttons (never, never plastic), rolled hems.

Turnbull and Asser shirting is usually distinguishable; the little checks and chic stripes are silent calling cards among the cognoscenti. A man's tie is the touch of the pure individualist. Any man who wears something other than a silk rep tie or a solid-color tie in navy, brown, silver, or black is a man with a mind of his own.

The most fashion-conscious wear colorful ties from Giorgio Armani and Missoni; the conservative trendsetter sallies forth in yellow. At some Manhattan stores yellow ties now sell in equal numbers with red ties. According to haberdashers to the powerful, yellow is the new look; it announces the arrival of a man in charge, a man who can afford to wear what he likes.

Shoes are the power giveaway.

One personnel director of a major corporation says that after all the psychological tests have been taken, after the interviews and the résumés—if you still doubt the capabilities of the candidate, look at his shoes. If they are shined and in good repair, you can assume that this is a person who pays attention to details, will have a neat desk, get his work out in orderly fashion, is detail-oriented—but may never be president. Men running for the top job are often moving too fast to see their shoes.

In New York the young men in communications and finance shop at Barney's because out-of-towners don't know that it has become the quality store for both conservative and far-out fashion.

But old or young, every man with an inner eye on underwear orders his linen at Brooks Brothers.

The Turnbull and Asser shop in Bergdorf-Goodman is shirt headquarters for those who don't even know how Jermyn Street is spelled. For the fussy shirt lover, however, measurements are kept on file in Turnbull and Asser's London shop, and a quick call from one's secretary sends an airplane load of made-to-order shirts or fabrics from which to select.

In the last ten years Hong Kong has become the well-tailored (and cost-conscious) executive's shirt store. An old shirt is taken to Hong Kong, fabrics are selected, and the shirt is copied. Once the Hong Kong shirtmaker knows your shirt size and style, you can keep on ordering forever.

In London one sees more dash and originality in the way men dress.

The English wear pattern on pattern; even when Americans try, most never achieve quite the same style. An Englishman always wears a vest or sweater under his suit jacket (no central heating in those chilly London offices and homes). They also wear bold, chalk-striped flannel suits and bar-striped dress shirts and accent them with patterned ties, a look few Americans are willing to risk.

And topping it all is that stylish English bowler.

When older and more conservative Wall Street men began wearing hats two years ago, the younger men gingerly followed. Wall Street is the one place where the old set the style. In almost all other fashion, trends begin with the young. Hats probably were returned to fashion by older men because as hair thins and heads grow cold, these former crew-cutted men now welcome a hat. The best-looking men's hats are Borsellinos (check the shops in Venice, Rome, and Milan). Younger men favor caps; the smartest come from Locke's in London.

And, even though no man will admit this, television does influence fashion. (Remember the Andy Williams sweater? Remember when Dan Rather was dressed in a sweater to humanize him on the nightly news?) Now Bill Cosby, whose cool and relaxed style catapulted him to the top of the ratings, has a hat wardrobe: four panamas, a homburg, a porkpie, a snap-brim, a planter's hat, and two felt fedoras. And since his show will probably still be in re-run in the year 2000, it is safe to assume hats will be worn by more men each year.

In the 1960s and 1970s facial hair was more important than a winning smile. Still, back then there were a lot of executives who considered whiskers an affront to American manhood. When Wyse was the agency for the New York Yankees, George Steinbrenner once banned one of our male copywriters from the locker room because the copywriter had a beard. Those, of course, were the days prior to the signing of Reggie Jackson and other bearded, hard-hitting wonders.

The briefcase is the most universal accessory in the world today. In all the world only the English banker is more likely to carry a black umbrella than a briefcase. But stand outside the subway in Tokyo, and during rush hour you will see armies of men in dark suits swinging briefcases emerging to go to work. You will see the same sight outside Grand Central Station, Charing Cross, and other metropolitan centers of the world where those who live in that city's version of suburbia commute for the work-day.

Briefcases, like CEOs, should never look new and unused.

A briefcase should look as if it has been places. A very good briefcase should be made of dark leather, have no designer imprint, and look as if it has been holding important papers beginning with the Treaty of Versailles. A shiny new briefcase from Gucci is carried only by a recent college graduate who is anxious to let his boss know that even though he doesn't have an MBA, he does have a briefcase.

The best first-class accessory for a man with his eye on a first-class ticket is a canvas sports bag with Nike shoes and a squash racquet. There is a story about one assistant cashier at a major bank who knew that one of his vice presidents took the same train to work every morning. He also knew that the vice president was a squash enthusiast. Each day the assistant cashier boarded the train with his sports paraphernalia. Finally one day the vice president caught up with him as they left the train. "I know we both work at Chemical Bank. Now tell me, do you really have time to play squash every day?"

"No, sir," said the quick-thinking young man. "I take my racquet and hope that one day I'll find the time."

Smiled the vice president, "I do play every day at the New York Racquet Club. Why don't you join me after work today?"

The two men became better acquainted, and, as a result, the young man is now better-situated. Although he is no longer with Chemical Bank, he still boards the train each day with his squash racquet. "You never know who you'll meet," he says.

Squash racquets are not the only status advertisements. A Cartier watch says something, too. It says quietly that while one could afford The Other Stuff, one has taste and judgment that permit rising above that glitz—but at the same time one is announcing that he is a cut above the digital dullards.

No man of style would wear a drugstore fragrance; the boys who used to wear Canoe have now moved up to Aramis, first choice among achievers, probably because most fragrances for men are bought by women, and Aramis (made by Estée Lauder) is sold where women shop.

While the American businesswoman would seem to have the greatest choice in clothes, she seldom takes it.

Dr. Leah Hertz of London, who studied the differences between female entrepreneurs in the United Kingdom and the United States, noted that the executive American businesswoman most often dressed in a suit with a bowed blouse.

On the other hand, her British counterpart wears pants, scarves, workclothes—whatever makes her comfortable.

Dr. Hertz concludes that the American woman dresses one step above the women in the office to show that she is different.

The British woman, on the other hand, dresses in a completely different way.

Still, each is saying with her wardrobe, "I am someone of importance."

The American businesswoman can have a varied and appealing look. Self-employed women (notwithstanding Dr. Hertz's comments) do dare to wear clothes as art. They wear jackets by Castelbajac, some of the Sonia Rykiel sweaters as well as statement-making Art Deco necklaces and bracelets.

Geraldine Stutz, the president of Henri Bendel, always has next year's haircut, today's clothes, and when a woman looks at her, she knows that she can trust somebody who looks like that to give her fashion direction.

Connie Boucher of Determined Productions in San Francisco wears bright red jumpsuits—just what you'd expect of a woman smart enough to think of a fashion show based on famous designers creating clothes for characters in the "Peanuts" comic strip.

It takes confidence to develop one's own style. Who besides Jacqueline Onassis would dare to walk into the trendiest restaurants in the world wearing black trousers and a black sweater? Most women need a little more dressing on the salad of life.

Surprisingly, the trendsetters for executive women are non-executive women. The best-dressed list rarely includes any woman who rises before noon to face her public.

It was Chanel who created the most-loved basic suit style for women and added the faux jewelry that has more wit than carats. Today that suit is done to a fare-thee-well by Adolfo for the Ladies Who Lunch. And it appears in boardrooms on some of the best backs (Robin Duke, Dina Merrill).

In lesser-known versions it is copied to retail at prices beginning at $49.95 in stores as diverse as Sears and Bergdorf-Goodman.

The successful woman can be recognized by her body, easily her best accessory. The best bodies are shaped regularly by experts at places like Gilda's (there are Gilda salons all over America), in aerobic dance classes which were originated and popularized by Jackie Sorenson, and in private co-ed health clubs like the Vertical Club. The person who comes to one's home for individualized exercise programs is part of the staff support of a number of successful women. It is not just movie and television people who live by their looks, but businesswomen like Ann Sutherland Fuchs (publisher of *Woman's Day*) and Isabel Stevenson (head of the American Theater Wing) who rely on the home exercise therapist.

The emphasis on health has made changes in executive fashion. It is now acceptable for women everywhere to walk to work in their running shoes; foot health is considered more important than foot beauty. At the office the woman changes into her sensible low-heeled shoes—but only after parking her bicycle outside her office.

Once a woman hits the six-figure mark, the bicycle must go—although the running shoes may stay.

Women have learned to dress for the territory. In the 1970s the pants suit was popularized and worn to the office and restaurant. In New York the most expensive French restaurants worried more over admitting women in pants suits than they did over fallen soufflés. But times change. And now that women know they can wear pants to the office, few do.

The executive woman carries executive purse accessories. Trussardi cosmetic cases (navy blue or black ones in winter, white in summer) are instant status as are any items from card cases to wallets to keyrings from Botega Veneto. Louis Vuitton is for the insecure. Ditto Gucci and anything else with distinguishing names, animals, or initials. Executive feet are shod by a myriad of Italian designers as well as Susan Benis and Warren Edwards (if you are high-fashion) and Helene Arpels (if the woman is not going feet first into contemporary cutes). Maude Frizon is for rock stars.

Women who work for banks, investment bankers, or other members of the financial community keep their jewelry confined to gold chokers or pearls (not too big, not too long, not too noticeable) around their necks, and on their ears, pearl, gold, or diamond studs. They wear rings (never big enough to become the focus of a meeting) on only one finger of each hand.

Dressing the woman who works has become a big business in the United States. There was a time when most clothes were sold for sportswear or dress. Now, with more than half of the women in the United States employed, stores and manufacturers have taken special pains to woo them.

Stores like Saks Fifth Avenue now maintain an executive shopping service; they keep a woman's sizes and clothes preferences on file. When she calls and says she is in need of some clothes, items are selected, a room is set aside, a time held, and the customer is treated in a businesslike way.

Other executives have their own shoppers, a service provided by those who go directly to designer showrooms with customers, select clothes, and pay wholesale prices. A fee is added to compensate the shopper; the theory is much the same as that of the interior designer. A first-rate shopping service does a full wardrobe plan for the customer.

A power wardrobe needs its highly charged special-events clothes, and it needs clothes to underplay situations.

As Lee Guber, the theater producer, says, "Executives should select clothes the same way costumes are done for a show. What you wear should be interesting enough to attract attention—and then fade into the background once the action gets underway."

Time Off

Power never takes two weeks off.

Power takes long weekends.

And Power goes skiing. (One never asks where. One simply inquires, "Here or there?" Here means the house in Vail; there means Gstaad the week that "everybody" is there. Everybody, in this case, is the best of Europe's power people as well as a few select Americans.)

As you can see, Power does not vacation like ordinary mortals.

Power holidays.

And Power holidays in more places than ski resorts, although Power does not go to Atlantic City or Las Vegas (unless it's a convention).

Power takes itself to Barbados in the winter, stays only in

private homes (Claudette Colbert or Marietta Tree are the preferred ones). Power also goes to Lyford Cay (pronounced Key)
when it's cold up north. Power holidays at its second or third
home in protected enclaves such as John's Island in Florida (Palm
Beach is too touristy, Miami is where foreigners launder their
money), and in seaside homes in Mexico and the south of France.
Real power never stays in hotels, and even when power children
are included in travel plans, Power will never stay in motels, unless
they are family-owned.

Power flies the corporate jet and is met at the plane door by
the company limo. And because Power never wastes time, executives like Thornton Bradshaw of RCA will, as they fly in from
East Hampton, call a favorite restaurant and say, "Expect me in
twenty minutes." Then when the small plane lands at the East
Side heliport, Power limos to its favorite eating places.

An important power consideration is time. Power is fond of
referring to time as money, and Power is fond of thinking this is
an original thought.

Although Power trusts luxury (only the middle class fears that
others may be offended by material excess), Power often travels
tourist class, particularly when Power takes its small children on
holidays.

Power style is never to spend money on something that can
provide equal results for less, and—as we all know—the back of
the airplane arrives at the same time as the front of the plane.

Power Gifts

Power does not give presents for promotions, birthdays, and special occasions.

Power gives gifts.

The biggest corporate gift-giving time is the Christmas season,
and Power runs up its corporate charges at Tiffany's and Cartier's
because the label is prestigious and also because Power gets a
discount at those stores. (Minimum corporate discounts at both:

10 percent. Discounts, however, can go higher depending on the amount spent by the company annually.) The power people delegate assistants or secretaries to cull the names and prepare the gift lists. Generally lists are done in groups according to title, current importance to the giver, and future importance to the giver. There is a price tag put on each group, and gifts are given without thought to the individual but rather to the group (e.g., everyone in Group One gets a silver Tiffany picture frame).

Not everyone in the corporate world is allowed to receive holiday business gifts.

The *New York Times* does not permit its employees to receive any gift at any time of the year, nor can *Times* men and women accept transportation, meals, or lodging from anyone in the covering of a story.

Maidenform, the lingerie manufacturer, sends a letter to all its suppliers in advance of the holiday season informing them that company policy precludes the receiving of gifts by any of Maidenform's employees.

Today nongiving is as much a part of corporate style as giving.

The usual gift practice is to give nothing to an executive that can be construed as too big or too important—no vicuña coats, oriental rugs, or other headline-making remembrances.

Instead there is a large assortment of cheeses no one eats, little tins of chocolate grasshoppers, and other "gourmet" items such as jellies, nuts, turkeys, holiday dinners, wine (not spirits). Spirits are given to service personnel (superintendents, mailmen) but are never given to executives.

If you are on a power person's A food list, you may receive fresh caviar, a crystal Baccarat caviar bowl, or tortoise shell caviar servers. Should you receive all three from one person, it would be wise to check all business dealings with that person, for if you as an executive receive this, what is your company's purchasing agent (who is undoubtedly responsible for that company's largesse) receiving?

Generally, however, food items are considered safe (a safe gift being one that cannot offend the recipient by its opulence).

All gifts, even though modest, are not safe.

One year a major advertising agency sent to its clients a silver Elsa Perretti pen from Tiffany. The only problem was that among the clients who received the Perretti pen was the client group that worked on Bic. No heads rolled, but faces were red.

Whenever appropriate, Power gives a gift of its own products. Bristol-Myers sends an assortment of it own analgesics and beauty products.

Some companies go beyond the Thanksgiving turkey in sending gifts to their employees. Needham, Harper & Steers chairman Keith Reinhard gives everyone in his office a birthday gift, usually an identical unisex present like an umbrella.

Gifts are all part of the reward system in today's corporate culture, and company manners are revealed in the ways thanks are given.

The written note, never a telephone call (unless it is followed by the written note), is acceptable company manners.

Although the typewritten thank-you on office letterhead is acceptable, the stylish hand-written note is preferable.

Notepaper or cards with one's name embossed are best.

The correct, conservative ones come from Smythson's on Bond Street in London where the individual die is kept on file. Reordering is done by one's secretary—by mail or telex for the organized, by telephone for the tardy.

The personal note is then written, not with a Cross ballpoint, but rather with a Mont Blanc pen, today's ultimate old-fashioned fountain pen. Never mind that you need a blotter and that your hands get full of the ink and that a fountain pen is simply not as convenient as a ballpoint—this is still the ultimate chic.

Personal stationery is always ordered from a fine stationer. Rag content should be high (it makes for easier writing), and the paper itself can be any color so long as it is white. One's name may be printed in blue (never black—that's for mourning), dark red, dark green, brown. The best stationers are available in the

United States at Henri Bendel or Dempsey and Carroll. Otherwise stay with Smythson's.

Benefits and Banquets

Back in the days when America had its great families of wealth and privilege, both cultural institutions and civic charities were able to raise funds without holding balls, selling tickets to a lecture series, a theater party, a testimonial dinner, or a banquet.

Those days are no more. Enter the charity affair.

Regardless of what the affair is called, it always seems to take place, at least in part, in a leading hotel with a banquet that offers not only a three-tiered head table and boring speeches but also features rubber chicken, watery baked Alaska, and dreary wines.

But the banquet is not about food and entertainment. The banquet is about power, for today a measure of power is (a) how many benefits one is asked to chair, and (b) how many benefits one is asked to serve as "honoree."

Many of the largest benefits are handled by a professional party planning company, and they are often responsible for picking the power person to chair the event, the person to "honor" as well as a list of vice chairmen (vice chairmen do nothing, but their names on a charity letterhead add prestige).

There are certain power individuals who need no professional assistance when it comes to organizing and running a benefit. Chief among this group are Washington's Pamela Harriman and Esther Coopersmith; in New York no one puts together a benefit with the panache of Phyllis Cerf Wagner, now the wife of the former mayor of New York, Robert Wagner. Phyllis Wagner is a major Democratic Party fund-raiser. She has raised as much as $1 million for the Democrats in a single evening. Her extraordinary organizational ability makes it possible for her to convince men and women of all persuasions to contribute to causes and events they never suspected they would support.

When Power is the honoree or chairman at an event, he or

she is expected to sell a lot of tickets. Typical honorees are bank presidents, chairmen of insurance companies, and department store executives. All are able to sell tables to customers. Honorees are rarely, if ever, persons who run companies that do not have a long list of people who are in one way or another beholden to the company. The best honorary chairperson is the president of the United States and/or his wife. On a lesser scale the governor and then the mayor.

It is difficult to decline the role of honoree with grace.

Robert Bernstein, the chairman of Random House, was once called and asked to be the honoree for an industry dinner. He thought for a moment and then said, "I appreciate this, but I really think a more deserving person would be Oscar Dystal." Mr. Dystal was then the head of Bantam Books.

"Oh," said the caller, "we already asked Mr. Dystal. He told us to call you."

Once one commits to being either honoree or chairman, one is honor-bound to buy several tables for one's own company and to sell tables to one's best corporate friends. This sets up what we have come to recognize as the contemporary corporate cycle of giving. From the time you sell your first table, you are obligated to buy tables for the rest of your corporate life—which means until death or retirement. At that time a new executive will come along with his favorite charity and so begin a new charity cycle. Various corporations have charities that suit their executives. Some are long-standing and do not change with each president. Seagram's, for example, has been a conspicuous contributor for many years to both the Boy Scouts and Cerebral Palsy.

Not all benefits accrue to the benefit of giver or receiver. A few years ago a partner in the accounting firm of Ernst and Whinney became involved in the Highway Safety Foundation and, with Sammy Davis, Jr., decided to do a telethon in a single market. Even though the telethon made no money the first year, the committee decided to do even more telethons the second year, the reason being that they were sure that by adding markets they would be successful.

And so they began the labor-intensive days that go into the making of any charitable event. By the time they were sure they were ready to go, Richard Baker, then the chief executive officer of Ernst and Whinney, was asked to take a close look at the numbers. What Baker saw appalled him. Not only would the telethon be unable to make money, but the committee was already down $6 million. Baker swallowed hard, pulled the plug, and made good on every dollar.

Chairing a banquet is often a thankless task. Power persons with about as much natural humor and visible charm as Khrushchev are asked to leave the privacy of their comfortable thrones and assume an unaccustomed role as host and raconteur. Very few have the necessary charisma. A notable exception is Anthony (Tony) O'Reilly, the chairman of H. J. Heinz Co., who often chairs Irish benefits.

Power tends to have little or no style when it speaks to large groups. The best chairpersons are those who eschew humor, keep the introductions short and simple, and end the program fifteen minutes ahead of schedule.

The most appropriate (and perhaps condescending) description of those involved in fund-raisers was given by Brooke Astor. At a luncheon honoring the mayor of New York, a luncheon which she chaired, Mrs. Astor introduced the mayor to the guests and described all those in the room as "the responsible rich."

It is never good business to turn down a charity dinner in which someone important in your business life is involved. If the person is on your "most wanted list," you take a table. Corporations may take two or more tables when they want to pay proper respect to the honoree.

One step down from the table buyer is the person who buys seats at a table (and if the buyer is truly courteous, he attends with spouse or friends and attacks the banquet chicken personally).

One never, never buys a ticket and leaves the seats empty. Tickets should always be given to a high-ranking associate if you cannot attend the event.

What some thoughtful persons do is buy tickets and return them to the committee for use among those who would otherwise be unable to attend the event.

The least one can do to express concern and interest is to send a check to the charity in the amount of one seat.

Sources of Information

Power reads the *Wall Street Journal* every day as well as the *New York Times* business pages. Power preferences in magazines are *Forbes, Manhattan, Inc., U.S. News and World Report, Business Week,* and *Fortune.*

But that is only a small part of what Power knows and hears.

Much is made of "the old boy network," and it is indeed a highly viable and useful tool for power.

Because it is "old boy," few corporate women and blacks have access to the information that the old boys have.

Women have tried to respond with the Committee of 200, a power network of women who run businesses of $5 million or more.

But men are the members of the Conference Board, those who run the most prestigious of the Fortune 500 companies. The only woman among the group is Kay Graham of the *Washington Post.* Other networking is done through directorships (a director of a powerful company is often a director of another powerful company).

Directorships today, however, are fraught with potential suits ranging from corporate mismanagement to environmental damage and product problems. Walter Wriston, the former head of Citibank and a director of many companies, has summed it by saying, "In the old days at director meetings, the director would lift his plate at lunch and find a $20 gold piece underneath. Now the director opens the door and finds twenty process servers."

Power congregates at key influential country and in-town clubs. These do not include the college or university clubs, but rather clubs like the Union League in New York, the Bohemian in San Francisco, the Duquesne in Pittsburgh. Generally these are *men only* clubs with limited membership. Today some have a few token women members.

Power plays squash. Power does not play racquetball (that sport is for the younger and less affluent persons in the corporation).

Golf is popular but is a power sport only when played at the right club.

The locker room is the single most important place for the exchange of confidential business information that will change the shape of world business. This fact, as much as any other, keeps minorities and women from scaling the corporate heights.

Power also whispers its secrets in the duck blinds of Georgia. Hunting in Africa is a used-to-be.

Polo came to the United States in the 1920s and is played regularly in Florida and at eastern clubs including the Sands Point Club where a key member is W. T. (Bill) Ylvisaker, the former CEO of Gould.

Just as tennis and golf have become major spectator sports thanks to corporate involvement and television, enthusiasts are trying the same kind of promotion with polo.

Should they succeed, polo will become just another game with horses and men because one of the trademarks of corporate style is limited knowledge of the existence of an activity, resort, restaurant, or hotel. Once "everybody" knows about something, "nobody" wants it.

Power Notes

Power keeps track of its life with the Filofax, a personal, compact, three-ring binder. This leather-bound organizer is chunky, slips into the executive woman's Kelly bag (the crocodile status handbag from Hermes made popular by the late Grace Kelly) or the executive man's briefcase. The Filofax organizer holds everything from a one-year appointment agenda to credit cards, passport, city maps, and special papers including one for a bird watcher's "life lists," ledger paper for accountants, music manuscript paper for composers, lined and unlined pages for corporate note takers and—for those who need it—pages for recording golf scores and a horse's stud record.

The cost of the Filofax (it is produced in England by Norman & Hill Ltd., who also produce leather accessories for Rolls-Royce automobiles) ranges from approximately $125 for an unfilled leather version to $400 for an ostrich counterpart. Outfitting the book with the proper pages for organizing one's life can add another $100.

Of course, not all men and women want to Filofax their lives.

Some Power prefers to take notes on small cards kept in a Cartier case which fits easily into the breast pocket of a man's jacket or a woman's evening bag. It was once a charming and impromptu gesture to reach for an old envelope or cocktail napkin to write names, dates, and places worth remembering. But those were the days when telephone numbers were written with old lipsticks.

All of that is now tacky, despite the romantic overtones. Style demands that you carry your own writing materials. The pen (unlike the desk pen) should not be a fountain pen but rather a cartridge pen of gold, elegant, thin, and always filled. Pencils are for the uncertain.

Portable computers used as word processors are the sine qua non, today's unmistakable mark of an indispensable executive.

The car telephone is now as much a part of executive life as a desk telephone, but the telephone in the briefcase is definitely for a salesperson or the president of the United States. No power person should ever be seen walking down the street talking into his briefcase—particularly if he runs a public company.

Power Talk

Power talk is positive.

It is not filled with modest expressions and self-doubt because Power is neither modest nor self-doubting.

Power is always the expert voice, and to the annoyance of non-Power, Power is generally right.

At a private screening for the movie *That's Dancin'* a film fan, aware that he was surrounded by Power and wanting to appear equally important, said to the man next to him, "This movie will make a fortune."

The man next to him shook his head, "It won't get a quarter at the box office." He was right. He was Bernie Myerson, president of Loew's Theaters; he didn't need the film fan's opinion. Power knows without asking anybody else.

The truly powerful avoid four-letter expressions as well as trendy language.

Power knows that unless one is a jazz musician, a teenager, or one who requires a security code, expressions such as "I dig," as well as computerese (the use of nouns as verbs), "Don't download that on me, Mr. Smith," are low-level management ploys.

Equally offensive is someone who refers to "my girl" when he is not speaking of his young daughter.

When anyone (Power or otherwise) refers to a female under 18 as a gal (the correct term is girl) or a female over 18 as a gal (the correct appellation is woman), take a deep breath and make a public correction, for usage will improve only when the well-intentioned learn from the knowledgeable.

The word "guy" is equally offensive. Males are boys (under 18) or men.

Power small talk differs from Power talk in that small talk is unplanned. Power small talk, therefore, is confined to those conversations that occur in executive offices while everyone waits for the cast to assemble and the meeting to begin, at elevators where Grand Power waits with Lesser Power for the carriage to arrive, and in unexpected meetings in unexpected places (the barber shop at the Regency, the bridal registry at Tiffany's).

The subjects for Power small talk vary depending on the occasion. Office talk is generally about activities of the past weekend, sports scores, and the weather. At the elevator the comments are brief, and questions are raised as to whether or not it is (a) raining, (b) unseasonably hot, (c) unseasonably cold. In the unexpected place one never asks, "What are you doing here?" but says instead, "I see we are both here on a little personal business. I'm sure I'll see you shortly back at the office." That conversation is equally appropriate for Lesser Power to deliver to Greater Power.

On no occasion should Power authenticate conversation with ". . . but my husband said" or "my wife thinks . . ." unless the spouse is an acknowledged authority in the area under discussion.

Spouses have an important place in executive life, but the middle of a business conversation is not it.

CHAPTER 11

The Art of Spousemanship

Back in the Middle Ages of Corporate Life, it was de rigueur for management to look at wives as well as men in selecting the next president of the Thumbtack Division. Would she be able to live well in Minneapolis? Would she get on the right social service boards? Did her dowdiness match the dowdiness of the other executive wifes?

But times have changed. Instead of executive wives, we now have consecutive wives, and in this world of second and third wives, no one is much concerned with what the Little Woman does and doesn't do in terms of the corporation. In addition, we now have an occasional female vice president or partner, and often she has a husband—which is the reason business now talks about the spouse instead of the wife.

But most of us dislike the spouse role primarily because:

Spouses Never Seem Important

Most spouses feel like a let-out hem in a 1979 suit.

That is because very few corporate executives make spouses feel like significant adjuncts to the company.

An exception is Sanford C. Sigoloff, who in less than three years pulled Santa Monica–based Wickes Builders Emporium through a difficult Chapter 11 reorganization. During the 33 months when the Wickes management team was working twelve to fourteen hours a day, seven days a week, Mr. Sigoloff organized the "Wickes widows," headed by his wife of more than 30 years. Mr. Sigoloff said, "I felt the success of Wickes depended on the ability of the guys who were married to have a normal home life. The heroines were the Wickes widows. They made it possible. They adjusted eating schedules and activities for the kids."

Wives also took part in comparative shopping projects with competitors in the marketplace. But when the turnaround was completed, the wives made their demands known: no more than two staff meetings a month, no weekend calls.

Another corporate exception to the expendable spouse philosophy is practiced by the Consolidated Natural Gas Company whose annual planning meeting with directors and key executives is always held at a weekend retreat where husbands and wives can mix and meet.

It is an important meeting in terms of what happens at the business sessions—and any executive who arrives spouseless feels like half a person. It is an occasion made and planned for husband and wife participation as well as company business.

But the reason so many spouses feel left-out and left-over is that their presence is required for infrequent state occasions, and they are on display rather than a part of a programmed life.

Those events that permit spouses to act more natural make everyone more comfortable and make both the company spouse and the company person more understanding of one another.

Spouse "Manners"

Always make your spouse look good

Walter Cronkite came up to my husband and me shortly after we were married and said, "Best wishes. I hope you like the champagne glasses we sent."

"But I just mailed the thank-you note today," I said in surprise. "How did you know what you and Betsy gave us?"

"Because," he explained, "Betsy always sends champagne glasses, so I'll know why brides are thanking me."

That anecdote symbolizes the essence of spousemanship, the gentle art of making one another look and feel good.

Never play down to the client's wife, the out-of-town spouse, or anyone else called "his wife"

Crystal and Ralph were the perfect corporate couple; he ran a large manufacturing company, and she was fashion director of a major store.

Just as Crystal was leaving her office one evening the telephone rang. It was Ralph. "Sorry to do this, dear, but we have a customer here from Michigan."

". . . but we have tickets for . . ." she began.

"I know. I know. But there's no way you take a couple from Michigan to the opera. Put on something not too glitzy, and meet me at their hotel at seven. We'll have dinner. I know they'll be boring, so we'll make it an early evening."

When Crystal met Ralph at the hotel, she looked around for the couple with the hayseed. Instead she saw a beautiful red-haired woman with what Crystal later described as "a diamond as big as the Ritz" and a distinguished-looking man, her husband. The midwestern couple were active in the arts, were opera buffs, and by the time their guests had finished ordering the wines and describing their last trip to China, Crystal wondered who the so-phisticates were and who the simple folk were.

Talk to a spouse as you would another person

Frances Lear remembers that she spent her California years as Norman Lear's wife. He was the producer. He was the celebrity. He was the famous one.

But she was determined to be her own person. She took an active role in the woman's movement, began speaking and writing for equal rights, and, by the time she moved to New York in the 1980s, had a strong sense of herself as an individual.

The difficulty in being the lesser-known spouse of a well-known person is that the spouse is considered not a person but a necessary appendage to The Great One, and conversation centers around the partner with public influence.

Indicate your comfort level in talking about your spouse

Drop a few clues.

Do you want to talk about your spouse, or would you prefer giving your own opinions and experiences and emerging with a personality of your own?

It can vary.

Although Moss Hart died many years ago, he is fresh in the memory and mind of his widow, Kitty Carlisle Hart. She does not wear her widow's weeds in public but keeps conversation lively with engaging reminiscences. As a result, people are always comfortable in talking about Moss Hart and his contributions to the theater.

She often refers to her husband as "a prince of the theater," and Phillip de Montebello of the Metropolitan Museum of Art, in acknowledging that description, introduced Mrs. Hart in her role as the chairman of the New York State Council on the Arts, as "a princess of the theater."

If you're a spouse with an identity other than "spouse," let people know

One evening at a dinner given by the Malaysian Ambassador to the United Nations, Zain Azraai and his wife Dawn, I asked my hostess to introduce me by my married name only.

Later that evening I found myself talking with a Standard Oil executive, and he asked what all men have learned to ask women these days, "What do you do?"

"I work in advertising."

"What do you do in advertising?"

"I am the president of the company."

He smiled broadly. "You're very modest. I know who you are. You're that famous Mary Wells."

Ever since that night, even though I may be in a nonprofessional situation, I have introduced myself by my three names.

Don't ever discuss your perception of a spouse's business contribution with the boss

The first time a wife told me how her husband sacrificed for the agency, I was made to feel guilty and uncomfortable. By the second time I had an answer. It was, "I really can't understand why he works that hard. Everyone else in that department seems to get his work done during the day. Maybe I ought to talk to him about the way he organizes time; obviously he's not doing a very good job."

Don't let anyone get you into a discussion about any other company spouses

It's always done with such cunning.

The person who instigates the conversation begins by talking about the terrific, fine, excellent, and superior spouses the company has.

From there on it's all downhill.

Before you realize quite what has happened, you find yourself on the listening end of the latest story about the latest spouse.

Enter the discussion, and you will be quoted and misquoted around the morning coffee. All of this will do your spouse no good, not to mention what it will do to your own peace of mind.

If you're not already employed by your spouse's employer, don't look for a job at the same place.

Some companies have rules prohibiting this.

Shearson Lehman Brothers, Inc., permits relatives—and that includes spouses—to work as brokers, but the brokerage company does not allow one to supervise the other.

Many companies do not permit employee-spouses to work in the same department. At the *Philadelphia Inquirer,* the rule extends to cohabitants.

If you do work for the same company, make sure that your responsibilities do not overlap

This is particularly important if you are business partners and are married. Each of you must have your own area of responsibility.

Very few people have the maturity, the time, and the patience to nurture a loving relationship under the same roof with two careers.

A recent college graduate decided it would be both romantic and practical if she and her boyfriend were to go into a film production business together. When I saw the young woman's mother recently, I asked how the couple was doing. "They are very successful," she reported with pride. Then she added, somewhat wistfully, "But they will never get married because there isn't any room for romance between them."

Patricia Kennedy, a New York psychologist, says, "Marriage, or even living together, has become every bit as much a business merger as it is an emotional commitment." And in writing of the perils of dual careers, Donald Bloch, director of New York's Ackerman Institute for Family Therapy, has noted, "People are turning themselves into pretzels to deal with the problems."

In a two-career family, decide how you will deal with finances

Money must be dealt with as politely as in-laws.

One solution in dual-income families is to regard the home as one would a club and pay dues.

Under this arrangement each spouse contributes his and her dues to the running of the family club every month, and one person is in charge of all the bills—everything from the telephone to the dinners out. This gives a sense of community as well as permitting each of the partners to hold on to money for individual obligations—contributions, gifts, clothes.

Other couples set up the Pool. Under this arrangement all money is pooled, and each draws as necessary.

The most important thing about money and marriage is not how you do it, but that you do it—that you do discuss the ways you will handle finances. It's a lot easier to decide who pays for the daily newspaper before you get married than it is later.

If you're a woman who just went back to work, talk about money before you go to work the first day

One woman who opened a neighborhood boutique talked about money with her husband before she opened the doors of the shop. They both agreed that if her business earned $x at the end of year one and $3x at the end of year two, her career would become the focus of their lives, and he would quit his job and manage the growth of the company. It did happen that way, but she feels that if that discussion had not been held before she went into business, there would have been hurt feelings.

Because, strangely enough, the presence of money can hurt as many feelings as the absence of money.

Become accustomed to employees responding to family pressures

As recently as the 1960s, the only time anyone in business talked about wives was when they had another baby, and the only time you heard about children was when they were graduated.

But now children are part of the office scenery.

Women editors come to work with baskets under the desk where sleeping infants wait for mommy and the next feeding.

Joan Lunden of "Good Morning, America" brought both her babies—along with a nanny—to the studio and tended to them between camera appearances.

And in offices all over America there are, seated in waiting rooms or at Daddy's or Mommy's desk, from one to three children waiting to be taken to the dentist, the circus, or simply "sat with" while the other parent is involved.

You may not like the idea of maternity leave, but it is here to stay. The pregnant woman no longer has to disappear from the office scene. Enlightened companies are granting paternity leave as well as maternity leave. Day-care provisions are being made by still other companies.

In order to attract skilled workers and maintain a high level of executive talent, it will become increasingly important to sweeten the executive package with parenting payroll promises.

Don't get mad.

You're not going to have a lot of options, so company manners would necessitate your doing it with maximum grace.

Don't cloud business meetings with references to your spouse

In a meeting with a client in the grocery business, the subject of couponing was raised. "Let me call in one of our vice presidents," I said. "He knows a great deal about this because he works with a company that is active in the field."

One of the client representatives said quickly, "My wife is the world's greatest coupon authority; she knows it better."

The next day the client called and apologized. "I realized what I did, and I thought how mad I'd be if someone did that to me. Please tell everyone how rotten I feel about this."

When I told the other people in our agency, they were relieved. Even the most secure persons in our group admitted being shaken by the words that inspire the greatest fear among agency people, a client who begins any sentence with the words, "My wife thinks. . . ."

Y.

Working the Party

Work is a twenty-four-hour-a-day event.

More and more the lines between social life and business life are blurring, and hosting is becoming a new business art.

A chief practitioner is Alexander Papamarkou, a Wall Street broker in his midfifties. He numbers among his dearest friends Ann Getty, the publisher and wife of the billionaire; James D. Robinson III, chairman of American Express; the royal families of Spain and Greece; Baron Thyssen Bornemisza, reputedly the richest man in Europe; former United Nations Ambassador Jeane Kirkpatrick; plus assorted Reagans, Rockefellers, Dillons, and Heinzes.

Papamarkou (known affectionately as Poppa Marco) reportedly spends as much as $300,000 a year entertaining friends, all of whom could afford to entertain themselves. Among his more lavish parties have been a week for thirty-six persons at the Golden

Door spa in California; a trip to Egypt for eighty-three friends complete with fancy dinners, private jet tours over the Sinai, and a barge voyage from Aswan to Luxor; and a glittering dinner-dance at the Metropolitan Museum of Art where the guest of honor was the First Lady of the United States.

That's *his* party style.

Party style in the company manner is seldom that lavish, although there are whispered stories about the cars and stereos and vacation houses that are bought, lent, and exchanged in the course of doing big business.

Generally, however, company manners dictate the kind of parties that are given and attended in the course of a business life. The party style changes with the location.

So, as one travels about the country, it is important to remember that what works at business parties in one city will not necessarily work in another. There are subjects one never discusses and subjects one is always prepared to discuss depending on what party you are working.

For businesspersons it is the hours between 5 and 8 P.M. that can be the bewitching hours of business, since it is the cocktail party that is the universal entertainment form. The cocktail party is the business way of getting a lot of people in a small space without spending too much time, money, or preparation effort. It is perfect for introducing products, saluting associates, and announcing events. It is also perfect for *contact sport*—the sport known as "making contacts" with people whom you had always hoped to meet but hadn't the proper entrée.

Parties from Coast to Coast

Since the place of the party is of primary importance, and since conversation and party objectives vary from city to city, party manners are dependent upon geography.

The New York cocktail party

If you are invited to a cocktail party in New York, it is generally assumed that you will go directly from your office. Therefore, the business-oriented cocktail party means wearing business clothes and taking your briefcase. (There will be a place to check it, but it is up to you to remember that you brought it.)

If the party is called for 5 P.M., you will never arrive before 5:30. You will stay past the closing time only if you are having a very good (which means profitable) time.

It is possible to fall in love at a New York cocktail party, but I have never met anyone who did. Usually there is too much noise, too much introducing, and too much overcrowding for anyone to feel relaxed enough to fall in love.

New York cocktail parties are held in discos (a favorite place for magazines, networks, and other communicators to entertain), a famous restaurant, a private club, or a midtown apartment. The midtown apartment cocktail is generally in honor of an author and a new book. There will be copies of the book placed conspicuously in the apartment. The host has provided these; discourteous guests will take them. A courteous guest realizes that the books so displayed are not for the taking.

A typical conversation at a New York cocktail party revolves around the price of cooperative apartments in New York, the availability and price of summer homes, anything that is hot at the moment—from the newest restaurants to the best-reviewed current plays to the smart new book no one yet knows. Nestled in this exchange of information and complaints may indeed be a good business lead.

Before going to the New York cocktail party you should have read the current issue of *New York* magazine, the current *Interview*, today's *Wall Street Journal* and today's *New York Times* from front page to book review to op-ed page, the entire Book Review of the past Sunday, as well as the Friday and Sunday Arts and Leisure section of the *New York Times*.

The food at New York cocktail parties is usually very good.

Almost every party features at least one sushi hors d'oeuvre. Among other favorites are small lamb chops, miniature baked potatoes scooped out and filled with caviar, clam bars, and oyster bars.

The Washington cocktail party

In Washington the get-together is not about cocktails, and it is not about party.

The get-together is about the guest list.

A Washington party is judged by the numbers of important White House, Capitol Hill, Pentagon, and State Department officials who are on hand.

There is always a bar, but there is not necessarily food.

The business of Washington is the cocktail party. It always begins on time and ends on time. No one comes fifteen minutes late. Everyone arrives at the same time. Come late, and you might miss the secretary of state as well as any power brokers who might be there.

Every Washington party is a company party because Washington is the ultimate company town. Everyone works for the government, so everyone is known to all the people present.

Bills are lobbied, cases argued at Washington parties.

Personal questions are never asked at Washington parties. It is assumed that if you are important enough to be at a Washington party—and you live in the city—you must be influential in the government.

Do not go to a Washington cocktail party unless you have read today's *Washington Post, New York Times,* and a third newspaper which may be anything from the *London Times* to the *Los Angeles Times.*

The Los Angeles cocktail party

Everybody comes in looking cool—real cool.

No men wear ties, only a few wear jackets.

Briefcases are carried only by men; cases are made of exotic materials like ostrich. The women are all dressed in something

very short or in something very tight—sometimes both. Every
woman looks as if she has just been plucked from a chaise at the
Beverly Hills Hotel pool, the pool best known as the home of the
nubile cuisine. All of the women at the party are accessories, not
women with power like those at the New York and, to some degree, Washington parties.

The food is always very California, includes sushi, Tex-Mex,
unusual fruits and vegetables.

No one ever comes on time. California realizes that it is always
three hours behind the rest of the world and will never catch up,
so why hurry?

Conversation centers on grosses, pictures with "legs"—and
women with considerably more—what's hot and what's not, world
rights of anything and everything that sings or dances or acts,
video cassettes, tummy tucks, face lifts, hairdressers, exercise coaches
who make house calls, the next spa, the next restaurant, the next
star, the next studio president, decorators, gardeners, real estate
prices, who's moving to California, who's moving back to New
York, who's moving out and who's moving in, Galanos, Bob Mackie
and Nike, kids, nannies, Grammies, and (most important of all)
who is taking what points on which film.

Reading material prior to the Hollywood cocktail party is the
daily *Variety, Hollywood Reporter,* and possibly *Billboard.* It is also
helpful if you know what the cover story of *People* magazine will
be next week.

Parties center around "the business," the business being the
entertainment business, and at each party there is a jockeying
among the power players for the bankable directors, stars, and
writers.

Everyone else is a supporting player.

The Midwest cocktail party

In the midwest business associates are friends, and the charity ball
is indeed a social event as much as it is a business event.

Business friends are entertained in suburban settings, and only for the out-of-town guest does the business gathering stop being a quasi-social event.

The out-of-town guest is frequently feted at a cocktail party held in a downtown hotel. Since everyone works downtown (and few live downtown), it is possible to get people together by 6 o'clock and on their way to the suburbs in time to join a family schedule at a reasonable family hour.

Advance reading for the cocktail party is the daily newspaper, the *Wall Street Journal*, and any business news magazine which has had a story about the host company within the past month.

The party is usually held to welcome a guest of the company who lives out-of-town. There will be a sprinkling of corporate executives, friends of the corporate executives, and the small list of friends invited at the request of the guest of honor.

Each group will move warily in its own concentric circle, rarely crossing the line to step into another's circle.

Food, when it is at its best, will include a shrimp bowl. Otherwise look for egg salad on soggy bread with plenty of mayonnaise.

Conversation will center on golf games, clubs, vacations, children and early admission to select colleges and universities, hobbies, mutual acquaintances.

The party will be primarily male. Any women present will be there because they are professionals associated in some way with the company. The wives present will be there (a) because that couple has plans to go on to dinner with the guest of honor or (b) because their husbands thought it would be nice to have "a few of the girls" around.

No one will drink too much, and within fifteen minutes of the announced end of the party, all guests will have departed.

Party Manners

No matter where you are, there are universal party manners that stand one in good stead.

No one should ever wait to be introduced to the guests at any business party. Part of the party manner is to approach strangers, introduce yourself, and learn the reason you are both there.

Always take a supply of business cards. It is much easier to exchange cards than to write names and addresses of people you want to see again. Further, card exchange is a kind of mutual agreement that you do want to meet again under less public circumstances.

Never stand at the bar too long (longer than it takes to get your drink is too long), and never hover over the hors d'oeuvres table. If you are talking to someone you meet at the hors d'oeuvres table or bar, move the conversation to a more private place, and make room for those still waiting to eat and drink.

If you find no one to whom you want to talk and you want to leave, it is not necessary to seek the host (particularly if he or she is busy) before you depart. When the gathering is very large and the host is otherwise engaged, get your coat and leave quietly. Be sure, however, to send a thank-you note the following day.

I'll Never Forget What's-His-Name

From the day you move beyond the little red schoolhouse and the neighborhood where everyone knew everyone, you're in trouble. And the trouble is pronounced what's-his-name. Someone comes up to you at a party or in a restaurant, and you get that clutching feeling in the pit of your stomach. What's his name, anyway? It's tough to remember all those names and all those people in all those cities and all those countries.

Sonny Werblin, the owner of Madison Square Garden, summed it for all of us who forget what we're supposed to remember. Mr. Werblin stood in a corner of a large cocktail party benefit and smiled benignly as person after person greeted him. "I'm in trouble," he said. "I had my eyes fixed so now I can see everybody, but I can't remember their names."

There are some remarkable people who can remember not

only names but also other significant facts. It is of tremendous value to them as people and of great value to them as business-persons.

But for many of us who whisper frantically, "Who is it?" there is little to do to help us remember at that awful moment, but there are things to do when memory fails.

1. *When you know you've seen the person before,* you can walk up, extend your hand and say, "I know we've met before. I'm. . . ." If you are lucky, the person will understand your plight and do the courteous thing which is to announce his name. However, there are times when the person simply acknowledges your self-introduction without giving a name in return, and then . . .

2. *It is necessary to be blunt* and say, "Please tell me your name once again."

3. *When you must introduce five or six people who are standing together,* do not try to be a hero and do all the names. Turn to the group and say, "I'd like all of you to meet Sally Jones. Now please introduce yourselves." To add a personal note, you can then say something about one or two of the people who introduce themselves should they have something in common with the person they are meeting.

4. *In a business meeting,* have a list of the persons in your own company who are attending, and be sure to include their titles and other pertinent data. In our business I have a tough time remembering titles like Director of Market Research Systems.

5. *When a number of people from outside your office will be attending a meeting with a number of people in your office,* use the good host trick. Put table tent place cards at the conference table, and on the side facing out, also put the name of the person seated there. It makes both sides grateful.

6. *Ask new acquaintances for business cards,* and have your sec-

retary file them alphabetically both by person's name and by company name. Then when you need a name from a particular company, you will have a ready reference.

7. *Before going to a convention,* ask the person in charge of reservations for a list of all company persons attending. Before you leave, check the list with everyone in your office who is acquainted with that company and knows the key names.

8. *When dealing with a new group of business associates,* study the names and titles, and keep a 3 by 5 card in your briefcase with names and titles so that you can review it quickly before all meetings.

But no matter how much difficulty you have remembering names, you will probably never equal the story of my friend who was at a convention in Los Angeles and was introducing a large group of people. She was giving names, titles, home towns and was priding herself on the fact that she was not missing a name or title. She reached the last person in the group, and then it happened. She went blank. Her face fell. She felt the blood rush from her face. She leaned against the table behind her.

The woman who knew her name was forgotten nodded understandingly. "It's all right, dear," she said. "I'm your sister."

Celebrations in the Office

In addition to the company parties where you are invited are the parties given by people in your office, parties to which you are invited as a guest.

If the people who work with you are planning a party and request your attendance; you must ask yourself:

Should I go?

If I go, what is my role as boss in this employee-oriented party?

Jane is having a baby, so we decided to have a baby shower

Now that babies are back in fashion, the working mother is no longer a phenomenon but an accepted fact of life. While you are undoubtedly tolerant and supportive when it comes to pregnancies in the office, there is no reason that a boss has to attend baby showers. If, however, one of the parents-to-be is someone with whom you have a close working relationship and strong office friendship, you may wish to make an appearance at a baby shower and leave quickly.

The presence of a boss is definitely not mandatory. Nothing stops the merriment faster than someone who has the power and the ability to judge the festivities.

Best suggestion: send a gift and your best wishes. Make your presents known, but not your presence.

A new disco opened, and a bunch of us . . .

Say no.

No, you do not go discoing with the people who work for you.

No, you do not go out after work with the people who work for you.

We booked rooms in Vermont, and a bunch of us are going skiing next weekend. Want to join us?

No.

No for all the reasons detailed above.

The only time it makes sense for a boss to become a member of the party is when it happens as an extension of the working day.

The best example I know in our office occurs when as many as 30 percent of our staff join the corporate runs in Central Park.

We arrange pasta and pizza afterward at the office, and we always make sure that someone from the Operating Committee of the agency is there to let everyone know that, as a company, we are pleased and proud that they participate.

We all know that what work is about is work—but the ability to party in style is a corporate plus.

CHAPTER 13

Shuttle Diplomacy and Other Travels

One hundred and fifty years ago it took four days to travel from New York to Washington, D.C.

For those who sit on the runway today and wait for incoming planes, outgoing planes, fog to lift, rain to end, thunderstorms to pass, and traffic to ease, it still seems like four days.

Taking the Shuttle

The airline Shuttle (on the East Coast it runs from Boston to New York to Washington and on the West Coast from Los Angeles to San Francisco) is a way of life for people who like to work in two cities and sleep in one bed.

Those who fly the Shuttle regularly have no rules concerning good manners; they move by custom. To be a Shuttle flyer, one need only understand the accepted, unspoken mores of Shuttle diplomacy.

The most famous people in the world Shuttle back and forth

between power desks in power cities. Television people have the East Coast recognizable faces: David Hartman, David Brinkley, Dan Rather; on the West Coast there are the movie star faces: John Travolta, Ann-Margret, Madonna.

Eastern Air originated the East Cost Shuttle in 1961. Until New York Air came along in the 1980s with its Shuttle, there was no real competition for the two-city business traveler. Eastern departs from La Guardia on the hour; New York Air on the half hour. New York Air, the upstart and newcomer, has attracted passengers by giving them complimentary copies of the *New York Times* before boarding and offers coffee and bagels en route; Eastern eschews the niceties. The fares are comparable, and so are the passenger loads.

The minipower Shuttle (sales managers, vice presidents, and members of congress) is Eastern's 8:00 A.M. flight from La Guardia to National. Heavy-power (presidents, chairmen, senators) are on the 9:00, or 10:00, or 11:00 A.M., depending on the time and place of their luncheon dates.

Once in the air you cannot tell William Safire, the *New York Times* columnist, from any of the other power hitters. They are all reading the same papers (the *Times,* the *Wall Street Journal*), drinking the same coffee from the same styrofoam cups, and all are studiously avoiding speaking to their seatmates.

Each person is absorbed in reading material; no one sleeps on the A.M. shuttle.

En route to Washington no one rubbernecks to see the Capitol or the White House, presumably because Shuttle people are those who work or visit these places with such frequency.

The few women who fly the power Shuttle are generally gray-suited, white-shirted, briefcase-carrying lawyers or other attendants to power (unless, of course, they are power reporters for the networks or a power woman such as Jeane Kirkpatrick or Elizabeth Dole.

Luggage is rarely carried on the Shuttle, and power can be recognized by the size of its briefcase. The thinner the briefcase, the greater the power.

The return power flights take off between 3:30 and 5:00 P.M. from National Airport. The returning power is much like arriving power: noncommunicative, self-absorbed, and involved in reading. The difference is the reading material. On the return trip passengers scan, read intensely, mark and clip the *Washington Post,* the news magazines, and papers with the letterheads of big-time law firms and bankers. No one of power reads a book on the Shuttle. All reading is either disposable or classified material. It would seem that the returning Shuttle is the world's largest flying homework team.

Although there is no conversation on the Shuttle, there is much conversation preceding every flight. All the telephones in the area adjacent to the departure gate are occupied by tense-looking men and women giving and getting messages. Behind them are other tense-looking persons waiting to make telephone calls that will let them know if there is a valid reason for their tension.

Did the order come in?

Was the call made?

Did the senator call?

The politics of politeness are not practiced at the public telephones at National Airport. Feet tap impatiently as hopeful callers wait to telephone. If they wait too long, they'll miss the first boarding call. And the first boarding call is important.

For politeness is not practiced in boarding.

The best seats are aisle seats up front. They are the first seats taken on both the morning and evening shuttles. The Eastern Airlines Shuttle has no reserved seats; New York Air offers reserved seats (the disadvantage is that one must call to reserve a seat and call to cancel).

The rush for seats, however, is a silent move. No one ever scrambles for seats; people move quickly and purposefully. Each knows exactly where he or she is going.

So, in the same silence they boarded their Shuttle flight some hours before, the many men and few women reboard for their New York dinners, Broadway shows, and suburban homes.

You cannot tell by looking who is going where.

Their faces are impassive. You do not know who won and who lost that day. You know only that some of them, on the flight to La Guardia, are relaxed enough to sleep and that none of them, awake or asleep, will look out the window to see the World Trade Center, the Empire State Building, or Central Park from the air.

The next day many of them will be back at the airport, this time for the longer trip, the convention or seminar or sales meeting or visit with satellite operations.

The longer trip, like the day trip or turnaround, is marked by a style of its own.

When Plans Call for Travel . . .

The business trip is one of the staples of the business diet. It is made up of one part pure business and six parts pure boredom. The boredom comes in down time, the hours spent hanging around airports waiting for late planes, the nights spent watching television in a dismal hotel room in a city you never thought you'd visit, and the hours spent circling in fog, thunder, and lightning as you wait to get back on the ground and safely home.

The good part of the business trip is in the results: if you get what you want and could not have gotten it without traveling, the trip is a success. If you don't get what you want, the trip is a failure.

But success or failure, nowhere are company manners more visible than when you take them on the road.

As a regular business traveler, there are certain things you know before you fly commercially. You know that it is always better to have an aisle seat (you have the freedom to move about the plane). You know that if you fly the Concorde, the best row is Row 11 because you have no one in front of you. You also know that if you fly to the United Kingdom, your return ticket should be purchased in pounds because that will save money. You know that if you fly to California on Regent Airlines, the sometimes posh airline that goes between Los Angeles and New York, the best seats are 4 and 5 because they are separate and swivel. You know that no one in his right mind ever plans to eat airplane food. You know that it is better not to drink alcoholic beverages when you fly because the alcohol affects you more at the higher altitudes. You know that it is important to drink water when you fly (particularly during long trips) because you will dehydrate more rapidly in flight than on ground.

Traveling by Corporate Jet

Just sitting there in the waiting room at the airport and giving the serial number of the plane you are awaiting is enough to set you apart from the rest of the world and make you feel special.

Few company planes look like a tycoon's dream aircraft; public companies don't care to give stockholders that kind of visible expense target. One of the last truly glamorous aircrafts was owned by Interpublic at the time Marion Harper, Jr., was chairman, and that was in the days before the company went public.

Even though many company planes are less luxurious than some first-class travel, nothing is better than private aircraft for efficiency because one does not have to deal with errant airline schedules to remote cities. Also, there is little waiting time, no delays for baggage, and there are no long hikes down endless airline corridors, no security checks, and no lines.

When you're okayed as a passenger on the company plane, it means that you are special to the business.

Respect for that specialness will keep you flying high in the company. So when you're invited to fly the corporate jet:

Do be on time

There is a scheduled departure time, and you had better be certain that a flight plan does not change because of your tardiness. The only person permitted to be late is the chairman, and he can be late only when he is delayed by the closing of a billion dollar acquisition.

Do take your own reading material

Most people on the corporate jet take paperwork with them. If, however, you decide to take supplemental reading material, make sure that your airplane reading is something more substantial than Jackie Collins's latest novel. It is not that reading Jackie Collins is below corporate taste; it just makes people wonder how deep you really are. Safest books for company plane travel: anything by Peter Drucker or Alvin Toffler; their books will prompt comment and conversation from fellow travelers. Do not take a book by Irving Howe or Saul Bellow; they smack of literary pretension, and only a few corporate executives can tolerate the literary mind. If you must take fiction, take a detective story by Elmore Leonard. People who run companies consider detective stories proper escapist literature. You can thank John F. Kennedy, who was a James Bond fan, for giving mysteries that cache.

Do not ask for an alcoholic beverage

Regardless of the hour you are flying, never ask for spirits or wine when you are asked your drink preference. Many companies have rules against serving alcoholic beverages in the air, and even those that do not often look askance at a nonfrequent flier on their airlines asking for booze. Besides, if you order first and ask for ginger ale, only to find that the harder stuff is being requested by the frequent fliers, you can always change your order. But the smartest move is to drink nothing stronger than grape juice.

Do learn the names of the pilot and copilot

And use their names when speaking to them. When you do, it indicates a respect for the company plane and its personnel.

Do make your own plans for getting to and from the airport

If you are traveling alone, always take care of preordering cars or taxis to take you to the airport.

When you land, you will probably find that your ground transportation will be arranged, and the car will drive on the field to the door of the plane in order that you may avoid inclement weather. Similarly, you will, in all likelihood, be taken back to the plane. When you return to your home city, arrange for transportation from the airport.

If you are with a group on the plane, the senior officer with the group will often take care of making the reservations (or his or her secretary or the company's travel department will).

Do not travel with thirteen pieces of luggage and your parakeet

Space is always limited on the company plane, and unless it is a golf, hunting, or fishing trip, your equipment should be limited to a single, easy-to-carry piece of luggage. However, if you are taking clothes for a change of climate and need a larger wardrobe, take two lighter-weight bags rather than one heavy one. Often the plane's pilot and copilot will be handling your luggage, and it is a consideration of their time and effort to keep luggage light.

Traveling by Commercial Jet

When you are going by commercial jet, there are other considerations:

Use the company's travel department to get the best deal possible

Don't try to outfox the company and make your own travel reservations through your cousin in Newark. If your company does not permit you to use your airline mileage earned on company business, comply with the request with good humor. Don't complain in the office, and tell corporate all about all your friends who get to keep the bonus miles.

If you do not belong to an airline club, ask your travel department to get you access

You will probably be told it is impossible, but it is not. And since you are a person who is both demanding and authoritative, you will not accept a no answer. Simply say, "Other companies can do it. Why can't you?"

Double-check all reservations before leaving the office

All boarding passes should be issued with tickets by your office. If you do not have a travel department or travel person in your office, make certain that the travel agency does this for you. No executive should be without a good travel agent. A good travel agent does not simply make reservations; he or she makes the trip and is as indispensable to life as a good barber or hairdresser. Best way to find one: ask somebody who travels a lot and is accustomed to dealing with demanding businesspersons.

Take carry-on luggage whenever possible

And do not use a carry-on luggage cart. This immediately marks you as a steward, a stewardess, or a vacationer.

Avoid conversations with anyone seated next to you

The ultimate chic is to speak to no one, unless you find you are seated next to someone you have always wanted to meet. Best ploy for avoiding conversation: take out work, become absorbed in it, and do not eat the rotten lunch or miserable dinner that is served on the plane. If you are traveling overseas, best advice is to have a picnic lunch packed by a take-out gourmet in your home city. On the return trip, ask your hotel or a gourmet shop in that city to do the same. Craig Claiborne, the *New York Times* food writer, never goes overseas without his own personal CARE package from Murray's Sturgeon on New York's West Side. The package includes caviar, smoked salmon, sturgeon, and thin-sliced rye bread. No one with a package like that is ever traveling tourist class, no matter what his ticket says.

If a seatmate persists in talking to you, be noncommittal in answering. A mumbled yes or no will turn most people off, as will a headset (the airline's or your own Walkman). One basic reason for avoiding conversation with strangers on planes is that almost invariably people delight in telling you about their close calls, their missed planes, hijackings, and crashes. If you felt slightly nervous when you boarded the plane, the stranger next to you is guaranteed to make you stark, raving mad.

Traveling by Train

No one travels by train today unless Washington is fogged in or Boston is snowed in. When that happens, the whole world rides the rails. The best way to travel to Washington is via the Metroliner. The Metroliner sells both coach and club car seats.

The club car is for people who never speak to one another; the coach is filled with friendly folk who exchange everything from barbecue recipes to notes about their gallbladder attacks.

To ride the Metroliner you need a reservation, and you must use Penn Station for the New York end of the trip. There are days when traveling to and from Penn Station takes longer than the trip to Philadelphia.

On the Metroliner are all the people one ordinarily sees on the Shuttle—a collection of senators, lobbyists, reporters—all of whom have company business in the United States's own company town.

Reading material for the Metroliner should include, in addition to the day's newspapers, a long book. One should always be prepared for track delays.

Taking Care of the Out-of-Towners

If someone is traveling from another city to see you, here are some of the courtesies that can make any meeting seem better than its outcome.

Be there!

Everyone has limited time, but those traveling have less work time. It is, therefore, an inexcusable discourtesy not to see someone who has an appointment and appears at your doorstep.

If you have a date with an out-of-town visitor and are called into a meeting, ask for a fifteen-minute delay. If you can get the time, use those fifteen minutes to meet face-to-face with your out-of-town visitor, explain the reason you must delay your visit, and either conduct an abbreviated meeting or arrange another date. If you can't see the out-of-town guest personally, then give your assistant or secretary full instructions to (a) make a date for later that day or (b) invite the visitor to have dinner with you that evening.

Under no circumstances permit a visitor from another city to make a trip to see you only to be told by a telephone operator that you were called away.

When the guest is a business associate . . .

There is no feeling worse than going into one of your branch offices and being made to feel like an outsider.

Anyone who works for your company (or is a client of your company) and comes to see you should be given separate-but-equal courtesies.

In our office we maintain a desk and telephone and offer secretarial services to our associates in other cities. Incidentally, the secretary you offer should be your own. Don't be generous with someone else's assistant.

Entertaining the out-of-towners

Don't be a tour guide.

Unless you work for American Express, you won't gain any points showing the visitors your city.

Still, there are many things you can do (short of taking visitors home) that will make them feel welcome:

1. Once, when I was appearing on a TV talk show in Los Angeles, I walked into the studio and saw a sign that said: Today our guests are—and then there was a list of six names, mine included, of out-of-town people who would be in the office that day. I thought it was a most helpful idea for the receptionist (as we all know, more than one person is at a receptionist's desk during the day, and this is a quick reminder of names to expect), and I breathed a sigh of relief. It meant I was in the right place, and somebody up there knew I was scheduled.

2. Make sure your company is known at three hotels in your city (either in different parts of town or those charging different rates), and make yourself known. Meet the manager, talk to him or her, and explain that your office frequently has out-of-town guests. Ask the hotel for special privileges: late check-out, last-minute reservations, rates. Sometimes you can get a corporate rate; sometimes you can't get a nickel's worth of anything except the assurance that you have a manager's name to use when reservations are tough.

3. Put together a visitor's guide to your city. Because we live in New York, a city I fondly call the restaurant capital of the world, we began a restaurant guide years ago that we give to guests on request. It was started when Liza Antelo was my assistant, and because she was a gourmet cook,

she had more than a passing acquaintance with all the good eating places in the city. It's a list that has names, addresses, and telephone numbers. Putting that kind of list together can be fun for a lot of people in the office who can contribute their own favorite places. It's also a good idea to include with the list that week's issue of your city magazine (if you have one) or cultural calendar.

4. If the visitors are in town more than one night, do not feel that you are responsible for entertaining them for more than one night. Keep the entertainment simple. Under no circumstances, take visitors to discos or other late-night spots where people you don't know well may do things you wish they would do only with people they know well.

   You will know that the evening has gone on too long if you are not at home for the 11 o'clock news.

5. If the visitors have a problem—anything from lost baggage to a nosebleed—use your office manager as your travel service, and offer on-the-spot help. Always know the names of nearby medical facilities.

6. No matter who the out-of-town visitors may be (guests from your own office branches or clients), pay the check when you are together. Never never permit an out-of-town guest to pick up a check when he or she is with you. You pick the place, and you pay the price.

   Incidentally, when you choose the place to dine, then you are also in control of the evening atmosphere, the kind of dollars that will be spent, and the hours.

7. Check with guests when they arrive at your office for a meeting; if they are going directly from your office to the airport, ask if they have arranged transportation. If they have not, call a cab or car service, and arrange to have wheels on schedule. It means everyone can work comfortably until the last possible minute.

Business Trips

Business trips are easier to take if you plan everything from reservations to packing to leisure time, and the easier you make the trip, the more productive it will be. Even a trip that results in no new business (or increased business) can be profitable if you take along airplane work or hotel work, the kind of you-alone work that can be done away from the pressures of your office and the interruptions of your associates.

Preplanning is a major courtesy; it not only utilizes your time better but also that of the people you will see.

Run your trip with 3 by 5 cards

Get a supply of 3 by 5 cards for your secretary and have him or her do the following:

1. One card should have all transportation arrangements made for the trip: flight numbers, confirmations to be called if necessary, hotels, rental cars, reservation numbers, telephone numbers (in case you are late, you can call easily and have a room held).

2. An individual card should be made out for each day with your daily schedule. Along with the name of the company you are seeing should be the name of the person, address, and telephone number. (Again, if you are going to be delayed, be sure to call.)

3. Cards should be supplied with the name of each company you are visiting, and the names of the individuals you will see. On the back should be written: Follow-up. It's up to you to decide the follow-up. Good follow-up is a letter written the day you get back to your office. Even better is the person who sends a note while still in the city—a handwritten note—thanking the host (remember, he doesn't have to feed you to be your host).

The biggest advantage of the cards is that they fit in the inside pocket of a suit jacket, a briefcase, a handbag, or a travel case. When you return to your office, the cards can be given to your assistant so appropriate action will be taken and a tickler file kept up-to-date.

Travel light

Unless you are the boss—or so talented that the world can't turn without you—take a cue from ex-president Jimmy Carter and carry your own luggage.

Nobody traveling with you or meeting you wants to look nervously at watches while waiting for your blue lookalike bag to come around the baggage carousel. Every man and every woman should keep in readiness (a) fresh undergarments for a two-day trip; (b) a toiletries kit; (c) nightwear; and (d) a packable daytime suit which is also appropriate for evening with a change of shirt or blouse.

On longer trips when it is necessary to check baggage, be certain to carry on board a small bag containing a change of linen, toiletries, and a fresh shirt because, despite the good intentions of all airlines, it is still possible for you to arrive in London at the moment your luggage is flying to Bangkok.

If you're traveling with associates, it's also wise to inform no one about any purchases you make. Often people who work with you do not have the same kind of disposable income that you do, and it's not only good manners, but good sense, not to remind them of this. Certainly you should not get on a plane with bulky packages that will discomfit your fellow travelers, and if you're a woman, never get into a situation where you make men feel like nasty old guys if they don't carry your overweight packages, luggage, etc.

Travel lean and mean. Translated, that means, "When you travel, lean on no one, and mean business."

Decide how to handle the expense account

If you and your traveling companion are with the same company, decide in advance who will pick up the checks for breakfast, lunch, and dinner. Then, when you are in a restaurant with customers or clients, there will be no discussion.

If the person with whom you are dining is a customer of yours and wants to pay the check, repeat your offer to pay. If he seems insistent (here's where your own good judgment comes into play), let him pay. Many clients like to feel that an association with suppliers is a partnership and—particularly if you have made a special effort to travel in order to make a meeting possible—they wish to show both the partnership aspect of the relationship and their thanks for your efforts.

Never offer to split a check.

No one on an expense account should be so short of funds that he or she would ever consider splitting a check. It's a high school offer and shows a real lack of sophistication.

Indeed, one of the least attractive things anyone can ever do in a restaurant is try to determine who will pay or try to divide a check.

Handling money professionally is the most businesslike thing any of us do. Fred M., president of a lumber company, met with two outside auditors at a breakfast and watched while they decided which of the two would be responsible for paying the check. "After seeing their inability to handle their own money, I decided I didn't want them to have anything to do with mine," he related.

When you entertain on a business trip, use an appropriate restaurant. An appropriate restaurant is not necessarily the most expensive restaurant in town—unless you're the CEO, it can turn out to be an embarrassment because your guest may think you have decided he or she can be bought with two drinks and a chateaubriand.

Even if you have a suite, never entertain just one person in your suite. If you have more than two people, a suite can be the ideal place. For a dinner in a suite, have hors d'oeuvres preordered and sent to the suite as well as a bucket of ice, mixers, wine, and liquor. (Many hotels today have stocked bars in suites.) If you're the host, make sure you get the last two people (other than yourself) to leave your suite at the same time. Why? Because one person, whether male or female, leaving your suite at a late hour raises suspicions. Of course, you are purer than Snow White. Sure, those other people are all big mouths who are lying in wait, dupes for gossip columnists and paparazzi. But why give them any reason to talk? Even though you desperately want to be famous by Friday, there are better ways—especially in your business.

Watch what you eat, drink, and say when you're on the road

When you take your act on the road, be sure you are in control.

It's never a good idea to eat foods that are strange, regional, or otherwise unknown. Nothing is worse than being sick away from your own bed and those loving hands at home.

Anybody who drinks more than he or she should deserves the headache and the stomachache that will follow. But think twice. Are you sure you will deserve the conversation that will follow because of your behavior when you are er—umm—uhhh—drunk?

Don't let the altitude go to your tongue because it really is not very mannerly to say something when you're away from the office that you would never dream of saying in the office. It's just not a good idea to tell the boss what you really think of his last memo. And the peer person with you doesn't really want you to blast him for the way he handled the order last week. We once worked for a company whose vice president argued his loyalty to the president to all of us who accompanied him on myriad trips. "If he ever leaves this company," said the vice president, "I'll be right behind him." So when the day came and the president left—and the vice president stayed—the vice president fired all those product managers who had heard his speech about undying loyalty to the president. But without that product managing group, the embarrassed vice president couldn't keep his act together. Eventually he, too, left the company, a victim of his loose talk.

No matter how much you may like/love him/her, don't do it

Business trips provide people with both the place and the time, so is it any wonder TRouble and TRip begin the same way?

Not only will the indiscretion not be kept secret (secret loves are secret only to those who are involved), but it will affect office planning because sooner or later the involved couple will begin planning their business life around their opportunities to be together.

Betsy and Kent worked together as merchandising consultants to corporations. Kent was a senior partner (there were four partners), and Betsy was a project administrator. Before anyone quite realized what was happening, Kent and Betsy not only were sitting side-by-side at staff meetings, they seemed to speak with one voice. And pretty soon they seemed to take all the same trips at the same time. In the beginning the other senior partners accepted the behavior—after all, Betsy and Kent were very good workers. But when two other project administrators objected, the senior partners were forced to talk to Kent. The affair has had its stops and starts since, but the partnership is now shaky. And the phrase "business travel" has fallen into disrepute at the company.

Get away from the business at night

You don't have to assume any responsibility for persons in your company who are traveling with you. They can be free to make their own evening plans, and so can you.

In fact, so should you. Both of you.

The best way to keep a business relationship on a business plane is not to let it get encumbered with late-night events.

Before you leave on your next trip, check your book for persons you know in the city you are visiting, call and set up your own plans. The politest way to do that is to say, "John, this is Jim. I'm going to be in your town next week and wondered if you (and your wife, girlfriend, lover) might be free to join me for dinner Wednesday or Thursday."

Conventions

Conventions, or sales meetings, seem to be a business staple. I have been to conventions where products were introduced and individuals reduced, where companies were honored and people dishonored, where careers were made and hearts broken. In short, I have been to conventions that make "Dynasty" look like *Alice in Wonderland.*

From all this convention experience, I have distilled certain basic truths.

First, if you are the convention host:

Don't use the company plane unless everyone of equal rank is going to fly the company plane

When Clairol used to have its annual convention (a practice they abandoned a few years ago), there was so much jockeying for position on the corporate jets that Bruce Gelb, a former Clairol president who moved up to executive rank in the parent company Bristol-Meyers, flew to the meetings on commercial jet. And he never flew first class.

Product managers and advertising agencies would ask one another, "Which is more politic—to fly the jet and hear the inside talk or to be on the commercial flight and let everyone know that you are as democratic as the corporate heads?"

If you are handing out invitations for the company plane, think twice about your list of invitees. Remember you are creating the political situation that many people will live with for many months.

If you are no. 1, be first

When you run the convention, be the first one to arrive at all meetings and social events and the first to leave. You create an attitude that is businesslike in a setting that rarely is. Most conventions are set amid exotic flora and fauna, and if you want to keep the conventioneers on target, it is wise not to be the last to come to the events and the last to leave the bar.

And, at each event, make sure that you circulate. Don't stand in a corner and wait for people to kiss your ring. Get out among the troops, and make them glad they came, glad they had a chance to talk to you. If your convention is so large that you do not know all your people attending, walk up and introduce yourself. It is a lot more gracious than depending on sales managers to take you by the hand and introduce you.

If, however, you do suffer from terminal shyness, pick a group of area managers from different parts of the country, invite each to be your "introducer" during meetings or the cocktail hour each day, and get to know as many of the people who work for you as you possibly can.

What many executives fail to realize is that they are a major topic of conversation in their employees' homes, and if an employee can leave the meeting and tell the folks back home, "You'll never guess what old J. B. said to me . . ." you will have a very loyal employee.

Follow the rules of good hosting

Assuming that the agenda has been set by others, supervised by others, and detailed by others—all of whom will report to you about events and your scheduled participation—it is important to your associates that you

1. Deliver a personal message at the first meeting.
2. Place-card your tables by region and/or name.
3. Rotate the persons who will sit at your table.

4. Scatter executives, and plan exactly where each will sit and with whom—seating order is an announcement of corporate standing in the pecking order.

5. Invite all persons who will play tennis and/or golf with you in advance of the meeting.

If you are the convention guest:

Pack for the track

If you are one of the persons with a major role at the convention, be sure that you take business attire for the session where you will be on the podium unless someone has told you in advance that this is a sports shirt and sweater meeting for all.

I have never seen anyone fired for dressing badly, but I've seen people so nervous about their clothing that they couldn't concentrate on the business at hand. So make sure that your casual sportswear fits you properly, stick to generally accepted apparel (navy blazers, white trousers—and, if you are from the North Shore of Long Island, green pants and pink T-shirts).

Women have a more difficult time deciding what to wear at conventions because women have greater choices. If in doubt and you have no one to ask in advance, take two cotton dresses for meetings or evening events, two pairs of trousers (one black, one white), white broadcloth shirts, colored T-shirts, and a wool blazer (if it gets cool in the evening) and a cotton jacket (if it doesn't get cool in the evening).

And, a special warning note: even if you've got it, don't flaunt it. Never wear a bikini or a low-cut dress or anything that is outrageous because of what it reveals rather than what it conceals.

Not only are bosses embarrassed by clothes that show too much, they assume that you are telling them something. And what you are telling them may not be what they are comfortable hearing. So even though there are tropical skies and other guests at the hotel are covering their vital parts with feathers and flowers, don't consider it for a moment. I've sat with too many men at too many conventions and listened to too many conversations that begin, "Wow! She's really looking for it, isn't she?"

Never mind that she isn't looking.

Just remember that gossip is about people; rumor is about events. And if you don't want to be grist for someone's gossip mill, keep your best parts under cover. And if you don't want to star in the rumor-of-the-week award, keep yourself undercover once the meetings and corporate socializing end each day.

Plan major maneuvers

At every convention you will find at least one good strategist who could give lessons to the CIA.

I can remember one time watching a salesmanager I'll call Ben. Ben knew that the company president was an ardent golfer, but his ardor for the game exceeded his talents; his first question each time he knew he was to play was, "Where's the practice range?" So when Ben arrived at Boca Raton for the company meeting, Ben immediately went to the practice range and dutifully hit buckets of balls. The second day his diligence was rewarded; he saw the president approaching. For the next two days they practiced together, critiqued one another's games—and, by the time they returned to the office, they knew each other well enough for Ben to approach the president on a new product idea.

That's the up side of a convention. If it works for both employer and employee, it makes each better at his or her job because it encourages better communication.

There is a down side. Sherry was an assistant in research and development, and the executive vice president of the division was tired of a procrastinating vice president in Research and Development. A good executive would have approached the vice president in R and D. But who ever said all executives were good? This executive vice president decided instead to quiz the research assistant at a two-day company meeting. Everywhere Sherry went, there was "that man." He put her at his table and talked to her for hours about his dissatisfaction with the division. Sherry, with this kind of prodding (who can resist bitching about a boss, especially when the boss's boss leads the way?), really let go. She told about the waste in the division, the favoritism, the play-it-safe attitude of everyone. And by the time she finished telling all, she was finished, too.

When the group returned to their offices in Boston, they found that R and D had been abolished and would be replaced by outside researchers.

Handle the expense account

At a business meeting all of your expenses will be picked up by management. That is, the rental car and the airfare and the transportation to and from airports. Your meals will be paid by the company.

As for the rest of the expenses, attention must be paid.

No one likes to see extravagant bar bills.

No one likes to see drugstore bills for toothpaste, dental floss, and other things you are expected to supply yourself.

No one likes to see room service charges.

So make a conscious decision. If you are entertaining at your company's request in a convention atmosphere, put it on your billable travel and expenses. But if it's just to add a little fun to a dull time, then it is better to pay your own way.

Sometimes it costs very little to buy a lot of respect.

And it takes very little to lose a lot of opportunity.

The group is going . . .

Any time that there is a group activity during a convention, be a part of it. One of the ways management looks at its people is in the way promising executives interrelate.

You may prefer reading under a shady tree, but if everyone is going together on a company-planned excursion, remember that you can always stay up late reading. But there are no replays on today's trip.

The only excuse for not accompanying the group is the need to (a) prepare for the next meeting, or (b) make calls necessary to the proper conduct of business.

Bring-a-spouse

If you are invited to bring a spouse, be sure that the spouse you bring is your own. Even in this day of mix-and-match husbands and wives, most corporations breathe easier when you arrive with a gentleman or lady to whom you are lawfully wed.

If you are gay, do not bring your live-in lover. This is more than many executives and their spouses are able to handle.

If you are heterosexual and single, do not bring your live-in lover. Same reason.

Nowadays when many executives may be females, the spouse group is not simply "our wives." If you are a male spouse (and therefore in the minority), relax and accept your role with the pleasures it is meant to offer. The more relaxed and convivial you are, the more you communicate your own sense of self and contribute to your wife's confidence in her corporate role.

CHAPTER
14

Is There Life After Work?

When Carl C. Icahn gained control of TWA, he was so jubilant that he reportedly put on the pilot's jacket of Harry R. Hoglander, the chairman of TWA's arm of the Air Line Pilots Association, and ran around his plush office in the borrowed jacket shouting, "We've got ourselves an airline."

There are days like that, days when the winning is bigger than the prize.

There are also days when you are sure that there is not enough money in the world to pay you for what you do.

There are times when you have to beg and cajole frightened people into accepting something you know is right.

There are moments when your whole life's work revolves around the next yes. And the answer comes back—no.

Those are the times when the burdens outweigh the rewards of the marketplace, the times when you have to take comfort from the built-in supports in your life.

*   *   *

For those of us who move on a fast track, there are bound to be times when the work is not as good as we want it to be. Some days we can bounce back better than ever. Other times nothing happens. And when nothing happens, we feel scared, spent. This is the start of executive letdown.

The symptoms of executive letdown are exhaustion, annoyance without reason at spouse and/or children, a feeling of hopelessness, constant boredom, and a reliance on alcohol and/or drugs.

Those who work in pressure jobs sometimes begin to think of themselves as superpersons.

They can stand the heat.

They can stay in the kitchen.

But no one can stay in the kitchen all the time.

Those who have moved ahead in a highly competitive and charged business atmosphere often try to live all levels of life at the same high-powered pace.

They have active social lives.

They accept community responsibilities and do everything from Boy Scout parenting to charity dinnering.

They believe the old adage that if you want something done, ask a busy person.

But even a busy person must sometimes say no.

People who make significant business contributions deserve something in return.

You deserve the right to treat yourself as well as you treat the supporting cast in your life.

The next time you wake up and say, "I wish I didn't have to go to work today," is the time to see if the getting is worth the giving, the time to ask what you can do to put the good time back in your life.

Sometimes it's a big step you need to take; other times only small adjustments need be made.

Relax, and Feel Good

Do you want to join a health club?

Then go ahead, and do more than join.

Use it.

Will massage make you feel good?

Book a masseur or masseuse.

If you have always wanted to go to a spa, take the time and go. It is your life. It is your body. You don't have to sell yourself—body and soul—to the company.

Just think about yourself as the machinery that does the job. You'd keep the machinery in good repair, wouldn't you?

When Gladys Justin Carr, Editorial Director and chairman of the Editorial Board of McGraw-Hill, was scheduled to participate in a big book auction, she knew what big book auctions were all about.

They were about staying in the office glued to the telephone; they were about being able to move bids, change numbers, and raise antes in order to get the Big One.

The only problem on this auction day was that Ms. Carr was scheduled to be on holiday in Long Island. It was summer; she was hot and tired and needed that Friday to herself. But McGraw-Hill needed her, too.

And then Ms. Carr figured a way to accomplish both objectives.

She went to her Long Island home and took her cordless telephone to the pool. Each time a call came in, she made her bid, then jumped in the pool to swim and think about her next move.

By the end of the day she had rested, relaxed—and won.

She was exactly where she wanted to be both in terms of her life and her job.

Stop Jumping Off the High Board

Some people gravitate to risk the way bees seek honey.

You don't have to be the biggest, the best, the hardest-working in the history of work in order to feel secure.

Sometimes it's even smarter not to try at all.

There are no-win situations in life, and you have to learn to recognize them.

When James L. Dutt was dumped as chairman of Beatrice Foods in a special Saturday morning board meeting, the media pounced on him the following week. He was hot copy. Instead of complaining and explaining, he said simply that he was not ready to talk to the media. He kept both his dignity and his privacy.

If you've been hurt so that everyone can see, why reopen the wounds?

Instead of going for the pain, go for the relief.

Take an Hour Off, and Do Whatever You Feel Like Doing

Don't be a slave to the desk.

Even if you cannot take a day or two for yourself, try to program your life so that you can look forward to an occasional hour or two.

One executive smokes a cigar a day; he looks forward to that hour, shifting it daily, to a time when he wants to feel relaxed.

One woman takes her mind off her desk by going shopping. In New York where things are often called what they are, a Madison Avenue boutique is named Therapy.

Play Tennis, Golf, Swim or Watch Your Favorite Team

Put sports in your life so that there is some physical energy programmed as well as mental energy.

Walk or run.

Swim.

Hike.

Ski.

Sculpt.

Paint.

But move yourself in ways that make you feel good.

Get tired doing something that isn't connected with your everyday work.

Take Some Days Off

Forget about two weeks with pay.

You are not in that category anyway.

Take a day here or there.

Pick a weekend, and then add a Friday or a Monday to your personal package.

One of the secrets of those who work hard and long is the frequent three-day vacation instead of week-long travels. If, each month, you can plan a holiday (even if you go nowhere), you may indeed find that the promise of the extra day keeps you more cheerful and interested at work.

If you really can't take an extra day, try arriving late and leaving early one or two days a week. Then take that extra time to do something you particularly like to do. Be selfish. Use the time to make yourself feel good.

Make Your Travel Time as Comfortable as Possible

If you must travel on business, then do the comfortable things that will make you feel better.

Join the airline clubs. Belong to the Admirals Club, the Red Carpet Club, or whichever airport clubs make the most sense for you. Because so many flights are delayed, you should have the comfort and the convenience of a living room atmosphere when you have to wait for airplanes. Further, most airline clubs have private meeting rooms. If you are going to fly in and out of a city, make life more convenient by conducting your meeting at the airport, and if the Puritan Ethic is really strong, you will find that one meeting will make the whole membership worth the money.

Use your frequent-flier miles on yourself. Decide at what times you will upgrade your usual reservations. Your health is worth that kind of comfort.

Should your spouse accompany you? Yes, if it makes you and your spouse feel better. Remember, of course, that you must pay for your spouse's airfare. You can, however, cover much of the cost of a hotel room because your business will pay for the cost of a single room, so all you do is pay the cost of the upgrade.

Use room service when it makes life more comfortable.

Buy the Best Home You Can Afford

And then, if you can, buy yet another. In another county, another climate, another state, another country.

Living well is indeed the best revenge.

William Levitt, the brilliant and far-sighted developer of Levittown, is now building a 25,000-home development in Florida. In each of the houses he is building, there is exactly the same number of bedrooms as bathrooms. If it is a three-bedroom home, then it also has three bathrooms. Says Mr. Levitt, "I am convinced that one of the greatest causes of stress is the lack of enough bathrooms. If I put enough baths in these homes, I am sure people will enjoy life more."

Program Enjoyable Spouse Time

Don't get so tied to business and social commitments that you never take the time to enjoy your spouse.

Arrange child care as you need it.

More important, arrange a dinner for two. Or theater. Or a

night together away from home. Don't let business permit you to grow away from the needs of the person who matters most to you.

And do not permit your spouse to become so involved with a career that marriage becomes an afterthought.

The two-career marriage requires greater courtesy and more thoughtfulness on the part of both partners. There are not many role models for that kind of marriage—so there is room for you to be the nonpareil union, a marriage based on the best of company manners.

15

The Five Keys

He runs a multibillion dollar public company.

He knows he will never be cold or hungry.

His marriage is as good as a long-running marriage can be, and his children are settled in careers they want.

"So what's the matter?" I asked.

He looked around the well-appointed office, the office with two Miros, a Picasso, and a Roualt. "I can't get what I want," he said with some anger.

"You can't get what you want?" I was confused. "If you can't get what you want, who can? What's your real problem?"

"There is someone I want to hire as a marketing director in one of our companies, and no one will let me bring him in. They say that if I do it will break morale."

"How good is morale?" I asked.

"I don't really know," he admitted.

"How good is the marketing director?"

"Fantastic. And the division needs him. But I'm worried about what will happen to the people."

When I left, he was still debating.

Would it be his choice for the job or would he still let present management make the decision?

Company manners makes us face that kind of decision in greater or lesser degrees every day.

Because company manners is really about human relationships.

When we talk about company manners, it is never about the cost of running the office or the problems with the Mexican devaluation.

Company manners is about the ways we survive the everydayness and the crises of business.

To survive and to endure takes a special kind of strength that underlies most of the anecdotes in this book.

It is a strength that is two parts courage and one part honest conviction.

In order to succeed in business today you cannot be a corporate clone. It doesn't work. If your brain functions at a gray flannel level, no one will notice you.

It takes the maverick, but it takes a maverick with honest conviction.

It is a lot easier to stand out in a small company than it is in a large one. It is simpler to take a little company and decide what you will do when you are the major shareholder than it is to take a big company where you are second-guessed on everything beginning with your luncheon choices.

But courage—courage to do what you believe—is the one true identifying mark of a real executive.

Wisdom, which is simply those things you have experienced and read distilled into planned action, will always be questioned.

There are many executives—like my friend—who operate with great wisdom and minimal courage.

Knowing is not enough.

You cannot pay lip service to the human relationships of business. You cannot simply call something company manners.

Company manners is the action we take and the action we do not take.

Company manners is really about choices.

So how do we make the hard choices?

First, we must remember that universal love is impossible in the corporate world. So we have to be realistic. It is not possible to have all our choices and decisions applauded. It is not even necessary.

Only those who can put the best interests of the company ahead of self-interest survive.

If you have the title, the responsibility, and the authority, listen carefully to everyone below you who talks about change. But, as you listen, remember always that they are not necessarily revisionists; many are protectionists.

Which do you want to be at this time?

Do you want to follow the revisionist with this action or the protectionist?

Once you make your choice, relax, and go on to the next problem.

You may solve that one differently.

Never forget that you don't have to be anything forever in business.

Indeed the most brilliant managers, those with the best company manners, are those whose personal and business flexibility increase.

But as you think about your own flexibility, look, too, at your long-time managers.

If you see the concrete hardening around their long-standing prejudices and preferred ways of doing business, shake them up. And if they can't be shaken up, then shake them out. Nothing brings old employees to new performance peaks faster than seeing that an employer has both the courage and wisdom to make changes in the lineup.

Try to remember where and how the last new idea in your

shop originated. Then think back to the one before that. And before that. If you (or only one other person) are the only continuing, dependable source of creativity and originality, you are either stifling your people with too much pressure and fear of failure, or you have people who don't have the talent you should have operating in your business.

Ask yourself who is opting for new ways to look at old problems. As a manager, you need to be questioned and challenged from time to time by people who either force you to defend your position or give you reason to abandon it. The status quo can become the status ho-hum if you are not continually watchful.

Stay on guard for new problems, and watch to see which managers recognize them and seize them as opportunities.

Make sure you reward anyone who cares enough to point out the opportunities.

Most of all, be sure that—unless you are a one-man business—you are not doing it all.

Don't be afraid to be tough on others. If you are, you will make good people grow, and the greatest reward in business is the satisfaction of making one's self and others reach full potential. No good people work for salary alone. But don't forget to reward the good people with more than titles—because good people don't work for applause alone either.

Managers have decisions to make each day.

We live in a business society that plays up the maverick—but more consistently rewards the conformist.

Managers are forced to decide almost daily which they want, the headlines or the cash rewards.

You need to decide how far you can go in expressing yourself as an individual before you look like a corporate mistake.

In America we have always loved the figure of the lone rider on the plains. But how far does the lone rider go in business?

Is independence a goal or a crutch?

Are you maintaining independence and thwarting growth?

In the end each of us is responsible for our own business failures and successes.

We become the authors of our own business lives.

The early chapters are often written by others, but managers write autobiographies.

As a manager you can decide to maintain the best of your independent thinking and still work and grow your people as a unit.

The power tool for this decision making?

Company manners.

For company manners provides the means to take your best ideas and translate them into action that results in both bottom-line and personal profits.

Everything that you want will happen once you determine your company manners.

The best-run corporations know that.

So do the best executives. For company manners is a code of ethics that truly means good business.

There are five keys to company manners, keys that will ultimately unlock your business talents and give you the confidence to develop and express the kind of dynamic, contagious, positive personal leadership that is within you.

1. *Know your marketplace*

Know the history of your company *and* the history of your business. Know the major events that have shaped the marketplace as it is today. And then know what happens day-by-day.

Use the history as a factor in decision making so that you will know when you are following precedent and when you are breaking it. Knowing the historical reasons gives you added confidence for any action.

2. *Consider all consequences before you act*

Who will benefit?

Who will lose?

Can you live with the winners?

Will the losers survive? More importantly, should they?

No one in business is a hero each day.

Business heroes are made by the moment, but the consequences are endured by the year.

Be certain before you take any action that you have carefully examined all ramifications, that all courses of action are compatible with your code of ethics and your company's ways of doing business.

3. *Act when action is needed*

Once the alternatives have been faced, make the decision.

Inaction is a choice of company manners as much as action.

Do not delay to act at critical times.

A promotion when it is anticipated can be more effective in building morale than it is if it comes two months later—and only because an employee threatens to leave.

A decision to close a plant is more humane when people are told in advance and given options—not at the last possible moment when individuals have fewer choices.

4. *Put responsibility, credit, and blame where they belong*

Assume credit when it is due.

And assume blame when it is yours.

Understand always the reasons for your actions. If you do, you will be better able to understand what others say and do.

If you are a manager who has the opportunity to ask for a similar assignment in a larger market and fails to ask for it, question yourself for the honest answer.

Are you saying blithely, "Oh, they'd never give it to me," when in reality you really don't want to be in a new place at this time?

The more you understand the reasons, the less you will say, "I can't . . . ."

The person who says he cannot ask for a promotion because he "can't ask for more than others get" may mean "I shouldn't . . . ."

There is a difference.

Recognize that difference.

You can ask for more when you give more.

When you do more than others, you can demand and get more than others.

Executives are rewarded for performance, not for hours.

5. *Share the dream*

Take your associates into your confidence, and tell them what you dream for the company, for them, for yourself.

Is it a dream for more offices, services, and goods?

Is it a dream to make something new that will make life better for others?

Is it a dream to change the way we think about one another?

Dreams are meant not only to be dreamed; they are meant to be shared.

For in sharing our dreams, we increase the possibility of their happening.

The person down the line who shares your dream may find the missing part that will put your whole puzzle together.

An associate may harness his dream to yours and help you dream an even bigger dream together.

The everyday value of the shared dream, however, is that it gives the company and all its people a sense of purpose, a common goal, a heightened awareness of their own importance in the scheme of things, a better feeling about themselves and their company.

For company manners truly is the dream of a flexible, living, breathing, changing spirit of success translated by you into a way of doing business.

And that is a dream worth sharing.

Acknowledgments

We all know that the only real work security we have is not pensions and welfare and unions. The only real security is our talent.

Company manners permits talent to flourish because the more we do to create a warm atmosphere, the more secure we feel in further exploring our skills. Company manners makes it possible for us to think, to grow, to enrich the best of us.

There are many people who have shaped my philosophy of business, particularly those who have let me share their vision for business at its best.

Among them are the family responsible for running the J. M. Smucker Company: Paul M. Smucker, chairman, his wife, Lorraine, and their sons, Tim and Richard. They have been a profound influence throughout my business life, and I am grateful each day that this is so.

G. J. (Jack) Tankersley, the chief executive officer of Consolidated Natural Gas Co., has provided unique business opportunities for me and our company, and he and his wife Mary are also valued friends.

There are many others to whom I am particularly indebted beginning with my agent, Edward J. Acton, who helped shape the concept of *Company Manners* and was consistent in both criticism and encouragement.

Gladys Justin Carr, McGraw-Hill editorial director, is an exceptional editor whose vision of the book never wavered and whose confidence remained undiminished, and both she and her associate Leslie Meredith made valuable suggestions.

My husband, Lee Guber, helped me communicate some of the things I believe most deeply—and along the way contributed some of the best show business anecdotes; my children, Robert Wyse and Katherine Wyse Goldman, and my nephew, Kenneth Wyse, gave me some special insights.

The people of Wyse Advertising have been valued associates and caring friends, and I have learned from all of them.

My ablest teachers have always been the clients of Wyse Advertising who made it possible for me to learn in the best of all universities—their companies.

To all of the above go my thanks and my appreciation.

My particular thanks also to the people who are mentioned in *Company Manners*. There are many others who were helpful in relating both personal and professional anecdotes, people I wish I could mention—my own company manners, however, prevent me from doing that.

Lois Wyse

New York
Spring 1986